CONFESSIONS OF A
FASHIONISTA

ANGELA CLARKE

CONFESSIONS OF A
FASHIONISTA

THE GOOD,
THE BAD AND
THE BOTOX

Virgin BOOKS

*To Mum and Mr Darling, who didn't want me to write
about them but let me do it anyway.
And to Dad, who didn't complain either way.*

2 4 6 8 10 9 7 5 3

First published in the United Kingdom in 2013 by Virgin Books, an
imprint of Ebury Publishing

A Random House Group Company

www.randomhouse.co.uk

Addresses for companies within The Random House Group Limited can
be found at www.randomhouse.co.uk/offices.htm

The Random House Group Limited Reg. No. 954009

A CIP catalogue record for this book is available from the British Library

The Random House Group Limited supports The Forest Stewardship
Council® (FSC®), the leading international forest-certification
organisation. Our books carrying the FSC label are printed on
FSC®-certified paper. FSC is the only forest-certification scheme
supported by the leading environmental organisations, including
Greenpeace. Our paper procurement policy can be found at
www.randomhouse.co.uk/environment

Designed and typeset by K.DESIGN, Winscombe, Somerset
Printed and bound by CPI Group (UK) Ltd, Croydon, CR0 4YY

ISBN: 9780753541197

To buy books by your favourite authors and register for offers, visit
www.randomhouse.co.uk

CONTENTS

Note from the Author

I worked for a variety of different companies in the fashion industry over a ten-year period, experiencing this weird and wonderful world first-hand. This is my personal story based on my recollections and experiences. I have changed, and in some cases created, characters, identities and events, including conversations and locations and other details, for narrative purposes and in order to protect the privacy of others. I hope you have as much fun reading it as I did living it (minus the sore feet from the heels).

Publisher's Disclaimer

This memoir is based on the recollections and experiences of the author. Names and descriptions of people and places, and details of events and conversations, have been changed, and characters created, as a literary device and to protect the privacy of others.

PROLOGUE

LONDON, EPICENTRE OF THE FASHION WORLD

I've been in the fashion industry for almost eight years. This is the other side of the velvet rope, an elite world where the beautiful faces from magazines and newspapers come to life. It's a charmed existence full of creative, fabulous people in head-to-toe purchases from Net-a-Porter, and it's all non-stop glamour and champagne. Right?

Not quite. I am standing in an industrial rubbish bin. It smells of rotten fish and sulphur. Alarmingly, my feet, which I've wrapped in two Tesco bags, feel warm as they sink into the squelchy mess. On the ground standing neatly next to the bin are two pairs of Louboutins. Their red soles stick out like tongues in disgust at the two women up to their knees in garbage in front of them. I roll up my 7 For All Mankind jeans a bit higher; I spent a week's food budget on these. It could be worse: the stylist in front of me is wearing a Balenciaga dress, worth, what, one grand? Two? Possibly more.

'Where is it? It's got to be here somewhere? I'm fucked!' she screeches. 'My career is *fucked*!' The stylist plunges two pale skinny arms into the mounds of rubbish, ripping open bags and riffling through shredded paper and carrot peelings like a demented hamster. This is the third bin we've been through in the last twenty minutes.

When I arrived at work earlier this morning, I found her desperately looking for a pricey necklace she'd borrowed for a magazine photo shoot. It should hardly be easy to miss: it's from a Bond Street jeweller and has a gemstone the size of a kiwi fruit.

I recalled that last night I'd passed the office cleaner in the hall as I clattered into my Addison Lee, the *de rigueur* private car company favoured by the industry, and wondered aloud if she might have put it somewhere for safe-keeping. I stopped the stylist reporting the cleaner for theft, and the poor woman in question was summoned.

After a large amount of tears, we pieced the sorry story together. The cleaner had mistakenly thrown the box containing the necklace away, believing it to be rubbish.

'What's she doing throwing boxes away?' The stylist's voice is shrill from panic and a forty-a-day cigarette habit. 'I still think she's stolen it! She's a cleaner, she's desperate!'

Desperate? She's not the one bin-diving in Balenciaga.

I grab at the top of another bin bag and heave it out of the way. 'Wait, wait! I think I found it!' Relief rushes through me. There, under the black sack, is a familiar-looking cardboard box decorated with congealed baked beans.

'That's it!' The stylist lunges towards me in a blur and forcefully grabs the box from my hand.

Her swiping action knocks me off centre. I flail my arms wildly to try and keep my balance, but it's too late. With a squelch, I land on my bottom. Instinctively my manicured hands punch downwards to break my fall and disappear up to the elbows. I think I might be sick.

The stylist brandishes the gaudy necklace in the air like the Holy Grail. Victoriously she beams at me, rescues her Louboutins and totters into the office.

As I slump back in the bin, I wonder – not for the first time – how in the name of Prada it all came to this.

A SIDE-PARTING
OF WAYS

WIVENHOE, ESSEX, 2001

'Where's the man could ease a heart
Like a satin gown?'

DOROTHY PARKER

I love lists. People who write lists are organised. Who cares that I never tick anything off? Just smelling that strawberry-scented neon-pink pen as it glides across the page makes me feel in control. I'm in my final year of university and my current to-do list reads:

1. Finish coursework
2. Pass exams
3. Find job
4. Graduate
   (Not necessarily in that order)

I'm pondering number three on a walk with my boyfriend.

'It's important to have a career plan; you need to be focused,' he says in a reassuring, fatherly tone.

I look at him. He has the classic good looks of a catalogue model. The type who stands on top of windswept country hills looking thoughtful with a faithful dog at his feet and impossibly neat hair. The type of man your mum will adore and knit jumpers for. Not that my mother's ever knitted anything but if she did it would be something traditional and sturdy, with a little matching jumper for his faithful dog.

He has classic mum-pleasing qualities as well: head boy at our school; a straight A student; attending a top ten university; and, in the last week, he has accepted a place on the graduate scheme at Barclays Bank. All this career malarkey is easy for him, he's got it all sewn up in a free corporate-branded bag. If I wasn't helplessly in love I'd probably hate him for being such a goody two shoes.

'Who said anything about a career?' I frown. 'I was aiming for a job. My list says "find a job".' *In strawberry-scented pen.*

A career sounds frightening. It sounds an awful lot like being grown up.

'What about becoming a teacher?' he suggests.

'I'd rather stick child-chewed chalk in my eyes – you know children freak me out.'

'Our children won't freak you out.' He wraps me in his strong arms.

We've been together for four-and-a-half years. I've sacrificed key uni experiences to keep this long-distance relationship going: the vodka jelly party where my friends ended up in the lake outside the library, girlie weekends away and drunken sex with strangers. On the plus side, I don't have to shave my legs during the week.

I reach up to ruffle his dark hair. He wears it neatly swept to the side but I can't help tousling it. It makes him look like he's just got out of bed, making me want to get back into bed with him. Soon we will no longer be apart. Soon we will both be in London, together.

The sun dips in the sky and overhead seagulls circle, calling morosely. He leads me to the local estate agent window. 'Perhaps we should buy as soon as we graduate?'

My heart does a little dance of joy. After years of living apart we could finally be together. Shall I add it to my list? 'Number 5: Buy a house!' This justifies a whole new list. I could buy a new pad *for* the new pad.

'The train goes straight in to Liverpool Street from here, and I could get to my new office from there.' He points at an adorable tumbledown rose-covered cottage.

'We can't afford that.' I drool at a photo of a cosy sitting room complete with a log-fire.

'It'll be tight, but with my golden hello – plus the amount Mummy should give us – we'll easily get a mortgage.' He squeezes me close.

'And hopefully I'll get a job – sorry – I mean a career, and then we can go shopping for furniture!' I fiddle with the eternity ring he gave me last year and imagine cuddling under blankets in front of the fire. I feel so warm, so protected. Our life is panning out beautifully.

***

A week later, and a week before St Valentine's Day, there's a knock at my student house door.

'Angela, it's for you!' calls my housemate.

On the doorstep is my boyfriend. A surprise visit! I fling my arms around him.

'I need to talk to you,' he says, stiffly. He's wearing a shirt and tie. He looks like he's going for an interview.

Wait a minute … We've talked about buying a house, he's driven three-and-a-half hours to surprise me, he's dressed smartly ... Oh my God! He's going to propose! I try to control my excitement as I lead him to my room. I wish I'd washed my hair this morning or worn something more appropriate than my scruffy jeans. I try to kick some of the debris covering my floor under the bed. This is the happiest moment of my life.

He puts his hands on my shoulders, placing me in the right spot, then steps back and clears his throat. 'I'm afraid it's not working out, Angela.'

'What?' The words he's saying aren't making sense. It's like walking in halfway through a TV show and trying to work out what's going on.

'We both know this isn't going anywhere,' he says calmly.

'But, but, what about the rose-covered cottage?' *This cannot be happening.*

'It's been fun,' his eyes don't meet mine, 'but really, it's just been a childish fling.'

'Four-and-a-half years?' I stutter.

'I think I was with you out of habit. I'm not even sure I ever really loved you,' says the stranger who looks like the man I love.

Shards of glass are cutting their way through my body. A strange gurgling sound comes out of my throat.

He smiles at me and takes my hand. *This has been some terrible mistake, a really badly judged joke. He's going to tell me it's OK, he's going to tell me he still loves me.*

'It'd never have worked out. All my friends are going to be bankers, lawyers and accountants. Sweetie, you just wouldn't fit in. Better to end it now before you feel really bad about yourself.'

He leaves.

I lie on my bedroom floor crying and staring at my eternity ring, breathing in dust.

Two days later (*oh really?*) I learn from a mutual friend he's started dating a trainee solicitor with a big nose (OK, it's not

that big – I just need something to get me through this. When
I can't sleep at night I imagine she has athlete's foot. Or halitosis.
She *can't* be perfect.) He dates his clever new girlfriend and
I start a serious relationship with alcohol.

I want to refer to him as The Heartless, Lying, Cheating,
Stuck-Up, Smug Mummy's Boy Banking Bastard. But that
seems like a waste of ink and paper so, for the sake of the
environment and being succinct, I'll call him Side-Parting (after
his ridiculously smarmy haircut).

I respond to my life detonating with great maturity
and strength: I refuse to go to class, I stop washing my hair and
I only leave my bed to dry heave in the bathroom. After two
weeks Jen, my oldest friend, stages an intervention. She arrives
from her university with an overnight bag, a bucket of ice cream
and a no-nonsense attitude.

She finds me gripping the edge of the toilet.

'Want some water?' She offers me the cup my flatmates and
I keep our toothbrushes in.

I look up from my sprawled position on the floor. I must look
pretty pathetic. Jen is tremendously tall and skinny with long
wavy red hair. She rarely wears make-up and yet looks like a
Disney version of Venus. She knows what she wants to do in
life; she's training to be a physiotherapist. She's sorted. I expect
bluebirds help dress her in her hospital scrubs each morning.
We met at school where we bonded over our scientific interest
in the opposite sex: we discussed boys during biology. (And look
how well that turned out). We're like sisters. By which I mean
we have wildly different personalities, opposite viewpoints and
we argue constantly. I would scream down anyone who dared
say a bad word about her.

'I'm OK.' I grimace. 'False alarm.'

'Paracetamol it is then.' She drags me up by the arm. 'Men are
bastards.' Jen pulls me back into my room. *That* we agree on.

'Don't let him do this to you, Ange. You have to pick yourself up, get on with your life.'

She has an infuriating habit of saying the same thing as Mum. I'm sure they swap notes. Sometimes I think I only keep Jen around because she can reach things from the top shelf. But sometimes – often, in fact – she's right.

'I will. As soon as I've had a nap.' I wonder how many bottles of shampoo it will take to clean the grease from my hair?

Jen returns to her university, leaving me the ice cream for sustenance. I set about my graduate job hunt with renewed vigour. I've made a new list, with one thing on it:

1.   Sort my life out

I'll prove Side-Parting wrong, the patronising git. *God I miss him.* Cue uncontrolled snotty weeping. *Get a grip girl, he was with you for four-and-a-half years and his great insight was to suggest you become a teacher. He's a spineless dick who annihilated your confidence instead of confessing he's porking some clever bird with a big schnoz.*

Internal pep talk over, I survey my options. What do I like? Books. I love books. I could be a librarian! Sounds a bit quiet. If I'd studied something sensible and vocational I could've been an accountant by now. I shudder at the thought. There must be something else I enjoy? *Drowning my sorrows in a bottle of wine?*

At the moment the thing I want to do most is shop. Shopping has always been my solution for everything. Stressed from exams? Buy a new handbag. Argument with Side-Parting? New dress. Money worries? Oh look, what a lovely pair of shoes. Look up retail therapy in the dictionary and there's a picture of me buried under receipts, my credit card still twitching in my hand.

That's *it*! I could be a buyer! A short amount of research reveals this involves spreadsheets. *No way.* My eyes bleed with boredom if I even open Excel.

I dejectedly mooch to the careers office. Out of the corner of my eye, I spy an advert for Harrods' graduate programme. A giant golden penny drops: I love shopping; I should work in a shop.

The day before my interview I decide to jazz up my mousey hair with a few subtle highlights. Getting your hair done always makes you feel better. Not this time. The dozy hairdresser mixes up the bleaches and I end up with a shock of platinum hair. There's no way to correct it. Touching it with anything stronger than baby shampoo will make chunks snap off. I'd look like an inverted stubbly chin. Harrods wouldn't hire that. In my fragile emotional state I decide the best thing to do is drink copious amounts of Tia Maria and orange.

I attend my interview and aptitude test (yes, they really do test you for your aptitude to operate a till), very hungover and looking like I'm wearing a dodgy Veronica Lake wig. Walking requires the concentration of every fibre in my body. I don't notice anybody else.

After the interview my eyelids stop making the sound of sandpaper being rubbed when I blink. Now seems like a good time to check out the legendary store itself.

Despite my dedication to consumerism I've never visited a luxury department store before. No matter how many times I dodge the question with vague references to the Home Counties, nothing changes the truth. I was born in Watford, I went to a local state comprehensive and I do not have a walk-in wardrobe. My hunting ground is cheap, local and smells of acrylic jumpers.

Harrods is a glittering giant jewellery box of polished marble, gold and mirrors. I take it all in like a spinning plastic ballerina dancing to a tinny 'Somewhere Over The Rainbow'. There are no toy beads, just real diamonds. What would Side-Parting say if he could see me here?

Drifting away from the gawping tourists, I find myself in 'The Room Of Luxury I: Handbags'. I always knew I had expensive taste. Elevated on individual mirrored podiums are clutches, totes and shoulder bags: miniature gods to be worshipped. This is a temple to style, handbag heaven. I've been aiming too low with strawberry-scented pens; here is true shopping nirvana. I fondle the soft leather of a red Lulu Guinness clutch shaped like a pair of lips. Releasing the soundless clasp I find the price, more than my month's rent. I put it down gingerly.

Lust explodes as my eye catches another gem: a black patent Burberry bowling bag here, a monochrome quilted Chanel flap bag there. I've watched enough *Sex and the City* to know what I'm looking at. Thank goodness my credit card is at home – working surrounded by this level of temptation would be disastrous.

'How did it go?' Jen's voice is on the other end of my mobile as I ride home on the train.

'OK.'

'Fingers crossed. Listen, I wanted to tell you – I've decided to go backpacking after finals. Thailand, New Zealand, anywhere else my ticket will stretch to.'

Everyone's abandoning me!

'Why don't you come too?' Jen's voice splinters through the phone. She already sounds far away.

Travelling won't prove I'm someone to Side-Parting. 'Cockroach-infested hostels aren't really my thing. How long are you going for?'

'Six months,' she says quietly.

Fields streak past the window. Half a year without my best friend. Something catches in my throat. *Must be a dusty train, I'm FINE.* 'What an adventure – you'll have an amazing time!'

'Hello … hello … Ange … can you hear me? Hel …' The phone goes dead.

Stupid train. I text Jen to tell her I'll call her later to discuss immunisations and whether there is such a thing as an attractive rucksack.

Back at my student house, the landline's ringing. Is it Side-Parting calling to say he's made a terrible mistake? That he's heard I've been interviewed by Harrods, sees now I'm a dynamic, go-getting retail powerhouse and wants me back?

'Hello,' I say in my best impression of a relaxed and confident woman.

'Hello, Angela?'

Damn. Not Side-Parting. 'Yes?' I struggle to place the voice. Is it one of the guys from the student union?

'Look, I know it's a bit strange me calling after what's happened …'

Oh God, it's Side-Parting's Flatmate! 'Oh hi, sorry, caught me on the go there! How are you?' I say at a hundred and fifty miles per hour. What does he want? Nice boy, but we never really spoke much beyond the usual pleasantries. I always had the feeling he didn't really like me. One of those who disapproves of their housemate always having their partner stay over and using up precious electricity. Perhaps Side-Parting has made him call? Perhaps he's been sent to spy?

'I'm good, thanks, Ange. I know this is a bit odd, me calling up, but me and the others are a bit disappointed with, well, *his* behaviour and I just wanted to call and say we always really liked you and we're sorry about the break-up.'

'Thank you,' I stammer. I thought Side-Parting's friends felt the same as he did; that I'm something to discard, that they're all moving on and leaving me behind, that I'm not part of their plans. I'm touched Side-Parting's Flatmate decided to call.

Now, though, we're suspended in an awkward silence. I claw for something to say. 'So, what are you going to do this summer?' God, that's the kind of question a hairdresser asks. I may as well have blown raspberries down the line and confirmed every assumption Side-Parting made about me.

'I've got an internship at an economic consultancy,' he answers.

Everyone has amazing plans, apart from me. But he only said internship. That's not a full-time job, not the beginning of a great career. Side-Parting's Flatmate is also struggling with his life strategy. 'And then what do you hope to do?' I ask innocently.

'I'm going to Oxford for a master's in October.'

'Great, great,' I say. 'It's been great to talk to you. Let's keep in touch.'

It's official: I'm a failure. I have no career, no prospects, no round-the-world ticket, no hope. I showed up at my first interview with a hangover to rival George Best's. I'm destined to stand in the street dressed as a giant sandwich handing out leaflets for the rest of my life.

SHOP GIRL

'Without gay men, I am nothing.'

JANICE DICKINSON

The last months of university pass in a cocktail of emotion-numbing alcohol and exams. In one memorable incident, my friends have to remove a bathroom door when I pass out inside. Well, it's memorable for them; my recollections are a little hazy. Apparently I was lying on the floor, skirt round my waist, hugging the toilet with some guy who was equally unconscious in the same position on the other side of the loo. Classy. I've hit rock bottom. I've been using alcohol to dull the pain of my break-up from Side-Parting.

But then, to my surprise, Harrods offer me the job. Suddenly I'm riding the high of my graduate employee status. I don't need a box of wine and a straw to get me through the day. I pack the detritus of my uni life into Asda grocery boxes and move back in with my parents. It's a fresh start. No more moping. No more vats of ice cream. No more drinking. Mum would be furious if they had to take the bathroom door off its hinges, so best behaviour guaranteed.

***

I've only been home a week and it's my first day at Harrods. I'm excited, nervous and up very early. I'm wearing my new Next trouser suit, which crackles reassuringly with static when I walk. And I've polished my black Oasis pleather handbag with Vaseline till you can almost believe it's never been used.

I leave my trusty rusty Metro at the station, looking sorry for itself among the 4x4s and sleek sports cars, and I squash onto the train, giving my fellow commuters accidental static shocks. I stand all the way into London, change onto the tube and finally walk into the staff entrance of Harrods. People do this every day?! I'm exhausted before I've even started work.

A receptionist gives me directions to a room. I trudge up the concrete back stairs, growing sweaty and hot in my suit. In a rectangular magnolia-painted meeting room stand all the graduates. It's a sea of women. There's one token guy at the back, a tall black man surveying his twenty-four new colleagues with the expression of a lottery winner: all the female graduates are stunning. None of them look hot from climbing the stairs. The majority are blonde.

I smooth my rough-dried hair. Have they hired me because of my bleach disaster? These are professional beauties; all straightened hair and flawless foundation. I don't belong here. I need to find a bathroom and correct my rather haphazard eye make-up.

I shouldn't worry. Over the next two weeks Harrods, with its strict dress code, moulds me into the (visually) perfect employee. There's a helpful two-page guide for female graduates. It contains such gems as:

Jewellery   One earring per ear. Pearls or diamond studs
            preferred.

Make-up   Full make-up at all times: base, blusher, full
eyes (not too heavy), lipstick, lipliner and gloss
are worn at all times and maintained discreetly
(please take into account the store display
lighting which has a 'washing out' effect).

It's like being groomed by a beauty queen on steroids. You must
wear head-to-toe black. You must wear a suit, preferably a skirt
suit. Your hair must be blow-dried and worn down; ideally it will
be blonde. You must wear make-up. You must have manicured
nails. You must wear heels. You must be slim. You must be pretty.
You must suck breath mints at all times. Unless you are a tall
token male employee, in which case you only get given one page
of dress code enhancements. Which you really don't need,
because you're so beautiful rich housewives would give up their
private tennis coaches just to have you hand them their shopping
bags. I'm getting distracted, where was I …

I didn't realise then, but this visual fascism, coupled with an
atmosphere of elitism and a backdrop of wall-to-wall designer
goods, is the perfect training for a career in fashion.

My first fortnight is spent chained to a till during the sales.
Next, I'm due to complete a series of placements across a range
of departments. I'm not sure if the managers sense dissent in
me? I'm finding it hard to adjust from being in a feminism
lecture a few weeks ago to now looking like shop-floor Barbie.
But they opt to assign me to Direct Mail. For that I'm grateful:
it opens my eyes to a new world.

Tucked up in a little office on the roof, the Direct Mail
department is a small team with a slightly more relaxed attitude
and dress code. My gay male boss even wears jeans to work,
heavens! We also only work Monday to Friday, which is a relief
after the torture of the seven-day week, all-hands-on-deck
approach to the sales.

I report for duty in my stiff black trouser suit on a roasting August day.

My new boss, with his over-plucked eyebrows and thinning hair, utters the words that change my life: 'Lose the jacket, Blondie, we're off to a photo shoot.' I had no idea Harrods, like most retailers, shoots its Christmas catalogue in August.

At a country house location somewhere within the M25 I stumble out of the taxi and into the blazing heat. I think I'm hallucinating: the Capability Brown garden is covered in more snow than Narnia. The sweeping undulating hills are all a brilliant white, the glassy lake winks in the sunlight. Snow blankets the floor in deep whirls, sitting on top of trees and bushes like dropped dollops of wet icing. It's magical.

'Blondie, fetch me some water.' My boss disappears in the direction of a group of children who are having a snowball fight in what look like all-in-one Ralph Lauren ski suits.

I run my hands through the snow at my feet. It isn't cold. It feels powdery and disintegrates between my fingers, leaving a thin coating of plastic behind.

'Here love, don't do that, you'll muck up the lay,' yells a stubbly guy in ripped jean shorts and a T-shirt.

'Oh sorry!' I don't want to get fired for fiddling with the snow. I better find that water.

I come across a tanned lady in a pale blue sundress, carefully arranging a hamper in front of a camera and light rigging. Various items are laid out on the snow-covered table. A glass of champagne. A dish of chocolates. She takes out a small silver flask and adds dry ice to a ham, making it look steaming hot. Next to her kit is a pile of ice cubes. They couldn't be? I pick up a half-melted one. Plastic.

'This your first photo shoot?' She smiles at me as she wipes the sweat from her brow and takes a sip of water. She has no make-up on.

'Yes, I suppose it is.' I look at the beautiful illusion around me. My first photo shoot.

'You can keep that if you like.' She gestures at the fake ice cube. 'I've got plenty.'

'Really? Thanks.' I drop it in my pocket. (I still have it now. It reminds me of where it all started.)

She turns back to her work.

My first photo shoot. I try to memorise every glittering detail. I really could be standing in a snowy wonderland in the middle of an idyllic winter. Suddenly a shriek breaks my reverie.

'She's down! Quick, does anyone know first aid?' cries a voice.

People are rushing toward a dark shape on the ground.

'Get some water!'

'Get her off the snow, she'll leave a mark!'

One of the models has passed out. Well, she is wearing a fur coat and rabbit-fur earmuffs in thirty-one-degree heat.

***

The Harrods Christmas photo shoot lasts a week, but I've joined the team on the final day. Like arriving at a party late to find only a well-fingered sausage roll and the clean-up left. It's my responsibility to pack up all the clothes and props from the shoot and return them to the relevant store departments and PRs. This Herculean task takes place in an otherwise empty office building across Brompton Road.

To reach it I pass through Harrods' underbelly. Behind a suitably posh gold door on the lower ground floor is another door; grotty plastic hangs over it like a poor woman's version of the fur coats in the Narnia wardrobe. Push through and you enter a warren of storage rooms and walkways, which look like an inner-city concrete car park.

Down here you're away from the shop-floor staff, the sneering gargoyles in high heels who guard the high-end products from 'inappropriate' customers. The subterranean green-aproned team who push the stock around in big trolleys are relaxed and fun.

'Can you point me to the tunnel?' I ask a lad about my age with a cheeky-looking smile as he wheels past.

'Sure, follow me.'

I walk quickly behind him and his rumbling trolley, noticing he has a nice bum. 'Cheers.' I give him my best flirtatious smile when we reach the mouth of the tunnel. He gives me a wink.

Side-Parting pops into my head. I squash the ache. He'll realise he's made a mistake and come crawling back and I'll tell him I've moved on: I work at *Harrods* now.

My heels click along the cavernous walkway that passes under Brompton Road and pops up the other side. A secret tunnel, the kind the Famous Five discover in large country houses, right here in Knightsbridge. I've heard rumours of a second tunnel, for the sole use of the chairman. I imagine him being wheeled down it in a large stock trolley, ex-SAS security guards in black suits and sunglasses running alongside.

I enter the building and stumble into an Aladdin's Cave of boxes, bags and crates piled precariously high and housing everything from the photo shoot. It spreads through two large rooms. I open a cardboard box to my left and pull out a mass of black taffeta, a dress. It's heavy and boned, with invisible underwear stitched inside. The label reads VALENTINO. I roll the dress in my hands like the word rolls round my mouth. Out of another bag comes a silky chemise, the silvery-blue material slithering through my fingers. Suddenly I'm opening everything around me, tipping the contents out, desperate to see what's inside. It's like Christmas, but with someone else's presents. I can feel the quality, see the fine stitching, the cut. I start to comprehend the power of designer clothes. I hold a black-and-white polka dot Moschino ballgown against me. Mosh-chino? Moss-chin-o? I'm not sure how you pronounce it, but it's gorgeous. I wish there was a mirror in this damn office.

I grab hold of myself. These things are not mine. Even in my wildest fantasies I wouldn't be able to get all this on the tube and disappear into a designer-clad sunset. The ex-SAS security guards would be on me before I'd walked two metres outside. *'I don't know what came over me Your Honour, I've never done a bad thing in my life before, but when I saw the Valentino I just snapped.'* I take a deep breath, smooth the Mosch-however-you-say-it dress lovingly and put it back in its carrier. I have to send them all back.

It takes two days to pack everything up. I tearfully wave the courier off and make him promise to look after the parcels as if they're his own firstborn. There's one bag left. A stiff purple paper bag, with the scrolling Lulu Guinness logo on it. If I could ever afford the red-lips clutch I saw on my interview day, I'd be given my purchase in this bag. If I could ever afford the red-lips clutch I saw on my interview day, I would take it to bed at night and sleep with it like a child does a cherished cuddly toy.

I carry the paper bag as if it's made of glass back to the Direct Mail office.

My boss is sitting at his computer. He's wearing his own unique version of the Harrods uniform: dark jeans, white T-shirt and blazer. It looks like he went a bit hair-gel happy this morning.

'This was left over when everything had gone back,' I casually say to his back.

'Mmmm hm.' He doesn't look up from the screen.

'Would it be OK if I, you know, kept it?' I act as if it's an entirely natural request.

He turns and looks at me, one eyebrow slightly raised.

He's going to laugh, call to the others, 'Look, this crazy freak wants to keep a paper bag! A bit of rubbish!'

'Sure.' He turns back to the screen.

I resist the urge to punch the air. I tote my bag with pride, as if it's a real designer one, not just a paper shell. I'll use it every day to carry my lunch into work, and my empty Tupperware home.

As I gather up my handbag and my prized paper bag to go home my boss calls to me, 'Hey, Blondie, you catch the train from King's Cross, right?'

'Yes, why?'

'Me and a couple of friends are going to a bar near there, we'll give you a lift in our taxi.'

A Lulu Guinness paper bag AND a lift back to the station in a taxi, this is the best day EVER. I trot behind him and out into the evening sunshine. I clamber into the back of the waiting black cab.

'This is my boyfriend,' says my boss. He sits next to a wiry guy with cropped brown hair. He looks like he's wearing girl's skinny jeans. He and his nose ring nod hello.

'Nice to meet you.' I smile and sit stiffly. What's the correct etiquette for sharing a taxi with your boss, his boyfriend and his friend? Do I shake hands? Ask them what they're up to tonight? Bow?

'And this is Lee.' My boss indicates the other man. He has a shaved head and a faint goatee. He's wearing a cardigan buttoned up over a T-shirt.

'Nice to meet you too,' I smile at Lee.

My boss and his boyfriend giggle.

I attempt polite small talk with Lee as the car winds across London.

'So how long you been at Harrods?' he asks.

'Only a few weeks, are you at Harrods too?'

'Yes, I'm at Harrods.' Lee smiles.

The giggles from my boss and his boyfriend grow louder.

What's so funny?

'So you into fashion then?' Lee says.

I think about the magic of the photo shoot, the siren call of the exquisite clothes and the empty paper bag at my feet. 'Yes. Yes I am.'

My boss and his boyfriend crack up. They start interrupting, talking across me. Somehow I'm the butt of a joke.

Don't underestimate me. I'm not some green small-town girl who comes to London and microwaves sushi, I know Lee's gay too.

The taxi pulls up at the bar and we all climb out.

My boss pulls me aside as he lights a fag, 'You know who Lee is don't you?'

'Yeah, he's your gay mate!' I answer triumphantly.

'Yes, otherwise known as Alexander McQueen.' He blows smoke through his grinning teeth.

Oh. My. God.

I wave as Alexander McQueen, fashion royalty, and my boss and his man, disappear into the bar. I shared a taxi with Alexander McQueen and didn't even realise. Alexander's charming and friendly; working in fashion must be incredible.

I dial Side-Parting's number on my mobile – I can't wait to tell him! It starts to ring and I remember myself. Side-Parting's no longer my boyfriend, he no longer cares who I meet. I hang up. Now he's going to think I'm calling him in some sad-stalking-ex kind of way. I wish Jen were here instead of off shagging Australians in various cholera hotspots. I bet Side-Parting's smart big-nosed girlfriend would never make such a childish mistake. But I also bet his big-nosed girlfriend has never met Alexander McQueen. Alexander McQueen! I smile to myself and swing my paper Lulu Guinness bag victoriously as I walk toward the train.

***

'That's one pound ninety-five,' says the local shop lady.

The joys of a lunch break: a snatched twenty minutes breathing gulps of fresh air – smog-drenched Brompton Road fresh air, that is – and scoffing an anaemic-looking egg salad sandwich so fast you get indigestion. I hand over my debit card.

'It says declined.' The lady eyes my Harrods black suit uniform and smiles smugly.

Having your card rejected in a shop in Knightsbridge? Priceless. I glance around to check there's no one I know in here. 'Gosh, it must be a bank fault, there's loads in that account,' I lie. 'Try this one,' I hand over my Visa.

Before starting at Harrods my wage sounded huge. But I didn't factor in tax, my student loan, or all the things I'd have to buy to resemble a Harrods employee and not a hair-bleached imposter. I've spent more on make-up in the last few months than I did over my entire three years at university. I'm thinking about petitioning the prime minister for a tax allowance on lipstick. How am I ever going to afford a proper designer bag? I can barely afford the token rent my parents charge me.

I'm not having a good day. The evil merry-go-round that's the graduate programme has ripped me, and my Lulu Guinness paper bag, from the comfort of Direct Mail and dropped me back onto the shop floor. I bet I'll never share a taxi with Alexander McQueen while working in Bed & Bath.

My new boss wears her hair in a bun so tight I'm surprised she can blink. You've heard of people who look like they're sucking lemons? Well, she looks like she's sucked the whole lemon tree, farm and packing factory. I resist the urge to scream when she complains about the intricate display of towels I've spent all day constructing.

'I asked for the towels to be one centimetre apart, Angela, these are nought point eight centimetres apart.'

She's so anally retentive I bet she measures her lemons are the *correct* size before sucking them.

After eight hours standing on a marble floor in heels, my feet feel like they've been repeatedly slapped with a concrete slab. Even fantasising about smothering my new boss with a Hungarian goosedown pillow doesn't make me feel better. I battle my way home on the tube and train before collapsing into my trusty rusty Metro and turning the key. Nothing happens. I bash my head repeatedly against the steering wheel until I hear someone tapping on the window. I wind it down to let the source of the tapping, a portly man in a suit, speak.

'You all right? Do you need some help?' he asks, leaning on the wing mirror. The wing mirror falls off.

We both stare at the wing mirror, which is lying in the mud on the car park ground.

'Can you give me a push?' I force a smile.

The portly man and the station guard push my car until it splutters into life. I shout thanks out the window, I'm too nervous to slow in case my trusty rusty Metro decides it's going to stop again. The amputated wing mirror lies on the passenger seat.

It's due to have an MOT next week. I'm no mechanic, but I think it's safe to assume it's going to fail. With my empty bank account and rejected card, forget a designer handbag, how am I going to be able to afford to fix my car?

I maintain speed over the roundabout, mouthing, 'I can't stop' at the oncoming cars. My phone starts ringing: Side-Parting's Flatmate. What does he want? I wedge my hands-free headphones into my ears. 'Hello?'

'Hello, Angela?'

'Hey, how you doing?'

'Yeah good, I just thought I'd give you a call. I heard you're working in London now.'

I wonder if he'll report back to Side-Parting? 'Yes, I'm at Harrods actually, on the graduate scheme, it's amazing.' *I spent six hours pricing up face flannels today. Totally fucking amazing.*

'Great! I'm glad you're doing well. Look I thought I ought to give you a call, let you know what's going on ...'

My heart leaps, and this time not from my suicidal car. Side-Parting's realised he's made a mistake. He's dumped the big-nosed girl and wants me back. His flatmate's ringing to smooth the way.

Side-Parting's Flatmate is still talking '... and, well, they've got engaged.'

My trusty rusty Metro swerves to the left, I clip the kerb, half spin. I see the panicked face of the white-van driver as he skids toward me. I close my eyes and brace.

MOVING ON

'I like my money right where I can see it …
hanging in my closet.'

CARRIE BRADSHAW

The van horn screams as the driver just misses the back of my
car. I shall never say a rude word about white-van men again.

I can't catch my breath.

Engaged. Side-Parting is engaged. He's going to marry her.
He's going to marry someone else.

'Angela, are you still there? Are you all right?' Side-Parting's
Flatmate sounds small and far away. My headphones have fallen
out.

'Fine. Got to go, speak soon.' I cut off the call.

My trusty rusty Metro chugs pathetically, half on the kerb
and half in the road. 'I know how you feel, mate,' I mutter as I
crunch the gearstick into reverse. I drive the rest of the way
home slowly, with the hazard lights on. Side-Parting is engaged.
I pull into my parents' drive, stumble out of the car and throw
up all over my dad's ornamental roses.

On my next day off work I take the eternity ring Side-Parting gave me to a pawnbroker's.

'It's not worth much, only twenty quid,' says the grey-haired pawnbroker gently.

'But it's a diamond!'

He looks uncomfortable. 'Sorry, love, it's only cubic zirconia.'

Fake. Like our relationship. I take a deep breath. 'That's OK, I have these too.' I hand over the jewellery, CDs, books and everything else Side-Parting gave me during our four-and-a-half years together. It comes to £197. I use the money to fix my car.

***

Shocked by Side-Parting's engagement, I fill the store shelves with fifty-quid bubble bath like a robot. I show no emotion. I don't talk to any other members of staff. The old lemon thinks I'm perfect. I'll win employee of the year at this rate.

Surprisingly, my fellow graduates still want to socialise with me. Perhaps if I kept my mouth shut more often, my life would run more smoothly. No opinions, no conversations, no boyfriends, no messy break-ups.

'Fancy a drink, Angela?' asks one of the girls on the graduate scheme.

Yes, yes I do.

One glass of Chardonnay later: *why has he got engaged?*

Two glasses of Chardonnay: *why doesn't he want me?*

Three glasses of Chardonnay: *why am I even drinking this Chardonnay? It tastes of rotten pears soaked in vinegar.*

Four glasses of Chardonnay: *I'm a failure, I'm unattractive, I'm stacking shelves with overpriced products for a living. And I'm drinking wine I don't like.*

Five glasses of Chardonnay: *when did we relocate to a club?*

Six glasses of Chardonnay: a tall dark handsome man is talking to me. He has amazing jet-black hair and intense eyes. He's gorgeous. I think I'm wobbling. I try to focus.

'You have such beautiful sad eyes,' he says.

I snort with laughter, spraying him with Chardonnay. 'That's the cheesiest chat-up line I've ever heard.' I brush white wine off his cashmere jumper.

'And that's the wettest response I've ever had.' He reaches for a napkin from the bar. 'I'm glad I amuse you. Can I buy you a drink?'

I look at the full glass of Chardonnay in my hand. 'Yeah, this is rubbish, I'd like a glass of Merlot please.'

I wake up with what feels like a bag of marbles in my head and a dead hamster on my tongue. I'm on the floor of my workmate's flat. I wonder if they've impounded my car at the train station? There are nineteen missed calls on my phone. Eighteen from my mother wanting to know why I never came home last night, and one from the man with the jet-black hair and intense eyes.

One sober-ish date later and I confirm the man with the intense eyes is gorgeous, sweet, rich and very indulgent. AND I learn he's a lawyer. *Your honour, I plead guilty to feeling a perverse pleasure from responding to Side-Parting's engagement to his big-nosed solicitor by finding my own legally hot lawyer.* Legally Hot speaks Arabic, English and French, he takes me for dinner in Knightsbridge, holds doors open for me, listens to old Frank Sinatra records and smokes like Humphrey Bogart. When he introduces me to his friends he says, 'This is Angela, *she* works at Harrods.' They all nod in appreciation. We have absolutely nothing in common. My relationship with him is summed up in the phrase: to get over someone you have to get under someone else. Except in my case it's not just under someone, it's astride, in front of, on the stairs, in the car, in the disabled loos in our favourite restaurant. The sex is fantastic. I'm honest with Legally Hot: I tell him I'm not over Side-Parting; I'm not looking for a relationship. This is just a fun distraction. He's happy to be of service.

***

Today I qualify for my Harrods discount, a limited number of 50 per cent off vouchers redeemable against 'uniform' items. In other words, anything as long as it's black. I should spend them wisely, spread over the next twelve months. *Sod that!* My work wardrobe consists of a poly-mix Next suit, a couple of New Look shirts and a pair of squat black heels from the market. I need all the help I can get. If, IF, I ever see Side-Parting again I want to look amazing: I want him to fall to his knees and weep over what he let go.

Casually I stroll to the Jaeger section and select a trouser suit, carrying it as a first-time mother would hold her newborn. The drop-front pant falls into a loose column over my shoes, giving the impression of long legs. The jacket nips in and highlights my waist. It even makes my New Look shirt look good. The lightweight material allows me to move and my skin to breathe. I'm not going to sweat in this suit. For the first time since starting at Harrods, I will make it to the end of the day without looking like a shiny polished cue ball.

With my discount it's £150. It's an investment. It's a necessity. It's my uniform. I can put it on my credit card.

I ball up my old suit and stuff it into my bag. Keeping the Jaeger suit on, I perform a brief dance to detach the price tag, then take it to the till to pay.

I should stop here. I have a new suit, a gorgeous new suit. There is nothing left in my bank account. No part of me is listening to my head. My feet waltz toward the shoe department. My hands are lifting up a pair of Tom Ford's Gucci black pointed pumps, caressing the soft buttery leather, feeling the strength in the metal spiked heel. My heart is singing. And so the internal argument starts.

– I can't afford them.

– *But they're so pretty.*

– I'll buy them after I pay my Visa bill next month.

– *They'll be gone by then. Someone else will be loving them. Look at this pair: Gucci shoe-boots with a skyscraper heel as thin as a pencil!*

– I don't know why I'm looking; I can't afford one pair let alone two.

– *It won't do any harm to try them on. JUST TRY THEM ON!*

The pumps hug my feet as if they were made for me. The pointed toe peeks seductively out from under my new suit leg.

The shoe-boots tip me so far forwards I worry I'll fall over. They're cut low to expose the anklebone, showcasing it like a Victorian erogenous zone. They look incredible. They scream power, they scream sex; my toes begin to scream in agony.

– *Compared to the shoe-boots, the pumps are a sensible buy.*

– Don't be silly. They cost £300!

– *That's AFTER 50 per cent discount. Really it's a saving of £300.*

– That is a big saving …

– *They're a bargain. You might never find a pair like them again.*

I hand over my Visa and the saleswoman hands me a bag containing a glossy box. Inside, the pumps are swaddled in their own silky brown shoe bag, the kissing Gs of the Gucci logo proudly repeated all over the fabric.

– I feel a bit sick. I've used most of my business dress vouchers. What if I need something else? I've spent all my money. How am I going to pay my rent?

– *Your own parents won't evict you if you're a little behind with your bills.*

– I can't afford to eat!

– *Pah! Who needs food? Just put them on.*

My old market shoes go into the Gucci box, the shoe bag folded neatly on top. I slide the box into my locker and go back to work in my Gucci shoes. Oh my God – I own a pair of Gucci shoes!

– *Feel better?*

– Yes.

At the end of the day I swish into the arms of Legally Hot.

'You look beautiful,' he purrs, twirling me round to admire my new outfit. 'I love those shoes, Gucci?'

'You should have seen the pair that got away. Shoe-boots, with—'

'What are "shoe-boots"?'

'A cross between shoes and boots obviously.'

He gives me an indulgent smile.

'They had the most outrageous high heels. Very, very sexy.'

'Let's go buy them.' He looks at me with his hypnotic eyes.

The saleswoman packs the boots into another glossy box, another logo-ed shoe bag. *Zero to two Guccis in one day.*

Legally Hot smiles charmingly as he hands the saleswoman a handful of notes. I give her the last of my business dress allowance vouchers.

'How lucky you are to have someone to buy you such a wonderful gift,' the saleswoman coos without taking her eyes from Legally Hot.

Legally Hot holds her gaze for a split second too long. I smile. *You can keep him, I'll keep the shoes.*

The next morning I climb into my trusty Metro to drive to the station. Slung over my shoulders is a prized charity-shop find: a Burberry trenchcoat. The Burberry department authenticated it for me, and suggested I could get £500 if I sold it to a vintage store. I paid £3.50 for it. I turn the key in the engine. Nothing happens. Again. This is the third time in two weeks my trusty, rusty Metro won't start. Not so trusty after all.

I wake my dad to help me jump-start it. He comes outside in his dressing gown, cursing the cold. As I stand there in my Gucci shoes, Jaeger suit and Burberry coat I realise my outfit is worth more than my car.

***

I'm working in the toy department. Against the backdrop of life-size teddy bears and huge wooden soldiers there's an incident with someone's hands and my bottom.

I quit.

My great retail career, over in six months.

Legally Hot and I amicably part ways when we realise opportunities for sex are limited now I don't travel to London every day. I picture him walking off into the sunset with the saleswoman from the shoe department.

If I bump into Side-Parting now, it'll look like I haven't moved on. I'm living with my parents, I have no job, no boyfriend, a stack of unopened Visa bills, a car that won't start and some very expensive shoes. I retreat to my bed to sulk.

After two weeks my mother has had enough. She marches into my room and wrenches the curtains open like a petite sergeant-major in a pastel-pink fleece. 'Jen's back, she's called twice.'

'Hnnhhph?'

Mum picks clothes off the floor and drops them neatly folded onto my legs. They say genius skips a generation, but in this family it's tidiness. Mum cleans instinctively, obsessively, like a Stepford Wife on speed. She has declared jihad on dust. Our house is free from books, ornaments, excessive soft furnishings and, often, people. She's a pioneer of OCD. They say minimalism began in 1960s America, but I have a strong suspicion it was born in 1950s north Hertfordshire.

'Ten more minutes, Mum.' I pull the covers over my head.

She taps her foot in a threatening manner.

Five minutes later and I'm up, trying to make my hair resemble hair and not fluff from the tumble dryer.

Mum stands in front of me, eyeing my Jaeger suit with suspicion. To her investing in something expensive and well made means going to Marks and Spencer.

'What are you going to do?' she asks.

'I'm going to get a job in fashion,' I tell her with all the confidence of a girl who has an obsession with designer goods and can think of no other way to build her collection. I'm five foot four, a size ten with an over-exuberant number of freckles, mousey roots where my hair dye's growing out and I wear glasses, so her response isn't a surprise.

'That doesn't sound very likely, what about a nice job in the local council?' My mum: ever the voice of reason. 'You don't have any experience in fashion.'

She has a point. I didn't study fashion. There was no Central St Martins College or London School of Fashion education. I wasn't obsessed by *Vogue* from the age of three. Mum didn't bequeath me a collection of classic vintage designer pieces to cut my style teeth on. My first and only clear memory of clothes is of a wine-purple velvet party dress with a white lace collar. I hated it. It itched.

But things change. I've changed. Fashion is fun and über-posh – it would impress Side-Parting.

'Yes I do,' I bluster. 'I shared a taxi with Alexander McQueen.'

'You can't put that on your CV. What about applying for a job at a bank? You could send them a photo? You might meet someone nice?'

'Mother, I want a job, not a husband.' I waltz out, imagining Side-Parting opening CVs with photos of pretty girls attached, and pick up the phone.

'Jen! Sorry I missed your calls. I quit my job. How was your trip?' I trill as I stomp toward the jobcentre.

'You quit? Are you insane? Why?' She sounds just the same: unwittingly backing up Mum and simultaneously making me feel like a loon.

'It didn't work out. I've decided I want to change direction. I want to work in fashion.' I like the way it sounds. Glamorous, exciting, interesting.

'You can't just wake up and decide to work in fashion, Ange!'

'Why not?'

'For one thing you have no experience.'

I wish everyone would stop saying that. 'You can't let things like that stand in your way, Jen.'

'Pah! And how exactly are you going to get a job in fashion?' she scoffs.

'I'm at the jobcentre right now. I'll call you later and let you know how I get on.'

Jen and my mum may be right. Annoyingly. It's not as easy to get a job in fashion as I thought. When the recruitment agent offers me a role at Asda, ''cause they sell clothes', I realise she's not going to be able to help.

The Direct Mail department at Harrods gave me a glimpse of a bewitching world where I could use my skills to be part of something creative. I want to work on glittering photo shoots with famous models. I want to be paid to drool over exquisite couture. All I need to do now is work out how.

NOT IN KANSAS
ANY MORE

'The most beautiful make-up for a woman is
passion. But cosmetics are easier to buy.'

YVES SAINT LAURENT

'You look nice, Angela, off anywhere special tonight?' my
manager asks, wiggling the knot of his navy tie.

'What?' I snap. 'Why do I have to be going somewhere? Can't
a girl just make an effort for work!'

His pale eyes look startled.

He knows. He knows! I can feel myself sweating. This calls
for drastic action. In an office full of men there's only one thing
for it: the same excuse that got me out of PE every week for four
years at school. 'Excuse me, my period's started.'

'La, la, la can't hear you!' He jams his fingers in his ears.

I flee to the bathroom. Staring back from the mirror is a
fully-made-up me, in a white shirt, new black pencil trousers
from Topshop and my Gucci shoe-boots. The boots I can't
really walk in but, I imagine, give me the height and gait of a
supermodel. I've been working in media sales for more

months than I care to remember, months of selling ad space to insurance companies, chipping at my Visa bills, trying to sort out my life. The work boys are lovely, but if I spend another Friday in the pub staring at the swirly carpet while they talk about football I will beat my brains out with my own high heels. Perhaps Side-Parting was right? This is as good as it gets. As good as I get.

I·shake the thought. The *Guardian* media jobs section has finally come up trumps. Tonight at 7 p.m. I have an interview with a creative agency that manages photographers, stylists, hairdressers and make-up artists. I *won't* blow it.

I arrive in Marylebone, where the agency is based, early. For an hour I pretend to study the ingredients of products in a local Italian deli.

At 6.50 p.m. I find the agency's office. I press the buzzer on the door and a male voice answers.

'Hello?'

'Er, yes, I'm here for the interview?' This red-brick building looks residential, not like the hub of an international fashion agency. I thought there'd be a louche photographer smoking outside, or some lanky models lurking about drinking martinis.

'Come up to the fourth floor,' says the male voice.

I pass through a hallway where there is post piled on a little table. Everything's addressed to individuals; there are no company names, no company logos. Is this a trap? I've read about men who pretend to be photographers and lure unsuspecting girls to their 'studio'. I hesitate for a second at the lift, then decide if the male voice turns out to be dodgy I'll attack him with my shoe. Note to self: remember to wrench shoe from predator before running (and then get it cleaned).

Inside the lift is a mirror. I have flour on my face – must be from the Italian deli breads I've been fondling. I scrub at it and smudge my mascara across my cheek. Damnit.

The lift pings and says in a helpful tone: 'Fourth floor.'

Damnit! Damnit! I rub at the mascara, making a red mark on my face. I hunt in my bag for a tissue.

'Door closing,' says the helpful lift again.

I jab buttons to try and stop the doors from closing.

'Going up. Doors opening. Doors closing,' says the lift.

The doors shudder and halt half open. The lift makes a whirring sound and then pings.

I freeze. *I've broken the lift! How am I going to get the job, I've broken the lift!* 6.58 p.m. I've no time to worry about it. I remove the stray mascara with the tissue and slither sideways out of the lift.

I reach the agency door. There's no sign, nothing to suggest this is the right place. What's the other side of this door? A dark dungeon? A damp prison? Gingerly I press the bell.

A man with bright pink hair opens the door. He's wearing a bright-green jumper and tight white jeans. 'Welcome to Charlie Monroe Management! See you later.' He minces past me and down the hallway

Hang on, wait! What am I supposed to…?

'Come in,' a female voice calls from inside.

A vaulted ceiling opens in front of me. A statuesque, youthful-looking woman in her sixties, with a chestnut bob and an origami of scarves round her neck, is standing there. 'I'm Charlie Monroe.' She holds out an elegant hand. Her nails are painted deep purple.

I shake it and remember to smile.

'This –,' she sweeps her arm round, '– is my agency.'

It's all exposed brickwork and high arched windows. Everywhere I've worked previously, even the Harrods offices, has been stuffed full of ugly mass-produced furniture and mounds of messy papers. This office is light, ordered, spacious, beautiful. There's lots of white: white desks, white chairs, white computers, white folders. A shock of colour is provided by the magazines piled neatly on the reclaimed-crate coffee table: UK *Vogue*, Japanese *Vogue*, Italian *Vogue*, *iD*, *Dazed*, *The Face*, foreign titles … I want to belong here.

'This is an amazing office!' I gush.

'It's a charming building. There's a photographic studio downstairs and a Hollywood star owns the penthouse for when he's in town.'

Your average workplace then.

There's a sound of quick-moving high heels from a corridor leading off the space. In stampedes a petite woman, messy white hair flying behind her. She's wearing an amazing combination of a Vivienne Westwood kilt and what looks like a bed sheet tied across her body. Clothes are heaped in her arms, hangers dangling from them. Balanced on top is a Roman officer helmet with red plumage.

'I'm running late, the taxi's outside. I'll be back tomorrow to fetch the rest!' She careers toward us.

I'm about to jump clear when she stops. 'Oh hello. You must be here for the interview.' She smiles warmly, her teeth no longer white, not quite yellow. 'I like your heels, Tom Ford for Gucci? Lovely. Lovely.' Then she whips up speed again and bowls out of the office.

Charlie nods at my shoe-boots and looks impressed.

We sit facing each other on the squidgy sofa – Charlie regally, while I squeak on the leather cushions. I try to stop my eyes wandering across the magazine covers.

'You're clearly interested in fashion, Angela. Tell me what you've been doing with yourself.'

I tell her about Harrods, how I discovered and became interested in photo shoots there. At the last minute I leave out the bit about Alexander McQueen in a taxi.

'And what about since then?'

I'm sunk. She must have had countless applicants with oodles of fashion experience and contacts. 'I've been working at a publication company.' With a bit of luck that'll sound like I've worked on a fashion magazine.

'As a sales executive?' She pulls out a copy of my CV.

Of course, she has my CV already. It's all down there in black and white. It's obvious my job has as much to do with fashion as a Trappist monk's.

'Yes.' I smile weakly.

'Do you have to cold-call people?'

It must be morbid curiosity. 'Yes I do.'

'Are you any good at it?' she pushes.

I'm about to lean forwards and stop the interview, like stopping a driving test after you've mown down three pedestrians and scraped the car down the wall of the local kebab shop. I've definitely failed. But she keeps going.

'Working as an agent involves rather a lot of cold-calling. It's your job to sell artists into magazines, ad agencies, clothing companies. Build a relationship with these people, persuade them to meet the artists, view their portfolios, book them. I've had nice girls, like yourself, before and they're too terrified to pick up the phone—'

'I can do that! I can sell! I could sell bum implants to J-Lo!' I clamp my hand over my mouth. *What am I saying?!*

She looks at me a little uncertainly.

I've blown it.

Charlie clears her throat. 'Once we've secured the work for our artists we produce the photo shoots for the photographers and the stylists: optioning and booking hair, make-up, assistants, the studio or location. Booking any equipment that's necessary, sending out call sheets ...'

My cheeks burn. I had a way in to the fashion industry and I've ruined it by making stupid remarks about Jennifer Lopez's arse.

We exchange the usual platitudes. Thank you for your time. We'll be in touch. But I know it's all over. I just want to get out of here.

I trudge down the stairs. There's a familiar diminutive woman pressing the lift call button in reception. Where do I know her from – university, work, Harrods? The last thing I need right now is to play social niceties with someone whose name I've forgotten. Come on brain, think. Where have you seen those cheekbones peeking out from under those shades before? That expensively highlighted hair?

'I think the lift's broken,' she says in a soft Australian accent. *It's Kylie Minogue.*

I blush. Not because she's Kylie, but because she's going to have to walk up the stairs because I broke the lift. My disastrous interview is karma. I've inconvenienced the princess of pop.

THE NEW GIRL

'You can never be too rich or too thin.'

WALLIS SIMPSON

'Oh my God. Oh my God. That was Charlie – I got the job!'

Mum peers over her *Woman's Weekly* at me. 'Thought you messed up the interview?'

'Apparently she was impressed with my confidence in my sales ability.'

'Perhaps she's a J-Lo fan,' she mutters.

My phone starts ringing again. I hope it's not Charlie changing her mind? No, it's Side-Parting's Flatmate. I press accept call. 'I just got a job in fashion!'

'Hello? What?' He clears his throat. 'That's good.' He sounds confused.

'Sorry to scream at you, but I literally just heard. I'm really excited!' I wonder why he's calling? He sends me the odd email and text letting me know how he's getting on at Oxford. Oh his master's! 'God you've finished your master's, haven't you? Congratulations!'

'Well, I don't know if I've passed yet, my exams were last week. I'm waiting for the results.' He sounds nervous.

Whoops.

He clears his throat again. 'Erm, I was ringing to ask you a favour, actually.'

My heart misses a beat. Irrationally I think this is going to be something to do with Side-Parting. 'OK,' I say hesitantly.

'Do you remember I did an internship at that economics consultancy?'

Not really. 'Yes.'

'Well they've invited me to their summer ball, and I don't really know anyone in London and I wondered if you'd come with me. As a friend?'

An evening with a load of economists sounds pretty dire. But this could be my opportunity to send Side-Parting a message about how well I'm doing. If I look amazing and talk about my glamorous new job in fashion, it's bound to get back to him. 'Of course, I'd be delighted.'

'Fantastic! It's black tie, I hope that's OK?'

All the better to show off the fashion fabulous me. 'No problem.'

'It should be fun, nice food, free drinks, it's in a posh hotel. You'd be doing me a big favour, I'm hoping they'll hire me.'

I write down the date; it's in just over a month. Perfect, I will have started work at Charlie's agency by then, I can tell him all the details.

'Who was that?' Mum doesn't look up from her magazine.

'Side-Parting's Flatmate, he wants me to go to some black-tie thing with him.'

'Another one impressed with your sales ability no doubt,' she says as I head upstairs to start trying on potential outfits.

***

Jen and I are in Topshop looking for the ideal fashion dynamo/office junior look. I had to promise to look at all 6,000 of her travelling pictures to get her in here.

'What exactly does an office junior in a creative agency do?' Jen trails behind, her red hair hidden under a cap.

'What about this?' I hold up an orange shirt.

Jen shrugs and leans against a mannequin. She's wearing her jeans and trainers, which she's accessorised with a look of boredom.

'Too corporate.' I put it back on the rail. Perhaps I could mould a dress out of *Vogue* covers. 'The agency represents freelance photographers, stylists, hairdressers and make-up artists. I think we help get them work. Charlie mentioned organising photo shoots, which will be amazing.'

'Trust you to get a job working with a load of fancy fashion types.'

'I read up on the industry before my interview ...'

'In case there was a pop quiz?' Jen holds a pair of trousers against her legs. The flares finish at her knees.

'It's good to be prepared. Did you know Coco Chanel is a feminist icon?'

'How does that work?' Jen looks at her watch. Again.

'She was a pioneering businesswoman. She liberated women from the constraints of corsets with her masculine-inspired tailoring. She was instrumental in society accepting women wearing trousers and cutting their hair short.'

'Remind me to thank her for the trousers.'

'She's a goddess. Oh. My. Coco! Look at this bag?' Black cord. Flower lining. It's perfect for my first day.

'Oh my Coco?'

'She's my god.'

Jen rolls her eyes. 'I need a drink.'

***

I can already tell you the best thing about working in fashion: the 10 a.m. start time. Bliss. I'd fantasised about a long luxurious lie-in, but in reality I used the extra hour to fiddle with my hair. I applied nine different products, massaged the roots and, like the magazines instruct you, hung my head upside down when blow-drying. I check the mirror in the office lift; my hair has the volume, vibrancy and lustre of a cotton thread placed over a boiled egg. Stupid hair.

My outfit's more successful. Jeans, a white T-shirt, Jaeger suit jacket and Gucci heels. Reassuringly expensive (no one need know I've reheeled these shoes twice and the T-shirt's from Sainsbury's). It's classic chic.

At the office door I pause. This is a moment to savour: the beginning of my fashion career.

The door flies open. 'Angela!' Charlie, in head-to-toe black, with more scarves wound round her neck, appears. 'I thought you were a courier.'

Not based on my appearance I hope.

'Come in, meet the team,' she ushers.

I click in.

'This is Pandora, the other junior.'

A cocktail stick wearing a white Chloé peasant dress and vintage cowboy boots steps forward. It holds out a splinter of an arm to shake. Pandora has long, sumptuous full hair, the colour of a polished conker. It billows seductively, as if a wind fan is permanently placed in front of her.

'Your hair is incredible,' I stutter.

'My mother is Indian royalty, and my father is Imperial Persian-Anglo,' Pandora peers down her beautiful nose at me.

Okay. My mother is from the Royal Borough of Hertfordshire, and my father is from the distinguished Elstree Massive.

'I'm an old hand. I've been here for over a year, so I'll get you up to speed.' Her diction is immaculate. She's like a posh Melanie Sykes.

Charlie nods, as if everything's under control. 'Right, I'm retiring upstairs to do some accounts. Angela, Pandora will show you what to do.'

I follow Pandora toward the desks, staring at her hair like a dog stares at sausages.

'You can leave your, er, bag here.' Pandora glances at what I'd thought was my fantastic Topshop find, then strokes her own Marc Jacobs tan handbag that hangs like a reclining sultan on a hammock from the coat pegs.

Note to self: start saving for a designer handbag.

'Who did you work for before?' asks Pandora.

I decide against mentioning my foray into advertising sales. 'I worked at Harrods.'

Pandora blinks with disinterested almond-shaped eyes. 'I worked with Alexandra at *Vogue*.'

'Wow, *Vogue*! That must have been incredible! What was it like?' I squeal.

Pandora stares at me. Blinking.

Should I repeat the question?

She keeps staring.

Maybe she's having some kind of fit?

'Mmmm,' she finally says, and turns away.

My stomach tightens. I feel uncannily similar to when Side-Parting dumped me: I'm not good enough. I need to win her over, impress her.

Pandora pushes on. 'I'm based in Chelsea, where do you live?'

Bugger. 'Erm, with my parents. In Hertfordshire.'

'Oh, I am sorry,' she says in an overly sympathetic voice, as if I've just told her my grandmother's died. Does she think I live in some workhouse squalor, where my parents and I all sleep in a broom cupboard?

I casually stick my shoes forward, as if flaunting a pair of Guccis at her will redress the situation.

'Girls, this is the new girl, Angela. Angela, this is Georgina and Ceci.' Pandora indicates each girl in turn.

Georgina steps forward. A wrap-dress-wearing waif with a porcelain complexion and painted red lips, she fixes me with a cool stare. 'Nice to meet you, darling,' she says, brusquely, as if I'm a terrible inconvenience.

'Nice to meet you too, darling,' winks Ceci, a leggy brunette. Her tan looks like she's picked it up from a yacht. Her jeans look like they're from Selfridges. Her smile approaches genuine warmth.

Darling? Darling. Got it. 'Pleasure, darling,' I reply.

I feel Pandora bristle next to me.

I shake Georgina and Ceci's hands, being careful not to be too firm in case I accidentally snap bits off them.

My weight's never bothered me, but standing with these tiny twiggy girls I'm conscious of my soft bits. I've dropped to a size eight – must be sweating it off on the tube – but my boobs and my bum have grown this morning. They're now so large I resemble a cartoonish caricature of a woman. I *am* the elephant in the middle of the room no one is talking about. These girls must be genetically thin.

Bad points so far: everyone in this office appears to be the shrunken offspring of supermodels with trust funds. Good points: if the prolific use of 'darling' is an indication of wider industry behaviour, my inability to remember names will never be a problem again.

Georgina and Ceci take their seats and tap on their Macs. I try to keep up with Pandora as she canters across the office.

'The artist portfolio books are kept here.' She points at white custom-made pigeonholes, as I breathlessly arrive at her side.

She pulls a large black leather-bound book out and opens it on the white table.

The portfolio is like a big photo album, with four magazine pages to each double-page spread.

'Today we're updating the tear sheets,' Pandora says stroking the book.

Tear sheets – what the hell are they?

Pandora drops a pile of magazines onto the table and looks at me expectantly.

There's nothing else for it. 'Sorry, but I don't understand what you want me to do.'

She stares at me like I'm a child who's asked for help using the toilet. Then audibly sighs, 'When a photographer, or make-up artist, or whoever works on a fashion story they are credited in the magazine. See here?'

She holds up a copy of *Vogue* and points, with a blood-red fingernail, to a small list of names at the bottom of a fashion page.

I nod.

'We cut their story out, neatly, and put it in the artist's portfolio. It's how we showcase their work. It's called tear-sheeting.'

'Thank you. I appreciate your help.' I smile.

'You shouldn't need it. This is basic.'

I hide my burning cheeks behind my hair as I get on with it.

I tear-sheet all day. I'm being paid to flick through magazines and cut out and arrange fashion pictures like a stylish *Blue Peter* project. If this is what it takes to make it in fashion, it's going to be a chic walk in the park. I ignore the uneasy feeling I have in my stomach about Pandora.

***

Charlie is just leaving as I arrive at the office for my second day.

'Morning, Angela, I'm off to a meeting with the art director for the ad campaign we're shooting Tuesday. They want to drop twenty-five tonnes of sand in the middle of the City to create an urban beach. I might be gone all day.'

I nod as if I understand the complexities of such a situation. *Jesus, where would you get twenty-five tonnes of sand from?*

'Keep going with the tear-sheeting and when I've got a moment I'll train you up on the production side.'

'Fantastic!' Urban beach here I come!

She's most of the way down the hall now, elegantly balancing the pile of coffee table books and magazines she's carrying. 'One of our New York fashion editors is in town. She's popping by this afternoon so you can introduce yourself.'

Ping. The lift doors close and she's gone with a rattle of bracelets.

I can't wait to meet a real fashion editor. Maybe she'll give me some tips on how to be stylish!

The day passes as I tear-sheet with Pandora and eavesdrop on Ceci and Georgina on the phone:

'I need a first class Eurostar to Paris. Now.'

'The shoot's with Madonna, for US *Vogue*.'

'We're looking for a young Naomi Campbell.'

I'm itching to get on the phones. *This is Angela, junior at Charlie Monroe Management. It's a fashion emergency, I NEED an option on Cindy Crawford. Yesterday.*

Around 3 p.m. the doorbell buzzes. The New York fashion editor's here! Pandora beats me to the intercom, so I wait by the portfolio pigeonholes to observe her arrival.

If I closed my eyes and imagined an archetypal New York woman, it would be this editor. Tall with honey-coloured skin and honey-coloured hair, Ms NY could be an extra from

Sex and the City. Her tight trousers and shirt are a shade of black you can't find on the high street, definitely designer. She looks just the type to give her card to VIPs at parties.

'Girls, you're all looking lovely,' she says with a professional smile. I can almost hear her repeating her mantra in her head: glittering white teeth, maintain eye contact, make them feel special.

We all titter.

She doesn't notice she's never met me before. We're all the office 'girls'. Interchangeable. Staff.

'This is Saffy, my London-based assistant.' Ms NY waves her hand at a woman behind her I hadn't even noticed.

Saffy's about the same age as Ms NY, but not as well maintained. Pale skin, long dark hair pulled into a rough ponytail, she's also wearing head-to-toe black, definitely not designer. Saffy holds a large white cardboard box.

Ms NY shoos her around like a small child. 'Put it down here. It's Saffy's birthday, girls, so I've bought her a cake!'

'How fabulous,' coos Georgina.

Ms NY lifts the lid of the box with a theatrical flourish.

Inside is the most sumptuous cake I've ever seen. Two feet long, a huge glistening white rectangle decorated with piles of frosted fruits. Saffy's name is piped in the centre. It must have cost a fortune. What a lovely thing to do for her assistant.

'Angela, don't just stand there gawping, go and fetch some plates and a knife,' Georgina says under her breath.

'Right, yes. Sorry.' Embarrassed by my homemade sandwiches, I've eaten lunch in the park the last few days so I haven't really been in the stainless steel kitchen. I fling cupboards open. One is full of herbal teas stacked in tonal colour order. Another is filled with wine glasses in regimented rows. One turns out to be the fridge, blimey, there's twenty bottles of champagne in here. A lone stick of celery lounges on a shelf.

I find Conran white plates, which match the Conran white everything else in this office. I pull a knife from a drawer of corkscrews.

'... Happy Birthday to yooou,' the others finish singing, and clap.

Ms NY cuts everyone a big slice and I pass them round. My fingers sink into the thick icing as I lift the cake to my mouth, close my eyes and savour the sweet goodness. Velvety chocolate sponge and sweet vanilla frosting dance across my tongue. It's the cake of dreams, the best I've ever tasted, I want to dive into the box and eat it all. I'm *so* ordering one for my birthday.

I open my eyes to see Ms NY, Saffy, Georgina, Ceci and Pandora staring at me in horror.

Is there icing on my nose?

'We don't actually *eat* the cake.' Georgina sounds disgusted.

'No one *eats* the cake,' adds Pandora.

'It's calorie kamikaze!' Ceci turns a funny shade of green.

'You'd need to run a marathon just to burn off a strawberry,' Ms NY frowns.

'Look,' Saffy says in a reassuring voice, 'you can just smell the cake.'

You what?

'That way you get all of the benefit and none of the calories,' she smiles.

All five of them close their eyes, raise their plates up to their noses and sniff.

A bit of icing drips from my finger and splats on the floor. *They are sniffing the cake. They are cake-sniffers.*

'See, don't you feel better now?' Ms NY shows me her glittering teeth as she takes my plate from my hand.

Wait – don't!

She drops the cake into the bin.

Oh my Coco.

All the girls step forwards to do the same. It's a sombre religious ceremony where the world's best cake is sacrificed to the rubbish-bin god. Georgina picks up the box containing the remaining cake and drops it into the bin as well.

I feel like someone's stabbed me in the stomach with a spoon. What kind of hell is this – where cake-sniffers smell food and throw it away rather than eat it?!

I fight the urge to scoop the box of beautiful cake from the bin and run screaming from the building. I fight the urge to cry.

Forget genetics, my new colleagues are skinny because they sniff food rather than ingest it. I surreptitiously lick the icing off my fingertips and ponder the sanity of an industry populated by cake-sniffers. Or rather, the sanity of working in an industry populated by cake-sniffers. Have I made a terrible mistake?

FINDING MY FASHION FEET

> 'What you wear is how you present yourself to the world, especially today, when human contacts are so quick. Fashion is instant language.'
>
> MIUCCIA PRADA

There's only so many ways you can work a Jaeger suit and two pairs of Guccis. My new colleagues have stepped from the pages of *Vogue*. I need to catch up.

We'll ignore my failed experiment with culottes and a corset shirt, which I thought channelled Jean Paul Gaultier, but actually made me resemble a drunken pirate dressed for a hen do. Instead, let's appreciate the intensive magazine research, charity-store sifting, eBay scrolling and cutting up of my existing wardrobe. To paraphrase *the* professor of makeovers, Henry Higgins, 'by Giorgio Armani I think she's got it!' A frothy white lace 1950s underskirt, an off-cream shirt and a bright scarf knotted into a necklace.

I flounce into the office.

'You're a vision of loveliness,' squeals Pandora. Then looks quite put out about it.

'Thank you, darling.' Warm smile.

This outfit's so good the people I'm cold-calling will be able to *feel* it through the phone. 'Good morning, can you put me through to the fashion editor please?' 'Putting you through to Tilly Kensington-Bolly.' The receptionist sounds robotic.

Where are all the Janes and Claires? Fashionistas' names sound either so posh you suspect they were christened at Westminster Abbey, or so crazy their mother must have pushed them out between hash hits in Goa. I talk to people called Kitty, Tallulah and Blue (no, really). The three girls on one mag's picture desk are Milly, Muffy and Daisy. Muffy? She could only work in fashion. *Meet my financial advisor, Muffy.* Doesn't work.

Pandora, who likes to demonstrate she knows everything about the fashion industry, explains it to me over an iced skinny decaf soy Frappuccino, no cream, which tastes suspiciously like a £4 cup of brown water. 'Your name needs to be memorable, it's your own personal brand.'

'Mmm.' I stir my brown water.

'Lots of people change or alter their name to make it suitable for the industry.'

'Like when Eleanor Nancy Gow became Elle Macpherson?' I occasionally like to show I do know something about fashion.

'Exactly. It's rife in the model agencies.' Every time Pandora says 'model' she flicks her hair like a nervous twitch. 'If there's already an Anaïs on the books, then any new girl joining called Anaïs will be rechristened.'

'Surely there can't be more than one six-foot skinny girl called Anaïs in London anyway?'

Pandora rolls her eyes.

'It must be confusing, imagine being called Angela all your life and then suddenly being told to answer to Mimi?'

'Ohhh, Mimi, I like that. You should use it!' Pandora enthuses.

'I like my name!' I draw the line at changing my name. And sniffing cake.

'Keep it if you must.' She shrugs, disappointedly.

Charlie's perfectly blow-dried bob appears from the corridor. She spends a lot of time in her office. I imagine her snoozing with cucumber slices on her eyes. 'I'll sit in on the model casting this afternoon girls.'

'It's only cause you're new, I could defo handle this on my own,' grumbles Pandora.

I've been calling real-live model agencies for Ms NY's beauty story. Giving them the brief, like a shopping list, over the phone: long blonde hair, great skin and a good body (there will be a bikini shot). The girls are to come to the agency at five o'clock, and we'll choose ten for Ms NY to pick from.

At 3 p.m. the door buzzes. Models are arriving early.

'Go away, come back at five,' Charlie trills into the intercom. *It's pouring with rain outside!*

Pandora shrugs at my appalled expression. 'This is a business. We're busy, they're just a commodity.'

I try to concentrate on my cold-calling, but keep picturing models huddling under bus shelters like drowned leggy kittens.

At 5 p.m. a mob of Amazonian girls pours into the office. They're all legs and hardcore heels, walking like Thunderbird puppets. They look fourteen. They sound fourteen. High-pitched screams, high-speed chatter and mobile phone ringtones drown everything else out. It's a teenage party, but with ridiculously expensive clothes instead of H&M.

'Shush! Shush!' Charlie moves between them, like a dog herding sheep.

'Where's the toilet?' a dark-fringed girl with a heavy Eastern European accent asks.

'It's out of order,' replies Charlie.

I'm about to say no, it's working fine, when Pandora jabs me.

'She doesn't like them using the bathroom, she's caught too many of them doing coke in there,' she hisses.

They look fourteen years old.

'Shush! Time to begin, there'll be a bikini shot ...' Charlie's voice silences them.

The models start taking their clothes off.

I'm sitting on a sofa looking at a group of prepubescent girls in their bras and pants. Pandora and Charlie don't bat an eyelid. Uncomfortable, I busy myself doodling rose-covered cottages on my notepad.

The first girl hands me her book. According to her card her name is Daphne, she's 5'10.5", her bust is 33.5" B, waist is 24", dress size UK 8, her hips are 35", she wears a size 7 shoe and has dark-blonde hair and green eyes.

She's not how I expected a model to look. She has an amazing figure and legs as tall as I am, but she's not traditionally pretty; with her wide forehead and tiny chin she looks otherworldly. I open her book and my eyes are opened.

Daphne's strong features come alive on the page. The light illuminates her cheekbones, her eyes shine like emeralds, she's an angel in *iD*. Mesmerising. There's no point looking at any of the others, this is the girl we should use.

'She's got spots,' says Charlie.

Pandora scrawls 'BAD SKIN' across the face of Daphne on her card and drops it into the reject pile. 'Next!'

Girl after girl steps forward. So many. When I close my eyes tonight I shall still see them advancing, like a gorgeous army of underwear-clad fourteen-year-olds. The objections keep coming:

'Her hair's too dark.'

'Fat hips.'

'Weird nose.'

After dismissing over fifty girls with unidentifiable flaws, I'm amazed we've found ten to show Ms NY.

I'm exhausted, almost tearful. The models smile, thank us for our time and jabber away as they leave. Strangers highlighting your imperfections while you stand in your underwear is just part of the job.

'Modelling's a bit brutal isn't it?' I say to Pandora the next day as she's tucking into her lunch of chopped raw carrot and black pepper. (The black pepper tricks the brain into thinking it's eating a dish full of flavour, apparently.)

'Modelling is fabulous. If I were taller I'd have joined an agency. You just have to be a *good* model.'

Vain at all, darling? 'A "good" model?' I shovel a forkful of baked potato and cheese into my mouth.

Pandora tells me about one of the 'original models' from the sixties who refuses to start work before 11 a.m.

'Doesn't that piss off the rest of the team having to wait around for her?'

'On the contrary, everyone loves working with her. They get a lie-in.'

Jen would not believe this! Guiltily, I realise I haven't called her for ages. I'm just so knackered by the time I get home.

There's no time to debate the morality of modelling further as the agency door bursts open. In walks a guy in his mid-thirties who's dressed as if he's in his mid-teens: baggy jeans, baseball cap perched at an artificial angle and hair that looks like it hasn't seen a brush since the 1980s.

'Awight darlin',' he sneers at Pandora, planting a wet smack on her cheek when she goes in for an air kiss.

'Alfie, you're here early!' She blushes all the way to her eyelash extensions.

'Alfie, how are you, darling?' Charlie sweeps over to greet him.

Alfie embraces her in an awkward hug. 'Good guv, good. How's it been?'

Alfie is one of our top photographers. A London-boy-done-good, he's conquered New York and is now networking his way round the world. He comes back to London for those jobs he considers to be impressive enough (and to see his mum).

He speaks with an exaggerated cockney accent I can only imagine warms the cockles of American hearts in the way Dick Van Dyke's did in *Mary Poppins*. He sounds daft to me. A man in his mid-thirties shouldn't wear his trousers halfway down his bottom. *I can see his Calvin's!*

Alfie's in town to shoot Bling-Galore, a very European designer of very expensive clothes, for *Harper's Bazaar*.

'I could do with a spare pair of hands tomorrow, guv,' he says to Charlie.

I'd bet a monkey under all that mockney and stubble is an Old Etonian.

'Angela can go along and be your gofer for the day.' Charlie waves her manicured hand.

Pandora shoots me a dirty look.

'Wicked. Go for this, go for that, eh luv?' Alfie winks and nudges me.

I grin. This couldn't have happened at a better time; I'm going to that economics company ball thing with Side-Parting's Flatmate in three days' time. I can tell him I've been hobnobbing with Bling-Galore. Side-Parting can't fail to be impressed by that! This is so Robin Hood, er, I mean good.

***

What do you wear to meet a famous designer? My recent eBay trawl didn't turn up anything from Bling-Galore's label. I should wear something that demonstrates my fashion nous, but is still reasonably practical. I am going to be working, after all. My first fashion photo shoot! Seriously overexcited!

I opt for gold silk cargo pants tucked into a spiked-heel ankle boot I can run in, if necessary. I finish the look with a cotton T-shirt and lots of gold jewellery. Alfie's proto-gangsta style is rubbing off on me.

I arrive at the studio to find EVERYONE is wearing jeans and Converse trainers. Bugger.

The industrial-sized white-painted brick studio is packed. Sat on the B&B Italia corner sofa are the art director from *Harper's Bazaar* and Bling-Galore's PR. Alfie's two assistants, the stylist and her assistant, the hairdresser, the make-up artist and various other hangers-on I can't quite place are industriously moving about the room. Bling-Galore is having his hair done in the make-up area. Public Enemy's being played on the stereo. Lights are positioned in front of the colorama, a huge roll of white paper background. There are occasional flashes from test shots. Everyone's on their mobile, there's a woman in the corner on two.

'Thank God you're here, luv!' Alfie has a look of panic on his face. 'I'm havin' a right nightmare.'

I can see from his eyes something's gone terribly wrong, the shoot's hanging from a thread over a pit of fashion doom and disaster. I adopt a firm but reassuring look. Whatever it is he can count on me to fix it.

'I'm gagging for a coffee, but this stuff's Pony and Trap. Can you go to Starbucks?'

That's it? That's your huge crisis, that someone's served you a dodgy cappuccino? I'm a glorified waitress.

By the time I've delivered all the coffees things have settled on set. The team have moved to the edge of the studio, the focus is on Bling-Galore, who is sat posing in front of the colorama.

'I loved your last collection, totally fucking blew my mind,' says Alfie.

'Yes,' says Bling-Galore. His face doesn't move or wrinkle when he talks.

'I thought it would be wicked if we did some shots with you standing, leaning on the back of the chair!' Alfie enthuses.

'No.' Only his eyes move.

I clutch my hot chocolate like a life raft at the back. It's good to keep my hands busy. Everyone else has a role while I just wait for something to go wrong, or for someone to want another coffee. I've been waiting a couple of hours now. My hot chocolate's grown cold. This is the coalface of the fashion industry? I stifle a yawn.

To my right is a matronly lady in a navy blue shirt tucked into her jeans and clean white plimsolls. She looks incongruous among the cool kids, like a tea lady who's wandered in to have a look at the photo shoot. Is she Alfie's mother, I wonder?

'Hello, I'm Angela, I work for Alfie's agent. Nice to meet you.' I shake her hand.

'Nice to meet you too, Angela, I'm Pamela.' Pamela tells me she works for Bling-Galore. She offers no further information. We make polite small talk about the weather and how nice everyone looks. Thumping drum and bass plays in the background.

'Hey, luv, can you chase lunch? We're all starving!' Alfie calls.

I find the studio assistant and persuade them to bring lunch forward an hour. *It's vital for the shoot.*

'Saw you chatting to Pamela, luv.' Alfie takes an Ikea plate from me. 'She's wicked, isn't she?'

'Yes, very nice.'

'She tell you what she does?'

'No, not really.'

'She's 'is private nurse.' He nods toward Bling-Galore. He piles one of the many catering salads on his plate.

'Is he sick?' I whisper. Is fashion about to lose one of its greats to a terrible illness?

'No, ha! He's just done so much Bob Marley up his nose it don't work any more. Pamela puts it up his bum for him.'

In slow motion the words connect together in my head. Bob Marley. Charlie. Cocaine. Pamela, the nice matronly Pamela, administers cocaine up the bottom of Bling-Galore.

What does it say on Pamela's CV?!

It adds a whole new dimension to the phrases; blowing smoke up the boss's ass, brown-nosing, arse-licking. Oh good God, I shook Pamela's hand. I run to the toilets to wash my hands. Repeatedly. I'm not hungry any more. No wonder everyone in fashion air-kisses.

REALITY BITES

'I don't do fashion, I *am* fashion.'

COCO CHANEL

Back in the office I'm not sure I'm interested in attending a photo shoot again. I spent yesterday fetching coffee, arranging food and shaking hands with someone who inserts coke up their boss's bum for a living. It feels safer here, cleaner.

Georgina flies into the office in such a heightened state of excitement I can only assume there's been a one-penny sale at Marc Jacobs.

'She's coming up! She's coming up!'

'Oh my goodness!' Charlie jumps up.

Is she actually flapping her arms?

Pandora dashes around in a high-heeled haze straightening magazines, shoving portfolios in cupboards and covering my Topshop handbag with her Celine jacket.

Ceci stands, then sits, then stands again. She looks like she might cry trying to decide which to do.

Clearly I'm missing something.

'She won't come up, she *never* comes up,' my boss is repeating to herself like a karmic mantra, except she doesn't seem very calm.

There's a noise coming from outside. It sounds like ... scratching and barking? They all freeze.

The door flings open and the handle smashes a dent into the smooth wall. A six-foot-tall woman with ebony hair and glowing jade eyes stands there. Her sharp elegant features are set in a scowl. Lethal black python stilettos snake up into spray-on black trousers, which spread like liquid into her sculpted black top. Hanging off her shoulders is a white fur. Scampering at her feet is a dog. Well, I think it's a dog, it looks like someone microwaved a powder puff and it exploded. Time stops. I think there's some thunder and lightening. She looks just like ...

'Why have I been forced to come to this hellhole in person?' she hisses.

... just like ....

'I demand this be sorted immediately.'

... just like Vampira!

'I *will* have a taxi.' She's threateningly calm. 'Right. Now.' Vampira turns on her snake heels, leaving a visible groove in the floor, flicks her fur over her shoulder and sashays off.

The dog sits in the open doorway staring at us.

We stare back.

'Come!' screams Vampira.

It yelps and runs in the direction of the lift.

A shiver runs down my spine. 'Who the hell was *that*?'

'Oh my God, isn't she amazing!' Pandora looks like she might swoon into a nearby pile of tear sheets.

'Don't you mean insane?' I gasp.

'Don't say that,' hisses Ceci tugging at her hair nervously. '*She* might hear you.'

'She's amazing,' burbles Pandora. 'Iconic. The best photographer in the world. I've followed her career for ever. She's worked with everyone who's anyone: famous designers, supermodels, *the* best magazines. I can't believe I'm getting to work with her. She's the reason I came to work for Charlie's agency.'

Georgina pats her hand like she's in a Regency drama comforting a sister whose beloved has just emerged dripping wet from a lake.

She does sound impressive, but she's clearly a nightmare in snake heels. I turn to Charlie for confirmation this she-devil is not really one of our artists.

'She *never* comes up,' she murmurs. She looks like she's seen a very stylish ghost.

'Amazing,' gushes Georgina. 'We're so lucky to represent her.'

Lucky?

Georgina sounds like a televangelist minister asking for donations. 'She earns more than all our other photographers put together, and the prestige! She elevates the agency, she raises us up, she's our star. Amazing.'

I won't be surprised if she starts singing Hallelujah any second now. Who's she trying to convince: me or herself? 'What does she want anyway? Did anyone understand that cryptic rubbish about a taxi?'

'Oh my God. The taxi!' Charlie snaps out of her trance. 'The shoot! We'll have to try again. I know he never allows taxis, it's a privilege to work for the magazine, but he *has* to understand she doesn't do public transport.'

What?? Did anyone understand a word of that?

They start manically running around, like a bunch of headless free-range, rare-breed chickens in high heels.

Gradually I deduce Vampira's shooting for a celebrity publisher's favourite magazine tomorrow. This is a great honour.

Something you don't get paid for. There's no budget for taxis. Most fashionistas would walk in bare feet over broken mirrors to reach this shoot. Vampira, who I learn is very wealthy from her successful advertising campaigns, insists the publisher pay for a taxi to take her to the studio. This is a battle of wills over a twenty-quid cab fare.

'Right, who wants to help?' Charlie speaks with false jollity.

No way, I'm not going anywhere near this madwoman. Let Pandora do it.

Pandora falls on her like a starving dog on a steak. 'Me, me! It's my life's dream to work with her!'

'Great, Pandora can liaise with her assistant, sweet talk the taxis and sort out the call sheet.'

Pandora looks like she will weep with joy.

'Angela, you can go on the shoot tomorrow and help out.'

'What?' Pandora and I cry in unison.

Did I just hit the same high pitch as Pandora?

'Georgina and Ceci are busy working on other productions,' she says missing the point. 'Jump to it, we've got lots of work to do!' She ignores my panicked breathing.

I can't work with Vampira, she's terrifying. *Did you not see the way she screamed at that dog?* I'm sweating just thinking about it. I glance at Pandora, who's cradling the penknife we use for tear-sheeting and has a deranged look in her eye. That's all I need – she's clearly obsessed with Vampira. She has that crazy-ass stalker vibe down. 'I'm sure Pandora, who has way more experience than me, would much rather go on set tomorrow ...' I plead.

'Enough. We don't have time to talk. She's our most important artist and I want this sorted. Get on the phone and get it done.'

I sit down with a bump. It seems formidable and experienced agents can be terrorised by powerful egomaniac artists.

Egomaniac artists like the one I'm going to spend tomorrow with.

I take a deep breath. Tomorrow night is Side-Parting's Flatmate's work thing. How am I going to transform into a black-tie fabulous fashionista after a day with Vampira?

***

I don't sleep properly all night. When I finally drift off I have nightmares about Vampira's white fur coming to life and biting my neck. I'm so nervous I can't stomach breakfast. This is why everyone in fashion's thin: fear.

After my overdressed appearance at Alfie's photo shoot I'm taking no chances. I'm wearing jeans and a pair of retro Adidas trainers (they used to belong to my brother when he was sixteen, worn once before his feet grew overnight to the size of small fishing boats). I'm carrying in a holdall my black-tie outfit and make-up for tonight. I've pinned my damp hair into a twisted bun, which will hopefully transform into soft waves later.

I'm so worried I forget to be excited about going to the famous magazine's studio. I'm here early and the only people around are suited businessmen hurrying toward the City. I take a few deep breaths and cross my fingers for luck.

Inside another large white room EVERYONE is in full-on heels and high-end outfits. One girl's wearing a lace bodysuit. Bugger. I stash my holdall out the way by the kitchenette.

I relax a little when I see the famous publisher. Greying hair and a black T-shirt and jeans. Reassuringly casual.

A compromise has been reached to stop Vampira launching nuclear shells from her handbag: the magazine's paid for one taxi to the studio. She's not here yet, but I think I spy her assistant. Yesterday, after she finally finished crying about not being allowed to work with Vampira on set, Pandora explained the über-photographer only hires assistants who could pass as models.

'She is a sensitive aesthete who likes to be surrounded by beautiful people,' she sniffed looking me up and down and breaking into a fresh bout of hysteria.

She's going to love my second-hand trainers.

The girl I've identified has long wavy dark hair and the sort of well-bred face that says Daddy's a landowner and Mummy's a show pony. Everything about her is immaculate: her make-up, her skin, her tanned lithe limbs and her Missoni wrap dress. All flawless, apart from her nails, which are chewed down. It's this tiny display of stress that makes me certain she's Vampira's assistant.

'Hi, I'm Angela, I'm from the agency,' I say.

'Hey, I'm Bonnie. Thanks so much for today – great to have an extra pair of hands. Awesome vintage trainers. Wish I'd worn mine, my feet are killing me!'

I like Bonnie.

There's a commotion at the entrance and Vampira appears. Despite entering a room full of models and fashion superstars, she towers a good foot over everyone else. The team part to let her through and she stoops to air-kiss the publisher.

'Darling, so wonderful to see you,' she says.

'Always a pleasure,' he concurs.

As they walk away from each other I see them both grimace.

Vampira's heading straight toward me and I start to sweat. I wish I'd worn different clothes. I wish my hair, just for once, would do what's promised on the shampoo bottle. Mostly I wish I wasn't here.

'You, take Binky.' She shoves the squirming fur ball into my arms.

Now's not the moment to mention my dog allergy.

She snaps her fingers for Bonnie to fetch her a chair and places it immediately behind the camera. She sits and directs the shoot.

'Bonnie, move the model's arm so it is more pronounced. Don't slouch, girl!'

The secondary assistants run round adjusting lights. One lad with strawberry-blond hair and mercifully strong-looking arms is assigned the task of human stand and has to hold the heavy metal light above his head.

'Don't shake; you'll ruin the shot,' Vampira barks at him.

Binky wriggles free from my arms and makes a break for the door. Vampira will skin me and turn me into a muff if he escapes. I race after him and pull the door closed just as he gets his nose to it.

He looks up at me, with sad soulful eyes.

'I'm sorry, Binky.' I feel like an idiot. 'Let's be friends.' I reach down and stroke his fluffy little head.

Binky growls and nips my hand.

The little bugger made me bleed!

Binky leaps forward and attaches himself to the ankle of my jeans. He's not much bigger than a hamster, but he's surprisingly strong.

I wrench my jeans free. 'You made a hole, you little ... good doggy, what a good doggy.' The make-up artist walks past giving me a strange look.

Binky growls and goes for the other side.

Bonnie runs over while Vampira's showing the model how to pose on all fours on the floor, literally.

'Here, he likes these.' She thrusts a bag of doggy chocolate drops into my hand. 'I always carry some. Here's his lead, try and get him outside so he can wee. Good luck.'

Don't leave me! I turn to see Binky humping a Fendi clutch on the floor.

Occasionally people try and pet Binky, but no one talks to me. One of the advantages of being a non-important person on set is you get to observe. I'm watching the work of a world-famous photographer, an industry-leading publisher and a well-known model. Not many people get to do that – even if the price is babysitting the devil dog from hell. I'm having a fantastic time. I can't wait to tell Side-Parting's Flatmate about Binky!

Binky makes a strange gurgling noise and goes rigid, one front paw held in the air.

Oh my Coco, what's wrong with him?

He exhales and a huge poo squeezes out his bum like toothpaste.

You have got to be kidding me.

Can dogs smile? Because I swear Binky's smirking at me. Nobody's noticed yet. We're near the make-up and hair area. I grab a huge wedge of the make-up artists' baby wipes. Closing my eyes is appealing but too risky. Urgh – still warm.

I'm tempted to dump Binky in the bin outside along with his 'present'.

I wash my hands, while he shreds every paper towel in the bathroom.

Back in the studio the lighting's being packed up and the make-up artist is clearing away her kit (peering quizzically at her diminished stack of baby wipes). My phone rings.

'Angela, it's Charlie.'

'Charlie! Great day, fabulous shoot, they haven't killed each other.' I eye my holdall; I'll get changed in the bathroom.

'There's a problem.'

I grip Binky's lead tight. 'What?'

'She won't leave until they pay for another taxi.'

Vampira is still sat behind the camera on her chair. The assistants are packing everything up around her. Her head is high and her arms are crossed.

I drag Binky into a corner so I can't be overheard. 'But they agreed the mag would pay for her taxi here, she would pay for her own car home?'

'She's changed her mind. She's insisting they pay for her taxi home too.'

'What do we do?' *Please don't make me to talk to her.*

'I'll speak to the publisher's agent and negotiate. Stay there till we get it sorted.'

But I've got to go. I've got to get ready!

Time ticks by. Occasionally the publisher talks to his agent on his phone, giving his opinion in a hushed tone. Vampira refuses to answer her mobile. When Charlie has news from the publisher's agent she calls Bonnie, who holds her phone against Vampira's ear so she can speak to Charlie. Neither the publisher nor Vampira discuss the situation together. They are less than two metres apart.

I turn my mobile over in my hand. It's been over an hour since the shoot finished. I was supposed to meet Side-Parting's Flatmate at 6.30 p.m. That was forty minutes ago. Vampira's still sat on her chair in the middle of the studio.

I send a text:

So sorry, still stuck at
work will get there
ASAP.

I imagine Side-Parting's Flatmate cursing me for being late, for mucking up his chances with the firm he wants a job with. What will he say to Side-Parting? My phone beeps.

OK. Dinner starts at 7.45.

I drum my fingers against my phone. What will I say if I can't make it? *Sorry I missed your career-defining black-tie party – I was babysitting a dog.* He'll never speak to me again. I imagine Side-Parting sneering, 'I told you she was a loser.'

The publisher strides over to my end of the studio.

Please don't ask me to speak to her, I can't move her, the UN wouldn't be able to move her.

He whips out his mobile. 'Charlie.'

He's called her direct. This has got to be bad.

'She's a fucking brilliant photographer, but she's so fucking, fuck, for fuck's sake, you know. Have the bloody taxi money. I'm going home.'

Vampira stands and glides elegantly out the door. 'Binky!' she calls and the dog breaks free from my grasp and scurries behind her.

I jump up and sprint across the studio, pulling my hairpins out with one hand, grabbing my holdall with the other.

Nineteen minutes.

I've got to try. I need to find a cab. I need a helicopter. I shove the studio door forcefully and fly into the hallway. What if I can't find a taxi? I should call a car. Halfway down the stairs I wedge my hand in my back jeans pocket and claw at my mobile, the holdall rocks and catches behind my knee. My legs wrap round the bag and I feel my feet disappear from under me. I'm falling.

I slam into the wall and land on my hip on the last step with a painful thump. I feel my hand twist and the tips of my nails snap. 'Fuck.' That hurt. Three broken nails. That's all I need. I pick my bag up, rub my hip and stumble out into the street.

Fifteen minutes.

I look up and down the road. It's empty, no cabs. I walk as quickly as my hip lets me toward the main road. *Please, I just need a taxi.*

Fourteen minutes.

I can hear Side-Parting laughing at me: 'All my friends are going to be bankers, lawyers and accountants. Sweetie, you just wouldn't fit in.' I'm not going to make it.

MR DARLING

'One is never over- or underdressed with a
little black dress.'

KARL LAGERFELD

Are my eyes deceiving me? Is that a brake light? No, it's a taxi
with its light on. Salvation!

I jump up and wave my hand in the air, like a schoolkid
desperate for a wee.

Thirteen minutes. I can still make it – my life is not a total
train wreck!

Fifty metres along the road a man in a mac, clutching a
briefcase, steps out and raises his arm. *My* taxi pulls over and the
man climbs in.

Who uses a briefcase anyway? Hasn't he heard of man bags?
I'm doomed, destroyed, devastated by a man with bad taste in
accessories.

Wait – what's that?

I squint.

I hold my breath.

'Taxi!'

He flashes his headlights: I'm in.

'Liverpool Street station, please. I'm in a hurry.'

My formal outfit, a black corset top with a lace-up back and a long black velvet skirt, looked like the perfect 'seeing your ex's flatmate' outfit last night. Now I have to change into it in the back of a cab, I can see it has limitations. I bet Vampira never has to do this.

The road bends round to the left and my holdall and I slide across the gritty floor.

The elasticated waist of the skirt slips over my jeans. The corset is going to be more difficult.

Can I pull it on underneath my T-shirt? I twist both arms inside it. My hands flap at my sides like a bad Flipper impression. I'm wearing a cotton straitjacket. Not working. Can I change when I get there?

Six minutes.

Shit.

'Have you got any children, mate?' I call to the back of the cabbie's stubbly head.

'Yeah. Boy and a girl.'

'How old is the girl?'

'Sixteen, love, she's taking her GCSEs.'

'Lovely, I hope she does well. I need to ask a favour. I'm not *that* much older than your daughter. And I'm late for this work do of a friend, which is really important, and I've got to get changed into this top … and … could you not look back here for a bit?'

It has come to this, bad burlesque routines in the back of a cab.

'My daughter's always late too, you girls and your clothes. You do what you got to, love. I won't look.' He closes the plastic divider.

Thank you.

I whip off my T-shirt and bra. I'm naked in public. *Get your tits out for the cabs.* This is not how tonight was supposed to go. I yank the corset over my head and pull the ribbon tight. No visible back fat. My make-up and my hair will have to do as they are.

We turn a corner and I see the mouth of Liverpool Street station.

'Thanks again.' I give the cabbie all the money in my purse.

'Cheers, love. Have a great night!'

Fingers crossed. This is it, my chance to send a message to Side-Parting: you missed your chance, buddy! I do a *Jerry Springer*-style sass wiggle in my head.

Side-Parting's Flatmate said he'd be outside McDonald's. People hurry past with their heads bowed against the cold. It's a pinstripe blur. I look for a short guy with glasses and messy hair. Perhaps he didn't wait.

Wow. Is that him? He looks completely different, taller, straighter, as if he was deflated before. I couldn't quite remember what colour his hair was, but I see it's a dark brown. He's had it cut into choppy spikes. It works – reveals his eyes. Such bright blue eyes. No glasses. I'm not the only one who's had a post-uni makeover. It must be the James Bond effect. All men look good in a tux.

'We're late.' He turns and heads away from the concourse.

Nice to see you too, it's only been two years. 'Sorry. I had a nightmare at work. Quite a funny story actually, involves a crazy dog.'

The sound of his dress shoes on the pavement echoes off the surrounding buildings. He's not stopping. *Come on, I'm giving you my best material here!* He must be really pissed off. By causing me to be late Vampira has managed to threaten his potential job as well. She's powerful.

I can't keep up with him. This skirt's a tight velvet column; it's like walking in a giant condom. There's so much friction between my knees I can see smoke. Scouts could use me to start campfires. 'Wait! These shoes don't go that fast.' I loop my arm through his, half for balance, half to slow him down.

He tenses.

It's going to be a long night.

'It's here.' He stops outside the entrance to a hotel. Tinted glass doors stretch upwards like the mouth of a cave.

I take my arm out of his.

The foyer smells of fresh lilies. There's a refined green marble floor and excessive swathes of gold curtains, hanging like Victorian knickers from every available surface. They should have kept their interior decorator on a tighter leash.

Side-Parting's Flatmate inspects an easel in reception. 'We're in the Blue Ballroom.'

'Up the grand staircase and on the left, sir,' simpers the concierge. His fake-tanned face clashes with his green-and-gold uniform.

'And would madam like to leave her *bag* in the cloakroom?' He eyes first my cleavage and then my holdall with distrust.

They're boobs, in a corset. I'm not a prostitute and this is not a bag of sex toys. 'It's my outfit from work. I had to get changed in the back of a cab.'

'Of course, madam.' His satsuma face is impassive.

Side-Parting's Flatmate is already halfway up the 'grand' staircase. *Sigh.* I catch up so we enter the room together.

There's chatter and laughter and groups of ladies in long dresses and men in black tie. A string quartet plays in the corner and waiters circulate with trays of champagne. I catch snippets of conversation:

'I hear they couldn't get the merger simulation model to work even with five workstations daisy-chained!'

Daisy what? These people are smart. Über-intelligent. They reek of PhDs. I'm severely out of my depth. *Pull yourself together. I may not be super-brainy but I would never have hung those hideous curtains in the reception. I have skills.* I grab a glass of champagne from a passing waiter. *I have alcohol.*

Side-Parting's Flatmate gives me a look that suggests he's regretting inviting me. He glances at me long enough to slightly raise his dark eyebrows.

A lanky man wearing throwback NHS glasses approaches. He wobbles slightly. It's safe to assume he's rat-arsed.

'Good to see you, so glad you could make it.' He grips Side-Parting's Flatmate's hand and claps him on the back.

'Great to be back.'

I've never noticed before what great teeth Side-Parting's Flatmate has. Perfectly straight. All the same size. I'm dying to ask if he wore braces.

'And who's this?' Mr Tipsy eyes me.

'This is Angela.'

I hold out my hand to shake.

Mr Tipsy pulls me in for an air kiss. With no air.

What if he asks how we know each other? I can't deal with hearing Side-Parting's name right now. *I have to explain.* 'We're old friends!'

'I bet you are.' He looks me up and down.

This corset was such a mistake.

Side-Parting's Flatmate tugs at his collar and looks at the floor.

'Come and say hello to Pete. I know he's looking forward to telling you about the High Court hearing.' Mr Tipsy weaves away.

We follow him through the room, and are deposited in a group of four men and a woman.

'Good to see you again, Rebecca.' Side-Parting's Flatmate shakes her hand.

When I'd imagined female economists I'd pictured bookish, mousey girls who never plucked their eyebrows. Rebecca's a statuesque blonde, poised and confident in an amazing full-length black dress which drapes over her shoulder and reveals a sweep of her toned back. It looks suspiciously like Alexander McQueen.

'I'm Rebecca, pleasure to meet you.' She shakes my hand.

Nice manicure. 'Good to meet you too.' I look to my right, but Side-Parting's Flatmate has disappeared. I can't believe he left me with the Heidi Klum of the economics world.

'Were you at Oxford as well?' Rebecca purrs.

Dreaming spires, billowing black gowns? I don't think so. I did go to university, but only because everyone who went to my school went to university. I'm not academically gifted. I clawed my way into Essex, a decent sixties university that's largely populated by international students and postgraduates who don't care about the white stiletto associations of the location. It's hardly Ivy League or whatever the UK equivalent is: dandelion fellowship? I suppress a laugh. 'No, I didn't go to Oxford.'

'Neither did I; I was at Cambridge.'

Figures.

'Which area of economics do you specialise in?' Rebecca smiles.

'I'm not an economist, darling! Thank God!' I clamp my hand over my mouth. I've just insulted her and Side-Parting's Flatmate's chosen career.

Rebecca blinks then opens her eyes wide and laughs. 'Economics is a small field, most people tend to date other economists.'

Date?

'What do you do then?' She smiles.

I think I got away with it. 'I work in fashion.' I like the way that sounds. *Glamorous.* No point revealing I make herbal tea for skeletal models and scoop up dog poo. 'I like your dress.'

Her hand flutters across her waist. I see a different look in her eye, one of magic and joy instead of the grit and determination of working in the financial industry. 'I treated myself to an afternoon shopping trip to Liberty.'

Common ground. 'It's beautiful, is it McQueen?'

'Yes! Thank you.'

Home and dry, baby, home and dry.

It's been ten minutes since I saw Side-Parting's Flatmate. This is either the longest bathroom break ever, or he's ditched me. Is there a mini-Rebecca who's caught his eye? Are they intently talking about fiscal policy in a discreet corner?

'Ladies and gentlemen, dinner is served,' a waiter in tails announces.

The party moves through to the next room. Who am I supposed to talk to?

'Sorry about that.' Side-Parting's Flatmate reappears.

'Back in time for the food, eh?' He keeps running his fingers through his hair. *It's still there.*

'Hey buddy, good to see you!' A woman in a plum wide-legged trouser suit puts a hand on Side-Parting's Flatmate's shoulder.

Well, that was a long conversation.

The dining room is really very pretty. White panelled walls, round tables covered in white tablecloths and white flowers. Mirrored droplets hang from silver candelabras. There's a seating plan. Side-Parting's Flatmate is on my right and an older guy with wiggly eyebrows is on my left.

Side-Parting's Flatmate shakes hands with everyone at the table, an assortment of faces and varying successful stabs at the black-tie dress code. Side-Parting's Flatmate starts what sounds like an in-depth conversation with a lady with a fearsome up-do.

At least the food is good. Smoked salmon and caviar to start. Roast beef and miniature vegetables for main. Champagne, white wine, red wine. I'm feeling better.

I spike a carrot with my fork. It flies into the air and lands on the floor with a buttery splat. *I'm Julia Roberts in* Pretty Woman*! Prostitution is the theme of the evening.*

'Don't worry, nobody noticed,' the wiggly eyebrows whisper.

'Thanks, darling,' I whisper back.

Side-Parting's Flatmate chokes a laugh.

After dinner there are casino tables and a disco room blaring Eurythmics' 'Sisters Are Doin' It For Themselves.' Several economists are attempting to dance. *I love this song! Let's show them how it's done!*

Side-Parting's Flatmate touches my arm lightly. 'I've got to get back to uni tonight, we ought to make a move.'

It's only 10 p.m., party pooper. Bye bye Eurythmics. 'I'll just pop to the Ladies.' What a waste of make-up tonight's been.

'I'll meet you downstairs.' He looks apologetic.

I'm a bad person.

Rebecca's reapplying her lipstick in the bathroom. 'Hello again, you having a good evening?'

'It's been very interesting to see how economists let their hair down. We're off now though.' I give a little wave.

'See you again.' She smiles warmly.

Well, that sounds positive for Side-Parting's Flatmate getting the job. Something good has come out of tonight. Unlikely I'll see her again. Unlikely I'll see him again after he's spent most of the evening ignoring me. I guess Side-Parting was right: I don't fit in with his friends.

Side-Parting's Flatmate is standing next to the cloakroom, my bag is on the table with his coat. He's fiddling with his phone like a drug dealer. Is he waiting for a message from his economics love interest? Or just anxious not to miss his train?

The tangerine concierge hovers like a bluebottle.

'Hi.' He smiles, and actually looks at me.

How did I never notice how blue his eyes were before? I must have been blind. Or blindsided by Side-Parting. 'Thanks for getting my bag.' I go to grab it.

'No problem, I'll carry it.' He picks it up and fakes a stumble. 'Jesus, what have you got in here, a complete set of the *Encyclopaedia Britannica*?'

'Why would I have encyclopaedias with me?'

'You were always reading when you came round to visit *him* at uni.'

'I studied literature.'

'I studied economics and I mostly read the pizza delivery leaflet.' He holds the door open for me.

'To investigate all those pizza monopolies.' I watch my step. I don't want to fall down the stairs twice in one day.

'Nice economics term there.'

'I picked it up tonight.' The pavement's wet from the rain. The Great British summer.

He laughs and the skin round his eyes crinkles. 'So what is in the bag then?' He makes a pathetic attempt at mimicking someone struggling with a heavy load.

'Knock it off. It takes a lot of kit to look like this, I don't just wake up in high heels and full make-up.'

This is fun. This is how we used to talk. Sometimes. I remember joking with him at Side-Parting's flat. He used to provide a running commentary of alternative silly voices for the films we were watching. 'Oh yes, fine sir, I can fight and kill aliens and still have perfect hair, but I'm terrified of spiders and no good at opening jars.' It feels like a long time ago. Before fashion, before I got my heart smashed.

I shiver. Despite my best efforts at ingesting vast amounts of wine I'm still cold.

'Do you have a coat or a jumper among this very important kit?'

'Sadly not.' I rub my bare arms. My goosebumps have got flocks of goosebumps.

'Here.' He slides his jacket off and hands it to me.

'Really?'

'I'm hot actually, it would be a relief.' He slips it over my shoulders.

I can smell his cologne. The jacket is still warm from his body.

He turns to look at me. 'I really appreciate you coming along tonight, I know you were a little late earlier ...'

Cringe.

'... so we didn't have time, but I had wanted to take you for a quick drink. To say thanks.'

And I thought you were ignoring me! 'That would have been lovely.' *Stupid Vampira and her taxi tantrum.*

'We could go now. If you have time?'

A drunk in the remains of a three-piece suit staggers past singing, 'Like a Virgin'.

'Don't you have to get the last train?' I ask.

'I'm getting the Oxford tube.'

'You do know there's no tube that goes to Oxford?'

He grins. 'It's a bus. It runs all night.'

'I see. In that case, let's go for a drink!' I loop my arm through his.

He tenses.

Perfect. We were just beginning to have a nice time and I overstep the mark.

I look longingly at each noisy warm pub we pass. My feet are screaming from these heels. *Won't this do?*

He stops outside a glass building with revolving doors. It looks like an office block. Is he lost?

'Good evening, I rang earlier, we had a reservation that we

had to, er, postpone.' Side-Parting's Flatmate approaches the bored-looking security guard.

Reservation? Rang earlier – is that where he disappeared to?

'Of course, sir, we've been expecting you. This way.'

'If I could just ask you to step through here, Miss?' The security guard indicates an airport-style metal detector.

Side-Parting's Flatmate is piling his wallet and watch and keys into a little plastic dish and handing over my bag.

'Thank you, sir. Here's your card, the lift is on the right.'

The lift has one button: 42. Is this some weird secret club, or a cult? Is he taking me to a board meeting?

'You're going to like this place, I promise.' He places his hand against the small of my back to guide me.

My stomach flips as the lift lurches up.

The doors open, we step into a neon-lit corridor. A uniformed man with soft jowls takes my bag and leads us through a doorway. We are in a bar, with floor-to-ceiling windows. It's very high up, I'm guessing 42 floors up. London is laid out like a curtain of fairy lights. I can see the Thames! I can see for miles! Look at the boats on the river! All the buildings! All the little people like ants!

'It's called Vertigo,' says Side-Parting's Flatmate from behind me.

'I can see why.' I walk into the back of the uniformed man. 'Sorry, I didn't realise you'd stopped.'

'This is your table, madame.'

It overlooks the illuminated dome of St Paul's. It's majestic. You could reach out and pick it up in your hands. There's a bottle of champagne and two glasses on the table. My stomach performs the same somersault it did in the lift. *Is this a date?*

Side-Parting's Flatmate clears his throat. He looks like he wants to run away. 'Thanks for coming with me tonight. It was great to have someone at the work do, but I also wanted to talk to you.'

Wanted to talk to me about what? Is Side-Parting breaking up with Big-Nose? Does Side-Parting have a terminal illness? Is Big-Nose pregnant? This *must* be about Side-Parting.

'I almost bottled it when I saw you outside the station …'

Is that why you stalked off?

'You look … incredible.'

This is all wrong. I can feel my jaw clenching. Side-Parting should be saying this.

'London obviously suits you.' He runs his hand through his hair. 'I used to really look forward to your visits at university, but I also couldn't bear to think of you with *him*. I never dreamt you'd split up. I know you were hurt and I wanted to give you time to heal …'

Legally Hot pops into my head.

'What I'm trying to say is: I've always liked you, maybe even been a little in love with you …'

Did he just say …? My champagne glass is shaking in my hand.

'… and, well, will you go out with me?'

I can't quite picture Side-Parting's face. The memory of him has diminished. And it's not the champagne. All I can see are Side-Parting Flatmate's piercing blue eyes looking at me. Waiting. Who asks someone to go out with them at our age? Old school. Preschool.

'Sure, fuck it, why not?' Not the most romantic response to a man who's just confessed to being in love with me for years, but I'm feeling overwhelmed.

'There's one more thing,' Side-Parting's Flatmate says.

Was this just some twisted test to see if I'm over Side-Parting?

'Next time you meet my boss, could you try not to call him "darling"? Economists aren't used to that sort of thing.' He grins. A dimple appears on his cheek.

'Of course, darling.'

And so Side-Parting's Flatmate becomes Mr Darling.

SAMPLING THE GOOD LIFE

'Women should look like women. A piece of
cardboard has no sexuality.'

ALEXANDER MCQUEEN

Jen was delighted when I told her what happened. She wasn't
so delighted I called her at 1 a.m. to tell her, but nobody's
perfect.

I'm humming 'Walking On Sunshine', as I reach the office.
'Good morning, Pandora.'

'What's up with you, finally lost some weight?' Pandora gives
my Oxfam acid-green snakeskin stilettos a disparaging look.

'I thought my jeans felt looser. Must be all those carbs I eat.'
No one can get to me today.

She flicks her hair and stalks toward the tear-sheet bench.

I pick up the ringing phone. 'Good morning, the Charlie—'

'Who is this?'

It's Vampira, sounding like she woke up on the wrong side of
the underworld. 'Good morning, it's Angela.'

'I will only deal with Georgina.'

Fine by me. 'Putting you through.' I wave the phone toward Georgina. 'She's asking for you.'

Georgina's chuffed. She checks her make-up in the little mirror she keeps on the desk.

She can't see you.

'Georgina speaking.'

'Don't take it personally, she once called a new junior a dirty pig on her first day.' Charlie appears behind me.

'Really? Why am I surprised! I find it quite amusing actually.'

Charlie smiles. 'Pandora, can you come here a minute? I want you girls to make some appointments today. We need to get out there, show people what our artists can do, get some jobs in the diary. Call everyone you know.'

I don't know anyone in the fashion industry. I could call Jen? Do physios have much call for stylists?

'Mills, darling, how are you?' And she's off. Pandora is gurgling into the phone. 'So looking forward to your summer party. Can't wait to get out to the country. We should catch up, I've got some darling books to show you – fancy coffee?'

My email pings. She's sent it to the whole office:

> I have an appointment with Millie Frothington-Whirl, assistant fashion editor at *Tatler* on Thursday 10th.
>
> xx Pandora xx

Who signs off with kisses in front of their own name? It's like kissing yourself.

'Great job, Pandora.' Charlie claps her hands together.

'Lorelai, this is Pandora. We met at Pippa's parents' ball last month?'

Urgh, not again. I have got to stop hanging out in wine bars with my real friends.

> I have an appointment with Lorelai Von
> Chewlittle, picture editor at *Glamour* magazine on
> Friday 11th.
>
> xx Pandora xx

'Fantastic Pandora! See it's really very easy.' Charlie stands, conducting an invisible orchestra.

It's easy if you went to school with/go shooting with/shared a nanny with the entire fashion industry.

Remember J-Lo's butt? I'm a badass saleswoman. This isn't even real cold-calling. I'm not flogging ad space in *Foot Fungus UK*, I'm making an appointment to show some pretty pictures. How hard can it be?

I open up the Diary Directory, which lists industry contacts, and dial.

'Hello, Alex Samson,' says a male voice.

'Hi Alex, this is Angela from Charlie Monroe Management. How are you?' *Keep smiling, people can hear it in your voice.*

'Busy.'

'I won't keep you long, I just wanted to tell you about this fantastic photographer we've got. He's based in New York and works for US *Vogue*, *Numéro* and *Purple*. I'd love to come in and show you his work if you have a spare five minutes?' *Pretty please, with cherry lip gloss on top.*

'Next Tuesday, ten thirty a.m.'

'I'll see you then.'

My heart thumps as I type out the email:

> I have an appointment with Alex Samson, art
> director of *Vogue* on Tuesday 8th.
>
> Angela x

'What!' Pandora's hair trembles.

'You don't just call up the art director at *Vogue* and ask for an appointment!' Georgina twists her chunky necklace like she's trying to kill it.

Why not?

'Impressive.' Ceci nods.

'Encore!' Charlie throws her hands in the air.

'What are you going to wear?' Ceci peers at me as if I'm under a microscope.

I hadn't thought of that.

'What are you going to do about your eyebrows?' Georgina releases her jewellery.

'Err …' *What's wrong with my eyebrows?*

'You'll have to lose weight,' says Pandora. 'You can't go to *Vogue* like that!'

They all nod their heads in sympathetic agreement.

Are you calling me fat? I try and sink lower into my chair to hide.

'You can be my project!' Ceci cries. 'Let's pool our discount cards, call in some favours.'

I am not a project. I am a human being who owns a Burberry mac and Gucci shoes.

'You should go to Giovanni to get your colour done,' nods Ceci. 'It's five hundred pounds, but once they know you're industry they'll give you a fifty per cent discount.'

'Five hundred pounds just to get your roots done?' I stick my head round the computer screen. They look like the Witches of Eastwick.

'Two fifty after discount—'

'Oh that's so much better!' I heap sarcasm into my voice.

'Defo,' smiles Ceci.

I'm not spending hundreds on my hair; I haven't got hundreds to spend. I refuse to be anyone's makeover experiment. This is not *Clueless*.

'And it's the McQueen sample sale tomorrow, we should go to that.'

'McQueen, you say ...' Maybe I'm being too hasty ...

They rummage in their handbags for branded plastic Visa-sized cards: Stella McCartney, Miu Miu, Browns, and a Topshop one thrown in for joy. Discount cards.

'I've borrowed this from Elspeth at *Elle*.'

'I got given this after I worked on the Look Book.'

Twenty per cent discount, twenty-five per cent discount, forty per cent discount. Think of all the things I could buy. No wonder I have outfit envy at work. These girls don't have wardrobes worth thousands of pounds, they have wardrobes worth forty per cent off thousands of pounds!

'Let's see what products we can call in. Georgina, haven't you just been sent some La Prairie Platinum?' Ceci's in full flow.

'It's worth six hundred and fifty pounds. I'm not giving her that,' huffs Georgina.

Six hundred and fifty pounds? That's more than a haircut! What could be worth six hundred and fifty pounds? 'Is it a bag?'

'Face cream. She doesn't even know what La Prairie is. It's a lost cause.' Pandora laughs.

'You paid six hundred and fifty pounds for some face cream?' I look at Georgina very closely. How good is this stuff? She looks late twenties to me; perhaps she's really fifty.

'Don't be stupid ...' says Georgina.

Finally someone's talking sense. A face cream worth six hundred and fifty pounds, it must be a joke. It's probably more like six pound fifty.

'... I didn't pay for it, they gifted it to me.'

'Huh?'

'The PR gifted it to me.'

'Why? Is it your birthday?'

Pandora throws the discount cards in the air in exaggerated frustration. 'When a make-up artist or a hairdresser works on a magazine photo shoot they credit the products they use. In exchange for that credit they either receive money or products. As agents we call in the credits and products, and so we have a great relationship with the PRs. If you've run out of Chanel mascara ask one of the make-up artists to request it alongside their other products. You can do the same with hair products, face cream, foundation, whatever you want.'

'We take twenty per cent and a little hair mousse on the side?' *This job keeps getting better.*

Pandora looks at me like I'm a bag lady. 'I would suggest you make friends with the hairstylists and PRs. Fast.'

***

I still haven't heard from Mr Darling. It's been a whole day. Is that a long time? Maybe he's changed his mind. There's no point watching my phone at 6 a.m. though, only milkmen and the psychologically unbalanced are up now. I shove my hands back in my warm pockets and look again at the uninspiring East End building we're queuing outside. A line of fashionistas in cashmere capes and fur coats snakes in front and behind us. Pandora's talking on her phone and Ceci's smoking.

Even with the promise of an Alexander McQueen sample sale I had to leave a trail of digestive biscuits from my bed to the door to guarantee I got up. The sale opens at 8 a.m. and ten people will be allowed in at a time. There are fifty girls in front of us and more keep joining the queue. There are many psychologically unbalanced people interested in fashion. Will there be anything left by the time we get in? What can you accessorise with frostbite? 'Do you think we'll be late for work?' I wave Ceci's smoke out of my face.

She pulls her faux-leopard coat tight around her shoulders. 'Maybe. Charlie knows where we are. Allowances are made for certain things: sample sales, getting your roots done, Restylane.'

'Restylane?'

'Injectable fillers.' She pushes her lips into a huge pout. 'It gets rid of lines on your face, like the crease that runs between your nose and your top lip.'

'Isn't that line supposed to be there? Without it you'd look weird.'

'Nah, you just need someone decent to do it.'

I'm going to be late in today, I'm just popping to Switzerland for a facelift.

'It's maintenance,' Ceci continues. 'There are some great time-saving treatments. You can have two people work on your hair at the same time, and someone else can be doing your nails. And there's that doctor who visits agencies on a moped and applies Botox at your desk.'

'A pizza delivery guy for botulism. What does he do, inject you while you're on the phone?'

'Yep.'

I look at Ceci's beautiful face. 'You haven't had Botox have you?'

'Not yet, do you think I ought to?' She touches her forehead.

'God no! I was worried you had. You're too young. I'm not sure you should ever have it, really.'

'Some of the girls start in their early twenties now, it stops the wrinkles from ever forming.'

'I'm not sure that makes sense. But then I'm not sure I agree with injecting poison in your face full stop.'

She leans in conspiratorially. 'When you've had it done you can't exercise, eat spicy food or have sex for forty-eight hours. In case your face freezes into the wrong position.' She screws her face up in an attempt to make it look ugly. She still looks gorgeous.

'What if you don't like needles?'

'You get a fringe cut,' she laughs and lights another cigarette. *Obviously.*

Pandora hangs up her phone. 'This is boring.'

'It's exciting! Think what we might find in the sale!' *Think what I'm finding out about minor cosmetic procedures.*

'I'm not like you; I'm not used to queuing,' she sniffs. 'I'm going to get coffee. Do you want anything?'

I scrabble for my purse. 'Could you buy me something to eat, a pastry or something?'

Pandora raises her eyebrows. 'You'll struggle to fit into sample size already!'

'I thought sample size was an eight?'

'Like a million years ago.' Pandora snatches the fiver I'm holding out.

Now I think of it the models at the casting weren't a size eight. More like child size. Under their warm layers I can see the women in this line are minuscule. I was so chuffed at the prospect of owning a piece of McQueen. I sat next to him in a taxi. I got up at five. This is like discovering all the brightly wrapped presents under the Christmas tree are Sudoku books. I should go home.

'Angela will be fine. Just stick to jackets, cardigans, tops and bags.' Ceci squeezes my arm.

Hallelujah for things that don't have to be done up!

There's movement at the front of the queue. Heads turn like fashionista meerkats. They're letting people in! What treasures will I find inside? Will there be any left? I'm picturing a beautiful room of full-length mirrors and racks of wondrous clothes, a Willy Wonka's Chocolate Factory of style.

It's a disused office. Grey/beige carpet tiles on the floor. Greige. Trestle tables lined up in rows topped with open boxes. Hardly Ange's Adventures in Wonderland.

A bony girl in a silk bomber jacket pushes past me. Everyone's running at the boxes. My base shopping instincts kick in. I will buy Alexander McQueen! I will own happiness!

I make a beeline for the shoes, pulling one amazing sculptural heel after another out. They're all size seven. I take a five. Even with two insoles that's not going to work.

'Are you getting those?' A girl with bleached blonde hair and some seriously scary eye make-up points at the heels.

'No, by all—'

She snatches them from my hands.

Two girls each holding one side of a black dress are arguing.

'I found it first,' the girl with a cut-glass accent and nose to match says.

'That's a lie!' the girl who resembles an angry bobblehead retorts.

'I need it for a funeral.' The cut-glass girl sticks her chin out defiantly. 'My mother's died, she would want me to wear McQueen.'

This is terrifying.

I step backwards and trip over a box on the floor. Out of it I pull a maroon silk shirt, with pleating and silk-covered buttons, and a black suit jacket with raised black cord shoulders. McQueen, real McQueen.

'There's more here,' a voice cries, before I'm shoved out the way.

These skinny girls are vicious. How do they train, hours of ninja Pilates? Where's the changing room? Pandora's standing in just her knickers, pulling a tight dress over her head. I can see my work colleague's boobs. I can see my work colleague's boobs. *Pull yourself together.* No changing rooms then.

I edge into a corner and gingerly take off my coat and jumper. I'm standing in my bra in a room full of stick insects. My tits contain more fat than all of them put together. This is worse than the school changing room after PE.

In the last few weeks I've seen semi-naked models, I've stripped in the back of a taxi and now I'm standing in a state of undress alongside my work colleagues. At this rate I'll be checking into a naturist resort by New Year.

I slide the cool silk top up my arms and feel it wrap round me. I breathe in, slightly, and get the buttons done up. Real McQueen. Sexy.

'Buy it!' Ceci shouts from across the room. She's wearing a dress, a pair of trousers and a jacket all at the same time.

It would be perfect for my date with Mr Darling.

The silk shirt costs thirty-eight pounds; the jacket ninety-five. There must be a mistake. These are originals. They should cost hundreds. My phone beeps. Mr Darling's texted!

> Do you like Italian?
> x

I'm so buying the top and the jacket.

> I couldn't eat a whole
> one, but I could share.
> Tomorrow? Ax

> Deal. On condition
> you don't make any
> more terrible
> jokes. x

What am I doing? I've never dated before. My first boyfriend and I rode around on bikes and then snogged on the way to school. Side-Parting and I hung around class and then snogged in the sixth form common room. Legally Hot and I met in a club and shagged everywhere. How do you date? Mr Darling sounded very proper when he asked me out. Is he going to arrive in a top hat and place his jacket over puddles? Will there be a chaperone? What will we talk about?

I grip the silk top in my hand. I *can* control my outfit. This shirt, my Topshop pencil skirt, Gucci heels and black fishnet tights – the ones with the small holes. I can do this.

*****

The restaurant is in a quiet back street between High Holborn and Clerkenwell. Thank God I printed a map. Christopher Columbus would struggle to find this with Sat Nav. My heels reverberate off the cobbles.

Mr Darling is waiting awkwardly outside a homely looking restaurant. He still looks good in his T-shirt and jeans. I was worried it was the tux. He looks nervous.

'Did you find it OK?' He holds the door open.

'Yes. Thanks.' *Say something else.*

The restaurant is terracotta with cane chairs, white tablecloths and candles in jars. Not a chain. Not wallet-weepingly flashy. Not a kebab shop. Good choice.

'I came here a couple of times during my internship. It's good.' He points to our table.

'Great.' *I should have read the newspaper. Prepared flashcards.* I pick the furthest chair so my back's against the wall. I can see all my escape routes.

'Shall we get some wine?' Mr Darling looks at the menu.

'Great.'

'Red, is that OK?' He offers me the list to see.

'Great.' I've only managed words of one syllable since I got here. 'So ...'

'Good evening, would you like to order some drinks?' The Italian waiter interrupts what would have been my fascinating observation about Parmesan.

'Chianti OK?' Mr Darling asks.

'Great.' *Shoot me now.*

The waiter smiles sympathetically. Mr Darling's on a date with a monosyllabic moron. Side-Parting was right, I have nothing to offer. I should go hang out with my equals. Maybe there's a nursery school round here, or a fish tank.

'So how was your day at work?' Mr Darling smiles.

'Great.' *No, shoot* him *now. It's the humane thing to do.*

The wine arrives. *Thank God.* I take a big gulp of the red. 'This is delicious.' A reasonably long word. I just need to stay away from the cheese topic.

'Glad you like it. I love Italian wine and food, and the country. It's so beautiful.'

'I've never been. I've always wanted to.' The wine is making me better. This is how I date: with alcohol. I take another gulp.

'You should go. You'd love it. The architecture is stunning. And the food, did I mention the food?'

'I want to see the art. The frescos. The sculpture. I love the Renaissance. Botticelli, Giotto, oh Michelangelo! And Baroque, I would love to see Caravaggio *in situ.' It's like I'm playing the word association game. At least I didn't say Parmesan.* The wine has freed my mind. I take another gulp. 'Good wine.'

'Glad you like it. Shall we get some food?'

'Oh olives! I love olives. Let's get olives. And garlic bread. Do they do garlic-stuffed olives? I love those. Wait: should you eat garlic on a date?'

'I'd forgotten how fast you talk,' he laughs and selects a garlic-stuffed olive from the dish on the table.

'Bad habit.' I toast my glass to him. *It's going to be OK. It's going well.*

***

Mr Darling stares at me as I scrape the final smears of tiramisu from my plate. 'You really like tiramisu?'

'Love it. Ate it for breakfast yesterday.' I could eat another now.

'How do you stay so slim?' Mr Darling looks like I've just carried fourteen Italians and a Giotto from a burning building.

'I'm not that thin. You see that breadstick over there?'

He glances at the jar of breadsticks on the next table. 'Yes?'

'She works in my office.' I pick the wine bottle up and tip it into my glass. Empty. When did we finish that?

'Want another drink?'

'Oh! Do they have Vin Santo?' I love that.

He signals to the waiter.

'I'm just going to the bathroom.' I stand. Whoa. The floor feels spongy. Perhaps I drank that red a bit too fast. In the ladies I push my hair back from my face and look in the mirror. I look great! Bad sign. It's guaranteed you're drunk if you think you look great in the mirror. I need some water.

'Your Vin Santo's here!'

'You hid your eyes for years. *Hid* them,' I say pointing at him.

'Are you OK?' Mr Darling throbs toward and away from me.

'I need some air.'

'Here, let me help you.' His hand is under my arm.

Suddenly we're outside. Two people lurch toward us laughing, like funhouse mirror reflections. 'I want to go somewhere quiet.'

'There's a park over there.' Mr Darling waves his hand about.

My ankle twists. Mr Darling's hands catch me as one knee comes in contact with the cobbles. That's going to hurt in the morning. 'Stupid cobbles.'

'Let's get you over here on the bench.'

'Parmesan.'

'You all right?'

The floor spins. My stomach is trying to escape. *Going to be sick!* I push him out the way and throw up into the flowerbeds.

***

Whenever I'm sick from alcohol I immediately sober up. Everything comes screaming back into focus. Right now this talent is a very bad thing. Right now I wish I were still drunk. Oblivious. Somewhere else.

Mr Darling's holding my hair. It's our first official date and I've just got drunk, fallen over and spewed over shrubbery in a park. 'I'm so sorry. I'm not usually sick. I didn't drink that much. I mean I've drunk way more than that and been fine. Not that I drink loads all the time. God, I'm sorry.'

'It's OK. Don't worry.' He's rubbing my back. 'Can you get up?'

My Topshop skirt is damp from the grass. Did I get puke on my McQueen?! No, thank Coco. 'I'm fine. Just hideously embarrassed.'

'Happens to the best of us. Do you want me to get anything for you? I ought to go back and pay for our meal.' Mr Darling sits next to me on the bench.

'God. We haven't even paid for our food and I've lost it. I'm so sorry. I was just really nervous.' Might as well be honest: he's never going to want to see me again.

'Me too. I thought I'd lost the ability to speak on the way here.' He smiles and his eyes twinkle.

'I was worried I'd talk about Parmesan.'

'That's why you said that! I guess that's a good sign.' He brushes a bit of grass from my hand. 'If we were nervous it means we wanted it to go well. And it did, I think.'

'Apart from the last ten minutes. I could have done without that.' I can't believe he's not running in the opposite direction screaming for bleach. 'Do you want to take my card for my half?'

'I'll get it. You can get it next time.'

Next time? I haven't completely blown it. Unbelievable. Perhaps throwing up in a park is part of the dating experience. I could write a self-help book: *Puking and Pulling*. But first, I need to find a breath mint... just in case.

IT'S A DOG'S LIFE

'The only rule is don't be boring and dress
cute wherever you go. Life is too short to
blend in.'

PARIS HILTON

'My ticket needs changing.' Vampira's voice cuts through my
hangover like a knife-wielding maniac.

I feel like I've been licking Ryvita crispbreads on a roller
coaster all night. Technically I lost all the alcohol in my system
– I should feel fine! 'Good morning!' I look around desperately.
Everyone's on the phone. 'Can I double-check which ticket
you'd like me to alter?'

There's a long painful sigh. 'I want to leave earlier. Then
I can lunch at my hotel.'

A hotel – it's a plane ticket! Or it could be a Eurostar ticket.
I scrawl 'S.O.S.' on my pad and wave it at Bonnie, who's in the
office scanning images for Vampira.

'Paris with Air France,' Bonnie stage whispers.

'In Paris!' I say jubilantly.

'Where else would I be going?' Vampira snaps.

Milan, New York, I'm pretty sure you went to Marrakech last week. 'Great.' Remember to sound perky. I flick onto the Internet and search for Air France's site. 'What about the 07.10 flight?'

'Business class. Binky needs a seat too. Next to me. This is taking up too much of my time.' She hangs up.

Boots should bottle Vampira and put her on the shelf next to the Alka-Seltzer: nothing cures a hangover quicker. 'She just made a joke.'

'Really?' Bonnie rearranges the hem of her faded Jil Sander shirt over her J Brand jeans.

'Yeah, she just said Binky needs a business-class seat on the plane. How hilarious is that?' I flick through my Rolodex for the travel agent's number.

'She's not kidding.'

I stare at her classically beautiful face. 'No way. She wants me to buy her dog a plane ticket?? Can you even do that? I thought you couldn't take pets to the continent because of rabies.' Binky's probably rabid already, that would explain a lot.

'He's got a passport,' she shrugs.

'Of course he has. And now he's going to have his own business-class seat. Does he get an in-flight meal?' I can barely afford my travel card and that mutt's being flown round the world first class. *A dog's life indeed.*

'I pack his organic fillet steak in a Tupperware box before they fly.'

'You do know this is mental?'

'It's not that bad. He stays in his Louis Vuitton carry case for the whole journey.'

I let my forehead bash against my desk.

Bonnie giggles.

The phone rings and I automatically answer. 'Hello, Charlie Monroe Management, Angela speaking.'

'And don't forget to book a suite for Binky!' Vampira hangs up again.

I look at Bonnie imploringly. 'Suite?'

'The client doesn't like dogs. Binky needs to be collected from the airport and taken to the Hôtel de Crillon. He stays in a suite while she works. Send another car to collect him at the end of the day.'

'Why doesn't she leave the dog at home? Kennels must be cheaper. I can't believe she wastes her money like this.'

Georgina looks up from the call she's on hold to. 'It's always billed to the client as expenses.'

'Because having her dog with her is vital to her creativity?'

'Precisely.'

Fashionistas don't understand sarcasm. This job gets crazier every day. What's next: a helicopter to take Binky from one end of the studio to another? 'I'm going on lunch.'

'I'll come with you.' Bonnie passes me my Topshop handbag.

I'm flattered. Bonnie's gorgeous and so sophisticated she doesn't bat an eyelid at a pampered pooch. Where will she want to go for lunch? An achingly expensive sushi restaurant where she'll eat a fingernail of fish and complain of being bloated? 'Where do you want to go?'

'I dunno. Boots to grab a cheese sarnie?' Bonnie pulls her long hair into a loose chignon.

Damn. I really fancied edamame beans.

'How you settling in?' Bonnie asks as we walk down Baker Street.

'Good thanks.'

She nods.

A guy passes, snapping his head round to see Bonnie and just misses a lamp post.

Bonnie doesn't notice.

Think of something interesting to say. 'Have you been away lately?' *Lame*.

'I was in Marrakech last week on location.'

I knew Vampira was in Marrakech! 'You're so lucky to travel with work. Do you sit beside Binky in business class and feed him slivers of steak?'

'I wish. I have to fly cattle.'

'That doesn't sound fair.'

She sticks her hands in her jean pockets. 'I'd rather sit on my own.'

'Where did you stay? It must've been an amazing country to see.'

'In a riad in central Marrakech. I saw out the taxi window to and from the airport. The rest of the time I was in the back of the location van with the equipment. It was intense. You want to know the worst thing?' Bonnie's eyes glint.

Fashionistas do like to gossip.

'She used both *her* and my luggage allowance. She changed twice a day and I only had two outfits and two pairs of knickers for a week. I washed my underwear in the sink every night.'

Vampira treats her dog better than she does her assistant. 'That's pants.'

LOSING MY VOGUEINITY

> 'A girl should start using a skin cleanser when she is 13. When she is older she can always buy a new dress, but she can never buy a new face.'
>
> ESTÉE LAUDER

My winning McQueen/Topshop combo is taking me to *Vogue*. I've had it dry-cleaned since my date with Mr Darling; I don't want to visit the fashion bible smelling of puke.

I'm carrying five oversized laptop bags that house the portfolios. Each book is updated, straightened and polished. These babies are flawless. They are also bloody heavy. As a junior I'm not allowed to take cabs. With each step the portfolios bump into my hips. The coarse straps cut into my shoulders. Torn blood vessels are flowering over my shoulders. Who needs the gym!

I was astonished my flimsy colleagues could lift a portfolio, until I picked up Ceci's handbag. Designer handbags are H.E.A.V.Y. Is top-grade leather made from fatter cows?

Big-boned bovine? Fashionistas may as well carry a colour-coordinated dumb-bell round all day.

Mulling this over distracts me as I weave painfully to the bus stop. I've been to Oxford Street before, *lots* of times, but never laden down with weighty, unbendable, precious bags. This is going to be interesting.

The bus lurches to a stop and I drag my portfolios out the door. Immediately someone bumps into me.

'Sorry.' I stumble sideways. I try to lift the portfolios onto my shoulders, but catch a lady in a biker jacket on her side, then back into a couple of girls who seem to be carrying twenty H&M bags each. 'Sorry, sorry.'

This is not working. I blow air up my face, check behind me and step into the road. I swing the bags up and walk along the gutter until a bus forces me into the crowd. Finally I reach Hanover Square, the home of *Vogue*.

It's only two minutes from the jabbing elbows of Oxford Street, but feels like another world. The street's wide, there are green trees and it's quiet. Vogue House is a 1950s brown-brick building with a double-height revolving entrance made from glass. My stomach contracts. I can't get these portfolios through a revolving door. I'll get wedged, stuck forever watching the fashion world literally pass me by, a whirling ornament to failed appointments.

There's a side door, a tradesman's entrance. Oh well.

To the right I spy a graceful girl with long, bare legs and a flippy dress. Her hair's so blonde it's almost white. She's carrying her tan Dior Saddle Bag like it's a bunch of freshly picked meadow flowers. She's heading toward Vogue House. She *must* work at *Vogue*.

There's another! A dandelion of a girl floating in from the other side of the road, drifting toward the glass doors in a wisp of an Isabel Marant dress (I know because I saw it yesterday in

Vogue). Stepping into this square is like stepping into another world, a world populated by flower fairies in designer dresses. I didn't think it was possible for girls to be thinner, wispier, and more highly polished than the girls in my office. I was wrong. These girls look like another species, mythical creatures from a time of light and air and blow-dries. These are the Voguettes.

I reach the door at the same time as the dandelion. Up close the skin on her face is tight. She's older than I thought. She looks startled at the sight of me. Then she wafts through the glass doors like a cool breeze.

Remember these people are normal. There's no need to be intimidated

The reception's smaller than I expected. Barely room for the security guard at his desk and the silver Condé Nast sign. It's very polished though, like a posh broom cupboard with a lift.

'Can I help?' The kindly security guards looks like my uncle Clive. Not fashion.

'I have an appointment with Alex Samson at *Vogue*.' I glance over my shoulder, I'm hoping for a supermodel sighting. Nothing. No one. Not even a measly reality TV star. Never mind, I'm about to enter the hallowed ground of *Vogue* and witness the high priestesses of fashion at work.

'I'll just see if he wants you to go up,' the security guard interrupts my thoughts. 'Sometimes they like to come down and go to the café.'

I queued from 6 a.m., spent money I didn't have on this McQueen top, dragged these portfolios here in high heels, and I'm going to end up in Pret?

'Yes, sir,' the security guard says into the phone. 'I'll send her up now.'

I could kiss him.

My portfolios and I shuffle into the lift. Imagine all the iconic photographers and models and actresses that have stood in this lift! *The* Condé Nast lift. A hand appears to stop the doors closing. In steps the most fantastically dressed woman, for 10.30 a.m. on a Tuesday. A McQueen circle-skirt dress, the kind of which I've only seen in catwalk photographs, black and white and nipped in at the waist. A large disc hat balanced like a dinner plate on the front of her head, partially obscuring her sunglasses. The graphic black of her hair is contrasted with the bright red of her lipstick. OhMyGod. It's Isabella Blow, fashion director of *Tatler*.

She stares forward.

It's taking all my self-restraint not to tell her: I'm wearing McQueen as well!

I step into *Vogue*'s office, drinking in the white walls, stylish glass divisions, gorgeous framed covers, and the tantalising racks of clothes being wheeled past by Voguettes. It reminds me of a long corridor. Or a runway. I didn't appreciate from the Voguettes I saw outside how tall everyone is. Another immaculately dressed giraffe stalks past.

Is being a minimum of six foot in your heels a job requirement?

A girl, who looks about fifteen, leads me through the office. A well-groomed, well-heeled schoolgirl who has pillaged her mother's wardrobe. I assume she's doing work experience, but she could be a member of the fashion team who's had amazing plastic surgery or uses the same £650 face cream as Georgina. She doesn't speak but communicates through raised waxed eyebrows.

She stops and stands to the side as more senior staff pass by.

No one talks to her. Intimidating.

Is this why some of the artists refer to it as Condé Nasty? It feels like a competitive girls' school. Do they flush your head down the toilet if you're wearing last season's Prada?

I'm shaking with nerves by the time we reach the art director's office. It's a small well-lit room, with a window down one side. Both the large table in the centre and all the walls are covered in pages torn from magazines, model cards, and printouts. It's a riotous collage of fashion. Energy pours from every image.

'Thank you.' Alex smiles at the silent work-experience girl. He's wearing a blue-and-white striped jumper and chinos; he looks like he's on holiday. 'Fancy a cuppa?' His manner is very 'boating on the Riviera'.

All aboard! 'Thanks, do you have peppermint?'

'I'll get the tea, you set your books up.' He taps the table.

Aye, aye captain! He's a delight. He's Condé Nice. I feel reassured of the work-experience girl's chances.

***

I've just left Vogue House when a man with bright green hair runs toward me with a wheelie case screaming, 'That's my book!'

It's the same guy who let me into the office for my interview. Different hair colour. I glance at the name on the outside of the case: Fraser. He's one of the agency's hairdressers. 'Fraser, hi! I'm Angela, we haven't formally met. I'm at Charlie's. I've just taken your book in to the art director at *Vogue*.'

Fraser's tanned face lights up. '*Vogue*, how super!' His arm drops onto my shoulder in a casual embrace adding to the already critical weight of the portfolios. 'I've just come off set, doll. Monstrous pop star, only ever eats boiled egg whites. Piles of the things in bowls all over the place. Fat little assistant scoops out the yolk and passes it to her. Stinks. Like working inside a room of a million farts. High-protein, low-anything-else diet. She does have rock-hard abs though, perhaps I should take it up?'

Pop star? Egg whites? 'It must be so cool to work with famous people.' *I sound like a groupie.*

'Oh, they're *so* draining.' He stops so he can use the arm that's dragging the case to gesture how draining they are. 'Models are much easier. Celebs are so whiny. They're all me, me, me! Don't they know their hairdresser is the real star? I'm off to do another one now, that pretty girl from that American TV show about the young rich kids boffing each other.'

'You don't mean Evelyn from *Spoilt and Sexy*?' That's only the most popular teen drama on telly. I'm totally addicted.

'That's her, doll. Round the corner at the Soho Hotel, why don't you come along?'

Yes, yes, yes! But the weight of the portfolios keeps my feet on the ground. 'I've got to get back to the office.'

'You can just come in and say hello.' He steers me away from Oxford Street.

We weave through Soho. A little road I've never noticed before leads off Dean Street to the hotel. Fraser wields his wheelie case with the confidence of someone who frequents five-star hotels. In the hotel's reception is an enormous fat black cat statue, as big as a car, squatting in the corner. I can see bars and lounges, occupied by bright cool-looking furniture and bright cool-looking people. Fraser heads for the lift.

People turn to stare at his luminous green hair. I'm struggling to keep up. 'How do you know which room to go to?'

'It's a press junket, she's been here for days. I come in and titivate her while the interviews take place.' He sounds matter of fact.

Everyone should know this. The fat black cat statue would know this.

We snake down corridors and arrive at a door. Fraser teases his AstroTurf, yanks his jeans up and knocks.

I try to look as elegant as one who is draped in heavy portfolios can. First *Vogue* and now TV superstars, I can't wait to tell Jen.

A woman opens the door. She's petite and the colour of a peanut. Her hair is highlighted and big. I would say she's in her forties, but her skin is suspiciously tight.

'Darling!' Fraser air-kisses her. 'How are we today? Did we sleep well?'

We?

He puts his arm round her shoulders and turns toward me. 'Doll, this is Evelyn's mother, though they could be sisters, no?' They both giggle. 'Darling, this is ...' he looks at me.

He's forgotten my name.

'... my agent.' He whirls the mother round and propels her into the next room.

I'm just the junior!

'She's just been in to *Vogue* for a meeting about my next shoot with them.'

Er, that's not quite *true.* I abandon the portfolios and scurry to catch up. Square windows run down the side of the lounge, plush sofas are arranged in a horseshoe. It has a very New York vibe.

I need to decorate my bedroom at Mum and Dad's.

Sat among the cushions is Evelyn. All arms and legs and black curly hair. She has huge childlike eyes. *Don't stare. Be cool.*

Evelyn eats a plate of fruit. Her mum and Fraser discuss the hair for the day. I stand awkwardly.

When am I going to get back to the office?

'Excuse me a minute.' Evelyn disappears into the bathroom.

'When do you fly out?' Fraser asks her mum.

A cough comes from the bathroom.

'Thursday, we're off to Paris, then on to Miami.'

There's a retch from the bathroom, and the sound of liquid cascading into the toilet. Evelyn's being sick.

I freeze.

'And when does filming start up again, doll?'

'Next month, we're just finalising contracts.'

They must be able to hear her?

I can no longer focus on what they are saying, just the mother murmuring away while her daughter makes herself sick.

SPANX ME

> 'Fashion is what you adopt when you don't
> know who you are.'
>
> QUENTIN CRISP

'I've had a life-changing experience!' I grab Jen as soon as she enters the bar. The place is packed with sweaty office workers out-boasting each other.

'You haven't joined a cult, have you?' Jen extracts herself and orders a beer.

I wait to continue till we've found a small space to stand between a gaggle of women in matching black shift dresses and a gang of men wearing pink shirts and braces. 'I've discovered Spanx!'

Jen spits her drink out. 'Ange, I don't want to know about your sex life!'

'They're underwear. Magic knickers. Arguably the least sexy pants in the world, unless you have a thing for shagging sausages.'

'What are you talking about?' Jen steps aside as the brace boys migrate toward the black-shift girls.

'Underneath this dress I'm wearing super-strength underwear. It starts above my knee and ends under my bra.' I move my hands up and down to indicate the affected area, and narrowly avoid spilling my Merlot. 'There's a wee hole in the gusset. Though it's a bit like when you were a kid and you pulled your ballet leotard aside to pee; I wouldn't recommend it.'

'Gross! Why are you wearing this contraption?' Jen wrinkles her nose.

'Because I've instantly dropped a dress size. Here, feel my stomach.' I press her hand against my side. 'I'm like a taut trampoline.'

'Urgh!' She steps back. 'Can you breathe?'

'Shallowly. They're surprisingly comfortable. Designer Dormouse introduced me to them.' Designer Dormouse was the petite stylist I'd run into on my first day at the agency. I nicknamed her the Designer Dormouse after the time she emerged sleepily from under a pile of Gucci dresses in what I thought was an empty office. She made me jump so much my fashion life flashed before my eyes: a blur of incredible clothes I couldn't fit into and shoes I couldn't walk in. 'I've ordered two more pairs. They're a bitch to get on and off, like squeezing your body into a rubber glove. But totally worth it.'

'I think I'll pass.' Jen is in her work clothes. Loose black trousers, skimming shirt, flat sensible shoes she can run and assist her patients in. And even if her outfit was tight and revealing her stomach is like an ironing board, the Spanx would be redundant. They'd fall off.

Imagine what I can wear though! My wardrobe has been liberated from VPL and bloating! I can't see any drawbacks. I take a sip of my wine. 'Excuse me, darling, I need to pop to the loo. I may be some time ...'

The next morning I wear my Spanx to work. I feel lean, sleek, unable to slouch.

'Angela, I'd like you to produce this shoot that's just come in.' Charlie looks up from the computer.

Me? These are lucky pants! This is the greatest moment of my career. I'd like to thank my parents for their continued housing, my bank manager for my Visa card ...

'It's a portrait shoot for US *Vogue*.'

Faints.

'Georgina will take you through the process.'

Every silver lining has a cloud.

I take my pad and pen and sit next to Georgina. She's looking particularly devastating today in a blue bow-fronted YSL jumper that looks like it would fit my little finger. 'So producing, hey Georgina?' I've no idea what that means. The girls are on the phone a lot?

Georgina fixes me with an eyelash-curling stare. 'How basic do we need to make this?'

'Fashion 101.' Joking will win her over.

She tucks her dark hair behind her diamond-studded ear and sighs. 'We need to organise the photo shoot. In this case, the magazine has picked our photographer, Zane, and one of their editors will act as a stylist.'

'A stylist calls in the clothes from the PRs?' See, I kind of know this.

'Yes, and selects what the model or subject will wear.'

I'll make notes for reference.

'The rest of the team will be picked by the photographer, though they can be chosen by the stylist or the client direct. You'll need to ask the photographer which assistant, hairdresser and make-up artist he wants.' When Georgina talks her nose wrinkles.

'You need to option the people the photographer wants. So say the photographer wants Vidal Sassoon to do the hair ...'

I've seen his TV commercials! 'We represent Vidal Sassoon?'

'No, I'm just using him as an example.' Georgina's nose salsas.

'Oh.' I add Vidal to my notes, just in case.

'You ring Vidal's agent and ask for an option. If they give you a first it means you are able to confirm Vidal for your shoot. If they give you a second, another client has the first option on him. Got it?'

'Got it.' First. Second. Gold. Silver. *I wonder if I can find bronze nail polish?*

'Good. If you cannot get a first on Vidal then option the photographer's other choices of hairdresser. OK?'

'OK.' Notes aren't going to cut it, I need a table, or a graph. I'm taking this to-do list to the next level.

'Our job is to chase up, confirm and release options as necessary. At the same time we will be giving options on the artists we represent to other agents and clients for the jobs they are producing.'

I think about my trip to *Vogue*. 'What does an art director do?'

Georgina sighs, more loudly this time. 'An art director oversees the visual look of a whole magazine, making sure it's cohesive. They will have decided how many pages will be dedicated to this portrait and how much pictures and text there will be. They may also have decided who the photographer will be.'

'I had no idea one little portrait had so many people working on it. You're so good at this, Georgina.' The way she's digging her nails into the desk is a hint she's running out of patience.

'Can we continue?'

'Yes, sorry.' I give her my best smile.

She rolls her blue eyes. 'You will need to get a list of the photographer's lighting and order it. Find out which studio he wants, option it and ...'

'... And if his first choice is not available option another?'

'Precisely.'

Gold medal and bronze nail polish for me.

'Then arrange catering. When everything's confirmed write a call sheet listing everyone's contact numbers and what time they are supposed to be where. I would suggest you double-check everything as you go along. If something goes wrong, say the equipment arrives at the wrong time, you will be held responsible.'

Stylist, hair, make-up, studio, lighting, catering. I grip my pen. This list is looking long.

'If the model is late, you will be held responsible. If the stylist doesn't have a steamer you will be held responsible.'

I'm responsible for a lot of things that aren't really under my control. I swallow.

'Make sure the shoot finishes on time; there won't be enough budget for overtime.'

'How do I do that, if I'm here in the office?' I'm beginning to sweat.

'Call them in advance; make sure they all know. Call them throughout the day. Make it happen.'

I can't handle all this. Can I escape out the bathroom window before anyone notices?

'Control when the film gets delivered to the client. Check the deadline and work backwards. The photographer makes his selects, the selects go to the editor at the magazine, and she picks which images she wants. They need to be printed and retouched by the lab and delivered to the magazine before the deadline.'

Georgina looks completely calm. Is she actually a robot with false eyelashes, able to compute vast numbers of tasks? 'Sounds like an awful lot to do.'

'Yes, and you usually only have a few days to turn it all around. I'm currently producing four different shoots.'

'How does your head not explode?'

'This is not the time for jokes. This is US *Vogue*, this is serious.' Georgina taps her pen against my pad. She shows no sign of wiring or the quiet hum of electricity.

'Sorry, I'm just impressed. I had no idea you were juggling all these things.' These girls aren't just gossiping to their old school buddies on the phone.

'You're in control of the budget. You have two thousand pounds.'

'That's a lot of money!'

'It isn't. The studio will cost eight hundred pounds. That's a reduced rate, because it's editorial.'

I keep scribbling.

'If this was a commercial shoot, advertising etc., it would be twelve hundred to fifteen hundred pounds per day instead. Lighting will be five hundred to a grand, depending on the brief. And as it's a portrait of a real person, not a model, you'll need to allow for more retouch.'

My budget's already been spent and I haven't even started. 'How much does the photographer get paid?'

'It's editorial so they receive fifty pounds, there's no fee for the hair and make-up or the assistants. They're doing it for the tear sheets, not the money. The stylist is obviously paid by the magazine.'

'They're working for free? Why do they do it?'

'Because it's US *Vogue*, it's the most powerful fashion magazine in the world. They will get work from the prestige alone.'

I'm working on a shoot for the most powerful magazine in the world. And I have no budget and no clue what I'm doing.

'Right, so you're good to go. The client ...'

I cough, piteously.

'... who in this case is the editor at the magazine, Lena. Call her on this number.'

'Georgie, Tallulah's on line four. She wants to know if you could build a crystal-studded pool in the studio,' Ceci calls.

'I've got to take this,' Georgina picks up the receiver.

'Wait, isn't it the early hours of the morning in New York?'

'Lena's already in London, the shoot is the day after tomorrow.'

Holy shit. My pad is full of illegible scrawls. I thought the fashion industry was all fun and sample sales. Bring back the cake-sniffers – all is forgiven.

I visit the toilet to breathe deeply for a few minutes. Where are all the brown paper bags when you need them? I completely underestimated Georgina, Ceci and Pandora. These girls are pro. They make things happen. *And* they have incredible dress sense.

> Having complete
> breakdown in bathroom.
> Been given production
> for US Vogue!!!! Don't
> think I can do this. Ax

My phone rings immediately. 'Jen! Thanks for calling,' I whisper.

'I'm between patients. You all right?'

'I've got to organise this whole US *Vogue* photo shoot. There's photographers, and lighting and hairdressers and film and I don't know what to do.'

'OK, breathe.' Jen's voice is steady. 'Ange, listen to me: you're the most over-analytical person I know. You think about everything in minute detail. You micromanage going to the pub.'

'That's not true—'

'Need I remind you of the time you CC'd me on your to-do list to coordinate going for a pint? It included recommended clothing.'

'The weather forecast said rain!' *I don't see how this is helping.*

'Organise this like you would anything else. Let your inner control-freak out.'

'I could write a list ...'

'Atta girl.'

'Thanks, Jen.'

'No problem. Got to go, I'm in A&E today.'

No understanding of real pressure, that one.

I stride purposely to my desk. I pick up the phone and dial. As it rings I write out a fresh, ordered to-do list.

'Hi Lena, this is Angela from Charlie Monroe Management. We represent Zane and I'll be producing the shoot.'

***

On the day of the shoot everything seems to be running to plan. The subject is a cosmetic surgeon. The American reader needs to know who to go to for emergency lipo if they get caught short sightseeing at Buckingham Palace. I check in with Lena, to find out how it's all going.

'We have an issue,' she says in her brisk American way.

The lighting hasn't arrived? Have I got the wrong studio? Hit me with it.

'The doctor will only wear black.'

'I don't see the problem?'

'Anna doesn't like black.'

The name rings through the phone like a bell. Anna. *The* Anna. Anna Wintour, the editor of US *Vogue*. People refer to her as Nuclear Wintour, in a rare example of fashionista wordplay humour. Isn't she supposed to be the basis for *The Devil Wears Prada*? 'I see ...'

'The pictures won't run if the doctor's wearing black. I've called in some awesome Marni, Bottega, Balmain, and she won't look at it.'

'Have you told her the pictures won't run?'

'I'll try that. Ciao.'

The threat of not being in US *Vogue* is greater than the threat of wearing colour: Lena persuades the doctor out of her black safety blanket.

Is Anna Wintour really as scary as they say she is? I call Lena again at 5.30. 'Hey, just checking everything's all finished on time?'

'Leaving the studio now. We got some good shots.'

'Fantastic!' I tick off 'no overtime' on my list. I might never get another chance to ask this. Worth a go. 'Lena, have you read *The Devil Wears Prada*?'

'I don't have to read it, I live it.'

That tells me everything I need to know.

***

'I thought we were popping for coffee?' Jen follows me into the Strada behind Oxford Street's Topshop.

'I'm hungry. And I deserve a meal out after the day I've had. The model on Ceci's shoot ate *all* the catering. For the entire team. That's like eight people's worth of food. I had to run across town on a mercy M&S mission to avoid mutiny on set.'

'Table for two, please,' Jen says to the waiter and pulls her cardi off.

'If anyone tells you models don't eat they're lying. These girls are teenagers. When I was that age I could have gone for a six-course meal with Ronald McDonald and still not gained weight.'

'You still eat like someone might steal your sweeties.' Jen hangs her handbag, which is as small as a wallet, off her chair.

'*And* she was four hours late. If I were four hours late to work I'd be sacked. But if you're a famous model you can show up when you like and eat whatever you like. I'll show you her billboard next time we pass it.' I take off my jacket, my jumper, and my scarf, and run my brush through my hair.

'Finished downloading?' she asks.

'Yep. I fancy Prosecco – shall we get a bottle?' I wedge my handbag and shopping bags under the table.

'Tap water for me. I'm saving money.'

'You're always saving money.'

'No, I just don't waste it on lots of junk.' She kicks my bags. 'I'm thinking of going to South America.'

'Travelling, again?' *But I'll miss you.* She's only been back a year.

'Want to share some garlic bread?'

'Sure. So how's the saving going?'

'Good. I've got the six hundred and fifty I need for the ticket.'

'Six hundred and fifty! You could spend that on face cream.' I clutch my hands in mock horror to my chest.

She ignores me. 'How's Mr Darling? Seen him since the infamous bush incident?' She closes her menu and leans on it.

'You deliberately made that sound rude. And yes, actually, we've been out a few times. Dinner, the cinema, we saw the latest *Harry Potter* – my choice – had a picnic last Saturday. It's been good. Fun. I wasn't sick.' I smile at the memory.

'Sounds like it's getting serious …'

My handbag vibrates. 'Hang on, my phone's ringing …'

'Saved by the bell,' Jen laughs.

I don't recognise the number. 'Hello?'

'Angela? This is Daffodil.' One of the agency's make-up artists. 'I've missed my flight.'

'Daffodil! How did you get my number?'

'Pandora gave it to me.'

I bet she did.

'She said you booked the flight.'

'Yes.' *Technically.* This is Georgina's production. I was helping out.

'Can you call the airline and get me on the next flight? I have to be back for my job tomorrow. And can you book a taxi to pick me up from the airport, I just want to get home.'

'Of course.' Where is she again? Which airline? Where does she live? 'I'll call you back.'

'Thanks.'

Why didn't I carry a copy of the flight details with me? I should save all the artists' addresses to my phone. I don't even have their numbers. 'Jen, I've got to make a work call. I'll be back in a minute.' If I can't get hold of Georgina I'll have to go back to the office. *This is a disaster.*

When I come back in, Jen's wiping her fingers with a napkin. 'I've eaten all the garlic bread.'

'So sorry that took so long. Total fail on my part.' Thank God Georgina had the call sheet details with her. 'All sorted now though.' *I won't make that mistake again.* 'Tell me more about South America ...'

The waiter puckers his thick lips at the card machine. 'I'm sorry, madam, your card has been rejected.'

Cringe. 'Try this,' I pass him my Visa.

Jen's nose has wrinkled. She only does that when she disapproves of something.

'It's no big deal, I get paid at the end of the week. I've just overspent,' I hiss.

'You didn't *overspend* during university.' Jen pulls her hair up into a ponytail.

'I've just had a few big expenses coming out of my account, that's all.' *Topshop. Cocktails. Zara.* It's been stressful starting at the agency, I need clothes for work and I deserve the odd treat.

'Be careful, won't you?' Jen hugs me goodbye.

When I get home Dad's still in his golf clothes watching a quiz show and Mum's asleep on the sofa. 'Night, night.' I tuck Mum's crocheted blanket over her knees.

It has been a while since I went through my filing. I have a standing order set up to pay a monthly chunk off my credit-card bill. That covers it. I only use it in emergencies anyway. I fish the pile of unopened envelopes from the bottom of my wardrobe and open the latest.

No. That. Can't. Be. Right.

£3,397.67

The numbers swim in front of my eyes. There must be a mistake. *Harrods. Trains. Topshop. Taxis. Bars. The underground. Hairdressers. Restaurants. Petrol. Space NK. McQueen. Cash.* It catalogues my life since the split from Side-Parting. But that was almost two years ago. The past. I'm over it.

There's a knock at the door.

I can't let my parents see this! I cram the bills into my handbag. 'Come in.' My voice sounds high and squeaky.

Mum yawns, stretches and unleashes her inner OCD. She starts picking clothes up off the floor. 'Darling, we're really pleased you're enjoying this new thing you're doing in London.'

'I work in fashion, Mum. I'm a junior.'

'Yes, that. But we were wondering when you might move out?'

Don't sugarcoat it. I'm in my early twenties, by rights I should be living in a grotty houseshare in zone 2. But where can I go? My closest mates are all travelling round the world, heading off to get life experiences, tattoos and STDs. I'd have to live with strangers. They'd eat my food and lick my shoes when I wasn't looking. Oh, and I'm forgetting I've got no money and I owe over three thousand pounds. 'I've been thinking about it too, Mum. Soon, hopefully.'

'Let me know how you get on looking for a place.' She leaves with four empty water glasses and some magazines I haven't finished reading.

Turns out I can run a production to budget, but I can't control my own spending. I'm going to end up bankrupt and homeless.

ET TU, BRUTUS?

'All I want is the best of everything and
there's very little of that left.'

CECIL BEATON

My first production was deemed a success. Even Georgina
smiled. Though maybe she just had wind. Now I'm in charge of
a £35,000 Christmas advert that Alfie's shooting. I'm going to
prove I can handle the responsibility. This is the new me:
budding production queen, lover of economists, sorter-outer of
finances. I will get round to tackling my credit card bill as soon
as I get a moment.

The shoot brief is: 'Candid shots of a Christmas rap video,
with one rapper and twenty-five extras.' The set will be opulent,
OTT and very bling. It is a little hard to think about being
austere when shoot props pass me like they're on the *Generation
Game* conveyor belt. Hermès bag. Diamond-encrusted milk-
bottle top. Cuddly toy!

It's also weird to be talking about Christmas trees,
decorations and roaring logs fires in July.

Ceci wafts in from lunch, bringing the sunshine with her. She's wearing long wide-legged trousers and a little vest top. Very 1930s cruise liner. Perfect for this weather. She pulls a thick wool coat out the boutique shopping bag she's carrying.

I've been staring at baubles too long – I'm hallucinating.

'It's divine, yes?' She wraps it round her shoulders.

'Why on *earth* have you bought that?' I'm hot and itchy just looking at her.

'New season.' Georgina comes through the door laden with bags. Out tumble cashmere jumpers, woollen dresses and even a pair of gloves and a scarf.

'But you won't wear it for months.' I fan myself with my notepad.

'All the good pieces get snapped up within a few days.' Ceci looks through Georgina's haul.

'Now's the time to start integrating new-season finds into your current wardrobe.' Georgina holds a black mohair roll neck against her.

'It's twenty-seven degrees. What about a knitted bikini?'

Ceci giggles.

Georgina rolls her eyes.

My email pings.

> From: Fancy Pants Advertising Agency
> Subject: Casting for two male extras.
>
> Brief: White guys that think they are black.
> Cheers.

Are you allowed to say that? I know fashion is visually reductive, blonde with no boobs, freckled girl etc., but this is a bit much. I feel uncomfortable. I forward the email to the casting agent, writing 'FYI' at the top. Someone else can deal with it. I swallow. I feel like a coward. I won't mention this to Jen.

**

I'm walking from the tube station to Fancy Pants Advertising Agency for a production meeting, slowly. It's so hot the pavement is melting. Or maybe it's my shoes. Either way the situation can be summed up by the word 'sticky'. My phone rings: the office.

'It's me.'

'Pandora?' Why is *she* calling? And why is she whispering?

'I need your help.'

Well, well, well. This is a turn-up for the books. I shan't gloat. I shan't crow. I shall graciously ...

'The airplane blades I sourced for Zane's shoot don't fit in the studio,' she interrupts my magnanimity.

'Oh. I thought you measured the room?' The airplane blades are key to her brief.

'I did, but not the doors.'

I wave hello to Alfie as I enter the meeting room. Fifteen people. Windows that don't open. No air con. Sticky. 'Can they take the doors off the hinges?'

'Still won't fit.'

'Is the shoot at Park Royal? They've got drive-in studios for cars. Ask to swap.'

'OK, yah.'

Well that's a first, Pandora asking *me* for help.

I join the brand owner, her team, Alfie, his assistant, five people from Fancy Pants Advertising Agency, the stylist and the props stylist brainstorming round a flip chart.

'You're bang on the money, honey!' Alfie's approach to the ultimate client, the brand owner, is excessive flattery. He fawns over her like he did Bling-Galore. He looks like he wants to lick her face.

'The tree should be twenty-four-carat gold.'

'The girls should be in bikinis and lots of jewellery.'

I scribble in my pad. Despite being the youngest and the least important in the room, it's my responsibility to make everything happen. *No pressure.*

'It would be super,' the brand owner strokes Alfie's chest, 'if we included Brutus.'

Brutus? Must be a model – I'll option him.

'Everyone says he's a natural in front of the camera,' she continues. 'I'll have my PA bring him in the car.'

Huh? Is Brutus her kid?

'He's a bulldog, right?' Alfie leers. 'Great breed.'

Oh no. Another dog. *Binky: The Sequel With Bite.* What is it with fashionistas and their dogs? *Puppies, for when you can't be arsed with a designer baby.* I snigger.

Alfie and the brand owner look at me.

'Sorry.' I pretend to cough.

They turn back to their flirt session.

Mental note: don't laugh about dogs in fashion.

I've booked a private Georgian house for the photo shoot. The location agent was a bit cagey about who owns it, but judging by the amount of gilt and marble in the hallway I would guess footballer or Russian oil baron.

The entrance hall is bigger than the ground floor of my parents' house. The ceiling's so high you could drive a double-decker bus into it. On the morning of the shoot I walk through mini-ballroom after mini-ballroom, a mass of knotted gold cornicing, mirrors and chandeliers. There's an expansive kitchen encased in acres of polished granite. Through another door is another kitchen covered in stainless steel. *Is this where the staff prepares food and the other kitchen is for show?* There's a courtyard garden. It's stately, brash and empty. What would it be like to live here? Echo-ey. The electricity bill must be huge.

'Hello? Lighting delivery!' A far-off voice drifts through.

I sprint back. 'Hi! Sorry! Big house!' I gasp to the hirsute deliveryman.

'No worries. Got your lighting here. Where do you want it?'

My phone beeps: a text from Mr Darling.

> Would you like to
> come over to my
> flat for dinner – I'll
> cook my famous*
> linguine? x
> *Fame is a relative concept.

An invite to Mr Darling's flat! Threshold moment. Not sure about the linguine though – from what I remember of university he lived mostly on lemon curd and Maryland cookies. I hope he's not putting those in the pasta.

> Not sure when the
> shoot will finish
> but could do tonight?
> Prepare the pasta! Ax

The morning's a blur of deliveries, people and props. Mr Darling confirms. I try to contain the hundred-strong team in two rooms. My mobile rings. It's the creative director's PA.

A Bentley is double-parked outside the house. A woman in her thirties, wearing a skirt suit and her hair in a bun, steps out the car and tugs on a lead. Brutus appears. Most of his squat body is brown, but his paws, face and one of his ears is white. There's no evidence of the frenetic energy or high-pitched bark Binky displays. He looks well behaved – he hasn't tried to hump anything in the last few minutes.

'I'll collect Brutus at six o'clock.' The PA passes me the lead.

'Good boy, come on, Brutus.'

'Angela, the steamer's broken! How can I prep the clothes without a steamer?' The stylist, who seems to be wearing a top made of safety pins, clatters toward me.

Erm ...

'Can we use the rooms upstairs? A bed shot with the rapper and all the girls would be wicked!' Alfie's wearing his trucker hat.

When did this turn into a Loaded *shoot?*

'What time is lunch? My account manager is vegan and allergic to nuts, wheat and gluten.' The greying art director from the ad agency marches over.

'One second, I'll be right back.' One of Alfie's assistants, Tom, nice lad, always wears a baseball cap backwards, is setting up the lighting on the main set. 'Tom, you going to be staying in this room?'

'Yeah, pretty much.'

'Can you watch Brutus?' I tie the end of Brutus's lead to a sturdy-looking light-stand. I wonder what colour Tom's hair is under that hat? Perhaps he's bald.

Tom strokes Brutus. 'Sure. You'll be fine here won't you, mate?'

'Thanks!' Time to tackle my ever-growing to-do list.

Locate and borrow a replacement steamer: done. Persuade Alfie to abandon tacky soft-porn shots: done. Find some fruit salad for the allergic vegan account manager: done. Regretting agreeing going straight to Mr Darling's without a shower: done.

Time for Brutus's close-up. He's no longer tied to the lighting rig. Where's Tom? Perhaps he's taken him for a walk?

Tom comes in carrying a large reflector.

'Hey Tom, where's Brutus?'

'He's right … oh. He was right there.' He points to where I'm standing.

My stomach collapses in on itself. 'Where is he?'

'Sorry.' Tom shrugs.

Is that baseball cap restricting oxygen to your brain? 'When did you last see him?' *Don't panic.* I've lost the client's dog. I may as well resign now. 'Brutus, Brutus! Here boy!'

He's not in the wardrobe room, not on the main set, not in the kitchen. I push my face against the glass surrounding the courtyard; not there. He could be lost for ever. He could have got outside. He could have been squashed under a London bus. My glamorous career in fashion is about to crash down around my ears. How will I pay my credit-card bill if I get fired? What am I going to do?

I've got to tell Alfie I've lost the client's prized pooch. I'm a substitute-baby loser. *Is that a tail?* Brutus! He's asleep behind a pile of exquisitely wrapped presents in the prop room.

What's that KFC Family Bucket of chicken doing there? Oh no, he didn't! That's a prop. He did! He's eaten the lot, even the baked-bean pot is licked clean. Aren't chicken bones dangerous to dogs? I'm sure I've read they splinter in their throats. Is he just sleeping?

I fall on to my knees and shake his warm body. 'Brutus!'

His eyes open in a languid gaze.

Thank God! 'Good dog, good Brutus, you are a good boy!'

Brutus eases himself up on to his feet, takes a step forward and vomits all over the carpet.

This is retching karma for throwing up in a public park. I don't have time to deal with this.

I grab Brutus's lead and the empty bucket of KFC. I stick a note on the door: 'ROOM OUT OF BOUNDS'.

COPING WITH
COUPLEDOM

'I can't concentrate in flats!'

VICTORIA BECKHAM

After work, Mr Darling and I walk through the communal foyer of his new-build apartment block. It's on Westferry Road, one of a line of developments bordering the Thames and stretching away from the dominant glass towers of Canary Wharf. It's very rich magnolia, like a lavish Travelodge, with less character.

'So what did you do about the dog puke?' He puts the key in his door.

'I've got to go back tomorrow with a mop and some Vanish. Working in fashion is endlessly glamorous.' I try and sniff my underarms while he's not looking to see if they smell.

'Welcome to my humble abode!'

I survey the laminate flooring, beige walls and obligatory glass dining table with dark high-backed chairs. You could believe this was a show home if it wasn't for the haphazard stack of newspapers and bottle of HP sauce next to the black leather corner sofa. 'Glad to see you have a ridiculously massive flat-

screen television: it really adds to the whole bachelor pad vibe.'
I spy a half-eaten can of spaghetti hoops with a fork sticking out
of it. 'Do you think this flat is identical to all the others in this
block?'

'Definitely. I looked at several along this road and they're all
the same.'

'Weird. Why don't you get some prints for the wall or some
cushions?'

'Never really understood the point of a cushion.' He takes off
his jacket and tie and drops them on the sofa.

'Colour, interest, personality?'

'This flat has *stacks* of personality – you can see the Thames
from the balcony. If you lean over and turn your head to the left.'
He opens the glass sliding door.

We watch two teenagers stand round a burning pile on the
slipway into the Thames. 'A charming riverside apartment with
quaint views of the local kids setting fire to things,' I say in my
best estate agent voice.

'They do that a lot. Last week whatever they lit exploded and
they ended up flat on their backs.' Mr Darling points at a TV
floating in the water.

'Local colour. Least you have a place of your own. I'm still
living with my parents.' *Loser*.

'You can stay tonight, if you want? It'll make it quicker to
get back to the dog puke.' His cheeky dimple makes an
appearance.

'There's an incentive for a girl.' I smile. I'm being asked to
stay over! 'I'd love to.' I'll stop at Topshop on the way to the
office and buy an emergency outfit. Can't wear the same clothes
two days in a row.

'Make yourself at home and I'll go start dinner.' He signals at
the sofa and TV. 'I reckon if I sieve the sauce it'll get rid of the
lumps.'

'I'll help. I want to live to see that dog puke tomorrow.'

'What you doing this weekend?' He fishes an alarming array of ingredients out of an M&S bag in the small and mostly stainless-steel kitchen.

Sleeping, stuffing my face with crisps and watching Spoilt and Sexy. 'Nothing that's fixed.'

'Want to spend the weekend together? We could picnic on strawberries and champagne in Hyde Park?'

'I think I can free up time in my diary.' I watch as Mr Darling attacks a tub of double cream. I have a boyfriend. Someone who wants to cook for me and spend time with me and take me on romantic picnics. I'd forgotten how good this felt. I jump clear as a blob of cream squirts into the air. I'll cook next time.

***

I admire the orange linen trousers in the Topshop changing-room mirror. They're identical to the designer pair I saw in last month's *Elle*. I can wear them again for my picnic date with Mr Darling on Saturday. He caught the tube in to work with me this morning. We were that really annoying couple snogging each other while all the other commuters tut and rustle their copies of *Metro*. It was fantastic. I wonder what Side-Parting would say if he could see his ex-flatmate and me all loved up? Mr Darling is no longer in touch with him, but he could have heard about our 'relationship status' through gossiping friends. Just the thought makes me laugh.

I look at the price tag on the trousers. It's not like £20 is loads of money – Pandora's just bought a £495 Marni clutch – but I don't really have it to spare. I glance nervously at my handbag, which still contains my Visa bills. I swallow. What can I do? I can't go to work in the same clothes as yesterday. Work! Christ! I'd forgotten about that, too busy mooning around like a lovesick idiot. No time to worry about the trousers now.

I bundle yesterday's clothes into my handbag, obscuring the threatening credit-card bills. I pay for the trousers, new vest top and new necklace (in the sale, so it doesn't count) and get my orange arse in gear.

I can hear raucous laughter coming from the office as I step out the lift. What is going on?

'Well I worked with a diva who wouldn't allow anyone to turn their back on her. You had to reverse bowing out the room like you were Japanese.' Fraser's tight-jeaned bottom bumps into me as he bows away from Daffodil and the girls who are sat on the desks. 'Oh, sorry doll!'

'Morning.'

They all crack up.

'Well that's nothing.' Daffodil, her bleached hair backcombed into a pineapple ponytail on her head, jumps up.

'What's happening?' I whisper to Ceci as I perch on the edge of the desk.

'They're having a goss-off.' Ceci wipes a tear from under her eye.

'It's hilar!' Pandora giggles.

'I once worked for a famous It girl who insisted I do her make-up while she was asleep. I had to sneak into her room and do it while she was in bed.' Daffodil shakes her pineapple.

'No way!' we all scream.

'Very creepy,' Daffodil grimaces.

Fraser takes the bait. 'Well, I once did the hair of a very well-known politician. In the government ...'

'... boring!' yells Daffodil.

'Wait for it.' Fraser puts his hand up in a stop sign and wiggles his head. *Uh huh girlfriend.* 'I was covering a friend who's been working with this politician for years. He's one of the cabinet and married with kids. But it's all a beard. He's gay. They all know: his team, his wife, everyone. Open secret.'

'Who is it?' Georgina cries.

'If I told you MI5 would probably kill you, doll.' Fraser winks. 'But he's in the news. A lot.'

I can't wait to tell Mr Darling all this on Saturday. He'll love the story about the politician.

Later in the day when Daffodil and Fraser have left, and I'm on hold to the lab about the film for Alfie's luxury-store shoot, I receive a text from Mr Darling. Bless him, he's probably sent me a mushy message.

> Sorry, problem with
> the project. I have to
> work all weekend.
> Another time. x

My picnic and pash-session plans crumble. What project? What could be so important that he has to work all weekend? Even crazy Vampira hasn't demanded any of us work over a Saturday. I have an awful feeling in the pit of my stomach. Is it an excuse? Maybe I've misread the signs, like when Side-Parting was talking about moving in together one week and dumping me the next. Maybe we weren't being soppy this morning, maybe only I was? Don't panic, play it cool. I text back:

> Sure.

No kisses, no lovey stuff.

'Sorry to keep you holding for so long.' The guy from the lab picks up the line and breaks into my thoughts.

I take a deep breath to make sure my voice doesn't sound funny when I speak. Mr Darling cancelling our date has really shaken me up. Maybe I should have waited a couple of hours before replying?

***

It's been four days and I still haven't heard from Mr Darling. Nothing. I couldn't sleep again last night. At 3 a.m. I got out of bed and organised my wardrobe; none of my clothes look remotely like the ones Ceci and Georgina have brought for autumn/winter. I finally drifted off just before my alarm beeped and then hit snooze. My trusty rusty Metro's joined the scrapheap in the sky and I'm supposed to get up half an hour earlier to catch a bus to the station. I've missed it, so now I'm late for work. I hate Mondays.

I fly through the office door expecting a barrage of dirty looks.

Ceci's sitting in her bikini filing her nails. I do a double take. The other desks are empty. Am I dreaming? It's 10.20 a.m. It's not a Bank Holiday. 'Where is everyone?'

'It's August, they're on holiday, darling.' Ceci switches hands.

'All at the same time?' What about the constantly ringing phones, the intense productions, how the hell are we going to cope?

'Everyone goes on holiday in August.' Ceci slides off her flip-flops and inspects her pedicure.

Ceci's wearing flip-flops! I've never seen her in anything less than a four-inch heel. 'Everyone in the agency has gone on holiday?' My voice echoes round the empty room.

'Everyone in the industry. Paris and Milan close for August and go to the Riviera. New York goes to the Hamptons. London winds down.'

Has she put reggae music on the stereo? 'We're still open?' Am I supposed to be here? I could do with a break or just a nap.

'Yeah, we run on a skeleton staff ...'

I won't make the obvious 'skeleton-thin' joke.

'... and we finish early. Five o'clock usually, sometimes lunch on a Friday.'

Score! 'Can I book time off?' The credit-card bills in my

handbag tug on my arm. I can't afford to go away. But Mr Darling could get some time off, and we could stroll along the Thames eating ice cream. If we're still together …

Ceci gets the office diary out. 'Charlie is away for the whole month. Pandora's in Monaco till next week, but then I'm off to stay on my friend's yacht …'

'You have a friend with a yacht?' I pull up a chair and rest my feet on the desk. Might as well make the most of it.

She waves her hand at me to signify she's concentrating. 'Georgina is back from her Italian spa in a week and a half, but off to a north Ibizan retreat the next day and, oh no, that's not going to work, both Pandora and I are away with friends in the country then …'

It's like she's reading from a list of Condé Nast Traveller's *hotspots.*

'… I'm sorry, darl. There's no time left.'

Oh.

She looks guilty. 'You've got to get in there early to get time off in August … because it's so popular.'

'That's OK.' I haven't got anywhere to go or anyone to go with anyway. Just call me Cinders. My feet slump onto the floor. My life sucks.

I switch on my emails. Nothing. I check the answerphone. Nothing. I pick up the phone and check the receiver is working.

Ceci's turquoise toenails have her full attention.

This is going to be a long, boring and depressing month. I press refresh on my inbox. Nothing.

***

I've tear-sheeted every magazine in the office. I've filed everyone's paperwork. I've cleaned and straightened every page of every artist's portfolio. I've even prepared a mail-out of artists' cards and labelled it up to be sent to five hundred industry contacts when they return in September. Yesterday I rearranged the cups in the kitchen. Times are getting desperate. Jen told me to keep busy. It's all right for her: she's taking a training course, which is eating up all her free time. All my other mates seem to be on beaches in Mallorca and Ibiza. My life is officially rubbish. It's been over two weeks since I heard from Mr Darling. I refuse to contact him – I keep rereading a *Marie Claire* feature I found about not chasing men.

I press refresh on my email. All I get at the moment are holiday snaps from Fraser. It's always white sandy beaches, azure sea, and cocktails in coconuts. Simon Cowell was in the background of yesterday's.

I open a new email and type:

> Hi,
> How's work?

I delete what I've written. What am I supposed to say to Mr Darling? *Gosh, isn't the weather warm and by the way do you still like me?* I need to stay strong. I should listen to Beyoncé songs about being a survivor and an independent woman.

'What ya doing?' Pandora's voice cuts through my thoughts. This is the worst week of August so far, because I am alone in the office with Pandora. We've been circling each other like tigers. She behaves as if she's my friend when no one else is around. A frenemy.

'Nothing.'

'You're emailing. I saw you! Is it your *boyfriend*? You never talk about him. Are you embarrassed, does he stack shelves in a supermarket?'

This is all I need. Boyfriend – ha! Mr Darling's probably forgotten all about me. 'There's nothing wrong with stacking shelves at a supermarket.' I minimise my screen.

'I knew it! He works at Asda!' She thumps her palm on the desk. Her pen pot, which is full of make-up, jumps.

I will not tell you anything.

'Does he have to wear that horrible green uniform?' She inspects her perfect hair for non-existent split ends.

'Actually he works in finance.' *Damnit.*

Pandora stares at me, tilting her head like a praying mantis. 'You mean he's a bank clerk?'

'No, an economist. He works in the City.' I may as well be talking about an imaginary boyfriend.

She sniffs. 'I don't think he's right for you.'

Apparently neither does he. I need to distract her. 'Where are you off to this Friday?'

'A friend's house in the country. Well, when I say house, I mean estate, and when I say estate, I mean castle.' She laughs.

How witty. 'And what are you going to wear?' All fashionistas can't help but talk about what they are planning to wear. It's like a disease. I've caught it. My wardrobe is planned for the next two weeks.

'I'm going to take my Matthew Williamson gown, my Missoni bikini in case the weather's nice …'

I start to zone out.

'… but then I heard there was potentially a second formal event and I haven't got anything to wear.'

'Pardon?'

'I said I haven't got anything to wear.'

Bingo! 'Would you like to go shopping? I can hold the fort here.'

'Really?' She looks like she can't believe I'm giving her a get-out-of-jail-free card.

'Of course!'

'OK, but this doesn't mean you get to swan off tomorrow.'

'Sure. No problem. Go forth and shop.'

She grabs her two-tone Marni shoulder bag and is off out the door.

Peace at last. I press refresh on my email and check my phone. Still nothing.

***

'I'm bored.' Georgina, who's been back in the office for one day, throws her copy of *Purple* across the floor. Even she is dressed casually. That linen Dries Van Noten barely has structure.

Being trapped in an office with a pissed-off Georgina scares me. I try the same trick as I did with Pandora last week. 'Do you want to go out?'

'No, it's too hot.' Her hair's still in flawless forties Hollywood waves. 'I know what we should do.' She leans toward me. She doesn't have the look of the cold girl I usually work with. The heat's melted her.

'What?'

'Let's have a casting!'

She's got sunstroke. 'We don't have any jobs ...'

'A men's swimwear casting!'

Cracked in the heat. Shall I call a doctor?

'We'll get a bottle of wine, hold it on the balcony and get them to take their tops off.'

Pecs, six-packs, bulging ... er ... muscles. There are worse ways to waste time. Now I get it; I bet Georgina was the girl who shimmied down the drainpipe at boarding school to go clubbing. 'Can we do that?' A bit of eye candy might distract me from thinking about Mr Darling.

'It's research.' She picks up her Rolodex.

'We can't!' Why am I whispering? Charlie isn't going to hear us from her Tuscany villa. Georgina ignores me and grabs the phone.

'Andi, darling, it's Gigi. Bit of a last-minute one this, do you have any boys in town?'

For the first time in what feels like weeks, I laugh.

My phone beeps. I hold my breath, it couldn't be? No, it's just Fraser:

> Land on Tuesday!
> London Fashion
> Week, doll!! Can
> we charge my airport
> taxi to my next job?
> xxxx

So the Tuesday after the bank holiday is fashion's back to school day. Then it's just two weeks till the shows. My first ever Fashion Week. At least that's something to look forward to.

You *Shall* Go to the Ball, Cinderella

'I base most of my fashion sense on what doesn't itch.'

GILDA RADNER

The fashion industry has exploded. Everyone is back, all at once. There must have been planes full of fashionistas flying in to London. I can just imagine them all clicking through the airports, laden down with duty-free Prada perfume, cigarettes and exotic jewellery they're going to work into their outfits.

There's a last-minute panic to shoot everything before the shows start. Fraser arrived into Gatwick one day and flew straight back out to New York for a job the next. He told me a shocking story about discovering the two fifteen-year-old models in flagrante with the production assistant. At the same time. Fashion can be worrying sometimes. I don't want to sound prudish, but where were these girls' parents? I thought everyone underage on a shoot was supposed to have a legal guardian with them?

Ceci and Georgina have started receiving invites for the shows, and even Pandora has a couple. Each day I add more to Charlie's in-tray. Nothing for me. But that's no great surprise: nobody knows who I am. I'm crossing my fingers someone lets me tag along to a show almost as much as I'm crossing my fingers that Mr Darling contacts me. Hopes for both are fading fast.

The office is buzzing today. The phone's ringing off the hook, emails are pouring in and there's a steady stream of artists coming in to show off their tans. The girls have gone into fashionista overdrive. The temperature is still in the mid-twenties in London, but Pandora, Georgina and Ceci are wearing their autumn/winter-season knitted dresses. Charlie's still wearing her trademark black when we see her, so everything's normal. By rights the girls should be pools of sweat on the floor, but they're as fragrant as ever. It must be years of hardened fashion training, or they've nicked Marilyn Monroe's tip of keeping their underwear in the fridge. I finish writing my Post-it note and stick it to my computer:

> September shows are spring/summer for next year
> – floaty dresses, bikinis etc.

> February shows are autumn/winter for the same
> year – coats, knitwear etc.

'What is that?' Georgina points at it.

'It's to help me remember the schedule.' I'm getting so confused. The autumn/winter collections that show in February are available in shops in August. And the spring/summer collections that show in September are available in shops in February. 'What are we supposed to wear to the shows: spring/summer, autumn/winter, this year or next year?'

'New season autumn/winter. But if there are strong trends coming through on the catwalk, then you can incorporate those into your look,' Georgina advises.

Trends I haven't even seen yet? What if I do get to go to a show? 'I'm not sure I can deal with working out what to wear *and* run productions.'

'Hardly anything gets shot during the fashion weeks, because the models are busy on the catwalk.' Pandora gives me her favourite disparaging look.

'We won't be producing much till after the shows, then the new-season samples become available for advertising campaigns, look books and editorial,' Georgina adds.

Can't we have one long continuous season? It would be easier. Another ten or so emails stream into my inbox. A familiar name catches my eye. Mr Darling. My heart starts racing. I hold my breath while I read it.

> Finally finished the project. Sorry I haven't been in contact. I've been working till 2 a.m. most nights. My manager sent me home yesterday because he said I looked ill. I've been living off of Crunchy Nut Cornflakes! Missed you, hope you're not still angry with me – your last text was quite abrupt! Dinner tomorrow to make it up?
>
> xx

I re-read it several times. He's been working till 2 a.m.? That's insane. Poor Mr Darling! Though he could have texted me. Just to let me know he was thinking of me; I've been miserable. I huff and angrily move my pad and pens round my desk. You can't just neglect your girlfriend for weeks because you're busy at work. I ignore the guilty feeling that I didn't message him either. I will go for dinner with him, but I'm going to play it cool. He's going to have an ice-cold blonde on his hands.

***

'The most exciting thing in the world has happened to me!' I rush up to Mr Darling in the gastropub we arranged to meet in. Forget the whole Hitchcock-blonde thing, this is too important. He's already at a table. I'm a little late.

'Hello, small tornado,' he says pouring me a glass of wine.

He has a huge grin on his face, he looks really pleased to see me. My tummy does a little flutter. I do feel guilty about ignoring him. We need to work on our communication.

'You know how it's London Fashion Week next week?' I hang my bag off the table clip.

'It is? It's my birthday next week.'

What! 'It is?' I freeze. *How did I not know this?* 'Your birthday is in the middle of London Fashion Week?' I slump on to the wooden chair.

'Apparently so.' He picks a peanut out of a bowl on the table and eats it.

'How can you sit there calmly eating nuts? London Fashion Week is the most important event of the year. The doyennes of the fashion world will be descending on town. There are rumours Anna Wintour might come this year.' I can't believe this is happening, it's like the universe is saying we're not compatible. I manically shove peanuts into my mouth. 'This is a disaster. There are fifty-two weeks in a year. How could you be born during Fashion Week?'

'You'll have to take that up with my parents.' Mr Darling raises a dark eyebrow. 'I'm sure it won't matter anyway. We don't have to celebrate.'

'Of course we have to celebrate!' *I've just spent the last few weeks ignoring you while you worked in an economics sweatshop, missing your birthday would kill our relationship.* My mind goes into overdrive. *I haven't got enough money to buy you a present! I'll have to cook dinner instead.* 'I'll come over to yours.

Make a special three-course meal. How does steak sound?'

'Tempting.'

Steak, sticky toffee pudding; this is not just a birthday meal, this is an M&S birthday meal. I'll stick candles in the custard. I feel a bit better. 'All this birthday talk has thrown me. I haven't told you my amazing news.'

'Ah yes, "the most exciting thing in the world".' He inspects the empty peanut bowl.

I place both my hands on the table and fix him with a stare. 'I have been invited to a show!'

He stares back.

'Well, aren't you excited?'

'Is that it?'

'*Is that it?* I've been invited to a fashion show. Little ol' me. Even before I wanted to work in fashion, I wanted to go to a fashion show. They're glittering events full of supermodels and designers and film stars. I've seen them in movies!' *What the hell am I going to wear?*

'I'm very happy for you.' Mr Darling is pulling his bemused face. The one that looks like I've just communicated through the medium of a squeaky toy. He's not getting it.

'I have an invite. An expensive, stiff, white, embossed-card invite. With my name written on it.' Well, it says 'Angele', which is close enough for me.

'Let's order dinner, all the peanuts are gone,' he says.

***

I'm still thinking about his response a few days later. How can you not be impressed by a London Fashion Week invite? Maybe Mr Darling and I are too different. But he's so sweet, and funny, and after we stopped talking about fashion we had a great time. He even had the restaurant ice 'Sorry' on my chocolate pudding to apologise for being so busy. He's been sending me texts and emails every day since then.

'Angela, can you get that!' Georgina signals at the ringing phone.

I look up and realise everyone's on other lines. 'Sorry!' I gasp. I've got to get my head out of the clouds, it's London Fashion Week for God's sake! 'Hello, Charlie Monroe Management, Angela speaking.'

'It's me, doll.'

'Morning Fraser, how's the prep going for the show?' He's backstage before one of London Fashion Week's biggest shows today. Über-important designer, oodles of supermodels. If Anna Wintour does put in an appearance this season it will be there. Lucky devil.

'Was going fab till the designer just lost it at the opening model. Don't blame him though: she waltzed in two hours late, all diva, snapping her fingers at the make-up artist. He was like, "Nobody's bigger than the show! Nobody's bigger than me!"'

'No way!'

'Honestly I thought they were going to bitch-fight. Miss Diva was all up in his face screaming, he's screaming back. He fired her. She quit. The place is in meltdown. The PR's in floods. The designer's locked himself in the loo. It's *fabulous!*'

'Oh my God! Are you all right?'

'It's been *very* trying. But I'm a professional. The show must go on, and all that, doll. As long as I get paid. Got to go – sounds like he's opened the bathroom door …'

'I'll see you tomorrow after the show!' I shout, but he's already gone. Fraser's heading the team for the show I've been invited to. He's the reason I've been invited – I told the PR controlling the guest list I needed to go 'for support'. Needs must.

Fashion Week is already exceeding my expectations – a bust-up between a supermodel and top designer! I love working in fashion: all of the gossip, none of the calories.

'More invites just in ladies – get your glad rags ready, we've been invited to *Outré Couture*'s party tomorrow night!' Ceci air-punches.

'Woo!' cheers Pandora.

Outré Couture is only one of the top glossy mags in the UK. A *proper* fashion party. With, with, I don't know what – proper fashion things!

'Storm and Models One parties later in the week,' chimes in Georgina.

Faints.

'I'm guessing wearing high street is a no-no?' I say to Pandora. She shakes her head. 'Designer or vintage.'

Vintage it is then. I'll pop to the shops after work. I squash the feeling of panic about my Visa-card bill. This is an emergency. I'll bring sandwiches from home for lunch and it'll even out my budget.

'God, I hope the traffic's better this season. Autumn/winter was a nightmare because of that *Blair Witch* protest thing,' sighs Pandora dramatically.

You what?

'She means the demonstrations against going to war with Iraq. They coincided with Fashion Week, screwed with the transport. All the shows ran an hour late. Carnage,' Georgina translates.

'*Blair Witch* – you meant Tony Blair?' I stare at Pandora. She *must* be joking. Jen will love this!

'Whatever.' Pandora rolls her eyes.

Back at home I show Mum my new fashion find: a gorgeous 1940s crêpe de Chine black dress, with a delicate lace collar and cuffs. Front-row fabulous, as Fraser would say. A snip at forty-five pounds for a piece of history. 'What do you think?'

'Lace? That looks itchy.' Mum rubs the cuff between her fingers.

'It isn't. It's perfect.' She'd probably wear her jogging bottoms to a catwalk show if she could. I must remember to text Mr Darling before I go to bed. Communication skills.

ALLERGIC REACTION

'I don't even think when I'm walking down
the runway. I don't really breathe either.'

ROSIE HUNTINGTON-WHITELEY

The show starts at nine. Fraser's call time was 5 a.m., poor thing.
The things we do for fashion! I must look eccentric waiting for
the bus in my vintage dress, neon-green heels and Burberry
mac, but I don't care.

Something's irritating my neck. Probably nerves. It's hot.
I take off my coat.

'Tickets please?' The train ticket inspector looks at me
strangely. He wrinkles his nose.

Yes, I'm wearing green shoes. Get over it.

He hands my ticket back.

I slide it under my lace cuff and scratch my wrist.

Oh no. No, no, no. Red spots, hundreds of them. A rash.
That's what the train inspector was grimacing at. I undo the stiff
buttons and push the sleeve back. It's spread up both arms! My
décolletage is angry and puce, it's growing up my neck. It's the

lace. I'm having an allergic reaction to the dress. Mum was right.

Keep calm. I can go to Boots on the way. Buy antihistamines. I roll the crêpe de Chine sleeves up so the lace is away from my skin. I close my eyes. Think of ice-cold water. Breathe. Breathe.

'Are you all right, dear?'

I open an eye. A middle-aged lady in an ill-fitting grey suit is staring at me. *You've got to help me, I'm going to a fashion show and I'm turning into an angry strawberry!* 'Fine, thank you.'

I'm in a cool mountain stream. I'm in a cool mountain stream. I'm completely fucked.

There's a Boots outside the tube station. Thank God for homogenous high streets. I scoop up cream and tablets and a bottle of water.

I use the make-up-section mirror to apply the cream to my chest. The rash has reached the top of my neck and is stretching round the back. It looks like I'm wearing a mohair scarf.

I fish my sunglasses out my bag and steel myself. The rash will go down.

As I near Somerset House's courtyard the crowd grows taller, thinner, and more extravagantly dressed. This is the fabled fash pack.

The pinpricks on my arms have mutated into lumps. I can see the entrance. My throat is tightening. It's five metres away. Am I going into anaphylactic shock? I can imagine Mum screaming at me to go to the doctors. I'm *so* close.

***

I turn and walk out of Somerset House. I need an alley. Bingo! This seems suitably deserted. I have to get the dress away from my skin. I undo the buttons down the front and roll it away from the rash. Over the top I belt my Burberry mac like a wrap dress.

I turn the collar up and adjust my sunglasses. Strippergram chic. I'm going to this show if it kills me.

The black-clad PR girl looks at my invite and her clipboard. *Why do PRs ALWAYS wear black?*

'Fourth row.'

My ears are pounding, no wait, it's just the bass from the music.

Neat rows of collapsible chairs line either side of a catwalk. It's not raised but just an empty, sacred space that people skip quickly across. Women, men, expensive clothes, stretched limbs, large leather handbags, bottled water, angular haircuts, faces I recognise from the magazines. If Pandora were here she'd know their names. If Pandora were here she'd probably know *them*. I'm relieved to note other people are wearing sunglasses inside. Quite a few, actually. *Avoiding eye contact? Hangovers? Bad plastic surgery?* Important sinewy women are escorted to their front-row seats by PRs.

Beyonce's 'Crazy in Love' shrieks out of the speakers. The lights flare. That's why people are wearing sunglasses! A model steps onto the catwalk, looking as if she's leaning back, her long legs bare and tanned. Massive gold patent platform heels are strapped to her feet, a delicate white smock dress billows around her like a cloud. Her hair, designed by Fraser, is in a walnut whip of a beehive, and her make-up is minimal. Glorious. Exotic. Stunning. This is the most amazing experience of my life. *I wish I didn't want to scratch my face off.*

***

'You've got hives,' says the doctor. 'To have had this kind of reaction to a dress you must have very sensitive skin. Keep taking the antihistamines and it should be gone within seven days.'

'I haven't *got* seven days!'

'I'm sorry, but that's how long it takes.'

Seven days, that's a whole fashion week! The magazine party, the office, I can't go to either looking like this. Mr Darling's birthday! How sexy, to be cooked for by a warty toady woman. 'You don't understand – I work in fashion. And it's …'

'… Fashion Week.' He turns toward me.

'Yes.'

'That is tricky. It *is* affecting your ability to work.' He's reasoning with himself. 'I could give you a treatment of steroids. That could clear it up quicker.'

'You'd do that?'

'Yohji Yamamoto is a friend of mine, I understand the pressures of your industry.'

As I walk home past the village cottages I call Jen. 'I got drugs because I work in fashion!' I whisper into my phone.

'What drugs? Are you all right?'

'Steroids. I have hives!'

'How?'

'Not important. What *is* important is the doctor gave them to me because I work in the fashion industry. That's what he said. Isn't that awesome?'

'So, if you worked in a shop or a bank you wouldn't have them? That doesn't seem fair.' Jen's voice has a touch of edge.

'This is a good thing. My prescription is the most important accessory this Fashion Week!'

She doesn't laugh.

'OK, well, I just wanted to share my news, that's all. Got to get changed now, got to catch the train back into town for *Outré Couture*'s party tonight.'

'You're going to a party when you have hives, I don't think that's a good idea.'

'I've got to, it's work.' I cross my fingers. Technically I don't *have* to go. It's only a little white lie.

'OK, well, let's try and catch up in person next week, if you can make time in your work diary?'

'Of course. I'll call you. Love ya, mate.'

***

I stare up at the austere building hosting the *Outré Couture* party. It looks better suited to housing public records than a fashion soirée. The stone steps that fan from the entrance are covered by a red carpet. Are there actual paparazzi outside? A group of three stunning young people pass me clutching invites. The man's wearing a red cravat, one girl has black netting over her eyes, and the other girl's in a midnight-blue cocktail dress. I'm in jeans and a 100 per cent cotton T-shirt: the least itchy thing I could find.

I swallow the saliva pooling in my mouth. I feel like a fifteen-year-old trying to get into a nightclub.

I wish Ceci or Georgina or even Pandora were here. They'd confidently stride in front of all these photographers.

I step onto the carpet. It's surprisingly deep. My stiletto heel digs into it, giving me grip. The photographers don't look up. *Is it so hard to believe I could be someone?*

Yet another black-clad girl with a ponytail, a headset and a clipboard is on the door: the gatekeepers of the fashion industry. *Can you be refused entrance to a party for a rash?*

She waves me past.

The ceiling stretches the full height of the building. The lighting's red. *Everyone* has a rosy glow. Result! I'm not going to stand out.

Through a door is the main dance area. A band plays on a stage, and the lights strobe, making snapshots of shoulder blades, long necks and collarbones. I scan the crowd for a familiar face. That's Penelope Cruz. An A-list superstar, right there!

'Darling, you made it! Hope the doctor was fine,' Ceci screams into my ear. She's wearing jeans too. Thank God.

'Look, it's Penelope Cruz!'

'Cool!' Ceci doesn't look.

'Shall I ask her for a photograph, to show my mum?'

'You're so funny, darling,' Ceci laughs.

Oh. OK. Acting like a one-woman pap is obviously not the done thing.

'Let's get you a drink.' Ceci takes my hand and pulls me to the black marble bar.

'Two glasses of champagne, please,' Ceci shouts to the barman.

That sounds expensive – wine would be fine.

The barman hands us glasses. Ceci steps away from the bar. *Does she want me to pay for both?* 'What about, er …'

'Free bar, darling.' Ceci raises her glass.

'I'll drink to that!'

'Chin chin!'

I spy Pandora, talking to a group of girls she probably shared a private obstetrician with when she was born. After an explosion of air-kissing she joins us.

'Was that Petal Ownmore? I know her sister.' Ceci fiddles with the chunky necklace she's wearing over her silk vest top.

'Yes, she's working on the Preen show. She's sending me an invite …'

I take the opportunity to study the room. Each time I spy a famous face I suppress a jolt of excitement. Tara Palmer-Tompkinson, Pearl Lowe, Sadie Frost, that girl from *Hollyoaks*, I wonder if Kate Moss is here?

There are empty wrought-iron tables and chairs in the corners of the room. *Is garden furniture stylish? Or ironic?* Wow. Look at that girl's shoes. How is she upright? That's a feat of engineering and strong core muscles. 'Why is no one sitting down?'

'It ruins the line of your clothes,' Pandora answers before continuing her conversation with Ceci: 'So I said to her she

shouldn't put up with it, everyone gets their nails done during
the day ...'

'Is that why they're not dancing either?' The dance floor's
empty.

'It's not cool to dance. And she said that he didn't eat anything
but melon for the whole six days ...'

No dancing and no sitting. *Not much of a party is it?*
A waitress walks past with canapés. I'm starving.

'Honey-coated sausages with a mustard-mash dip.' She holds
the tray forward. Slim girl, but in this room of waifs she's one of
the curviest. Apart from me.

I pop a sausage in my mouth. 'Can I have another?'

'Sure.' Her cheeks glow.

Pandora and Ceci stare at me.

'What?' I say with a mouthful of sausage.

'If you think it's OK to eat in public, that's up to you,' scolds
Pandora.

Not eat in public? That's just perverse.

'You never really know how many calories are in these things,'
Ceci adds softly.

I self-consciously chew my sausage. The cake-sniffers
strike again. Canapés: the riskiest thing you can eat in the
world.

Half an hour later the waitress has made it round the room
and back to me. Her tray is untouched. I help myself to another
sausage and eat it behind my clutch bag.

'Darling, how are you?' A sturdy blonde with a strong chin
grabs Ceci.

'Darling! Girls, this is Lulu, we went to prep school together.'
There's a surprise.

Lulu grips Pandora and me in a hug. Pandora stiffens.

The tactile Lulu works at one of the glossy magazines. She's
clearly taken advantage of the free bar.

'Did you hear about Seb? Totally dumped his wife and kids and ran off with the manny.'

'Manny?'

'Male nanny, darling.' Lulu erupts into a throaty laugh.

Pandora tries to hide her smile in her drink.

'And see her over there, standing with the model-agency girls? Apparently, she asked to do coke off the stomach of a male model on location. Utter scandal!' Lulu snorts into her champagne.

How has it got so late? Can you mix champagne and steroids? 'I'm going to make a move, long day,' I shout at Ceci's hair.

'OK, darls. Keep yourself fabulous!' Ceci spits into my ear.

By the door a gatekeeper hands me a fabric bag emblazoned with the magazine's logo. *Goodie bag!* 'Thanks.'

'Taxi, madam?' A guy in a long overcoat is at the exit.

'Sounds sensible.'

'Where you going?'

Mr Darling's? No, I'm still too rash-covered. Rash-y? Rashed? Even my own body is conspiring to keep us apart. 'King's Crosh.' *That champagne was strong.*

I tumble into the back of the cab and open my goodie bag. A full-sized bottle of limited-edition Vivienne Westwood perfume. Holy scent, how much would that cost? A Chanel lipstick. A Mont Blanc silver-plated picture frame. A bottle of posh-looking bath oil. A voucher for Brown's hotel. Three condoms in a small exquisitely decorated wooden box. *OK.* A mini-bottle of Moët. *What's this – bubble bath? No, posh mineral water. Who knew!*

This is incredible! All this must be worth … hundreds. Just for going to a party! That's Christmas sorted, I'll give each of these as presents. Much nicer than anything I could afford. Fashion parties rock. Who can I give the box of condoms to? Great Aunt Mabel? All the way home I giggle to the goodie bag and myself.

***

Day Two of Fashion Week. The good news: my hives have reduced from angry lumps to pinkish raised skin. The bad news: I'm hanging from a great height. Mixing champagne and steroids was not clever.

Why is everyone on this train breathing so loudly? I need a copy of the *Metro*. I have to block out the incessant noise of my fellow commuters. Bastards. Page three: cats make tea. I flick forward. This is more like it: Fashion Week coverage. There's a positive review of Fraser's show. No mention of the hair but a nice photo. And pap shots of celebs arriving at fashion shows and leaving parties. Penelope Cruz looking AMAZING. *I can attest to that.* There's a photo of a girl wearing just a top and tights, no skirt. *How embarrassing* ... there's something familiar about that strong chin ... *Oh my God, it's Ceci's friend Lulu!*

The caption reads: 'An unknown blonde made an unusual fashion statement when leaving the party.' *What happened to her skirt?*

'Ceci, have you seen this?'

Ceci's at her desk with her Givenchy shades on. 'What, I'm awake!'

I drop the paper in front of her.

'Oh my God.'

The others crowd round.

'Least she'd had her bikini line done,' says Georgina.

'I'm calling her, now!' Ceci picks up the phone.

I can't wait to hear this.

'... I see. Thanks.' Ceci hangs up. 'She hasn't shown up for work!' She picks up her mobile to call.

I pretend to read my emails until Ceci comes back in the room.

'She's too mortified to go to work. Someone saw it in the paper at like six thirty this morning and texted her. It was her

friend's skirt she'd borrowed for the night. She decided, God
knows why, to give it back before she got in a cab.'

'Total humiliation.'

'Awful.'

Mental note: be careful working in fashion; the outside world
is a little too interested in what we do.

BACKSTAGE BEDLAM

'For every two minutes of glamour, there are
eight hours of hard work.'

JESSICA SAVITCH

My wheelie case is knocking gently against my calves on the
train. At least with it being both Fashion Week and Mr Darling's
birthday I won't need to change; I'm already wearing my best
outfit. It's been difficult to find a moment to text him over the last
few days. I hope he doesn't think I've been ignoring him again.

I shift my weight from one heel to the other. At lunchtime I'll
pop into M&S and buy what I need for his birthday dinner.
Steak and chips: the route to every man's heart. Unless the man
in question is vegetarian, or doesn't like steak.

My phone rings, disrupting my thoughts. It's Designer
Dormouse. 'Hel—'

'Angela? I can't get hold of anyone. Emergency!'

'What's wrong?'

'Sacked her ... The day before the show ... Tomorrow ...
Can't do it ... Have to ... *Bitch*.'

'Slow down, I can't understand.'

'That designer, the bitchy one I worked on the look book for, has sacked her show stylist. She's asked me to do it instead. It's tomorrow. I've got to style the whole show in one day.'

Is she hyperventilating? Boho Bitch is a *big* designer with a fearsome reputation and a lot of money. Designer Dormouse can't turn this down as she's struggling to pay her mortgage. She styled a show earlier this week and had been working towards it for over a month. One day's worth of notice and prep is unheard of. *Impossible.* 'All the girls can help.' *They're just sitting in the office hungover.* 'What do you need me to do?'

'Go straight to Marble Arch M&S and buy twelve pairs of size twelve, flesh-coloured magic bodies.'

Not what I was expecting. 'Who are they for?' *Has Boho Bitch told her staff to have flat stomachs for the show?*

'The models.'

Has someone been feeding the models? 'Do they need suck-it-all-in underwear?'

'I'm unlacing the tops, so you can see the cups of the bodies – they'll look dishevelled. It *has* to look diferent to the previous styling.'

'Size 12?'

'I don't want any pinching. They need to be loose.'

Based on the models I've seen they'll definitely be loose.

'Buy fifteen pairs of white thermal Long Johns.'

This is the weirdest list in the world.

'And a few cans of hairspray.'

I'm not going to ask.

I find a doughy lady in the M&S lingerie department. 'Excuse me, do you have twelve pairs of these in size twelve?' I hold up the shiny stretchy bodies. *Honestly, I'm not addicted to shapewear.*

'You a stylist's assistant, love?'

Wow! This doughy lady has her finger on the fashion industry pulse. 'Sort of.'

'I get a lot of you in here, buying up all my nude thongs. I'll check out back and bring 'em round.'

There's no time to visit the food department for Mr Darling's birthday supplies. I've got to get to Boho Bitch's studio. I'll pop out at lunch.

'Hi, darling!' Ceci grabs me as I enter the long white room we're using for prep. 'Pandora and I are both here. Georgina's finishing up in the office and coming later.'

She's clearly taking the situation seriously; her hair, which is always down, is in a ponytail.

There are rails on wheels and piles of cloth. *Have they not finished making the samples?* Designer Dormouse's assistant, and two girls I don't recognise, are steaming clothes in the corner. There are other women with needles and thread and scissors making last-minute alterations. A hairdresser and make-up artist are working on a girl – they must be practising looks for the show. And what are all these boxes – invites or the show credit printouts?

'The previous stylist held a model casting, but that was it.' Ceci takes the M&S bags from me.

The door opens behind us. A model comes in wearing a Virgin-Limobike-branded crash helmet.

I hope she's going to take that off before the show?

'You! This way, we're trying looks over here.' Pandora appears with a clipboard from behind a rack of clothes. She also has her hair in a ponytail.

I need to put my hair up.

'I'm helping Pandora dress the girls. You can Polaroid the looks for the running order.' Ceci is picking her way round people and fashion debris.

'OK, let's do this.'

'Oh, Anna, that's your name right? Lovely long legs,' Designer Dormouse is smiling at the model who has now removed her crash helmet. 'I think Anna would be perfect for the floor-length Empire, don't you think?'

'That's already assigned to Carla B.,' Pandora checks her list.

'Try Anna in the dress. Call Carla's booker and get her back here – perhaps she could wear the bustier and cropped jacket instead.'

The running order is documented on a whiteboard covered in Polaroids. I take Carla's photo off and replace it with Anna's. She will now be opening the show. I stick Carla's on the bottom with the TBCs.

'We've got a make-up and a hair look for you to see now.' Ceci touches Designer Dormouse's arm.

Designer Dormouse picks her way over boxes and the legs of models who are sitting against the wall waiting for their fitting. She holds a cream gauze dress against the test model. 'Love the orange lip. Can we make the hair a little less perfect?'

'Good,' says Boho Bitch nodding her head of corkscrew ginger curls. She turns, dramatically sweeping her lilac kaftan like a cloak. She beckons to a model with freckles on her nose. 'You'd look great in the evening gown because you're so flat-chested.'

OK …

'Tick this girl off the list.' Boho Bitch stops to look at Pandora. 'You have very beautiful skin, are you a mongrel?'

WTF?!

Pandora's green eyes are wide with shock.

Boho Bitch wafts toward the girls adjusting hems.

'Are you all right?' I say to Pandora. 'That was completely out of order. Do you want me to complain?' *To whom? We're*

insignificant juniors in this multi-billion industry. There are
plenty of other girls desperate to get into fashion, waiting to take
our place.

'Doesn't matter.' Pandora swallows. Her eyes look glassy.

'I'll take over for a bit, you take five, have a cigarette.' Nobody
deserves to be spoken to like that.

'Thanks.' Her hands shake as she passes me the clipboard.

Georgina, her hair pulled into a ponytail, comes in carrying
a tray of sad-looking sandwiches.

The models head straight for her.

'You're hungry!' I say to a five-foot-eleven girl with a gap
between her front teeth.

'Got to get your food where you can during shows,' she
answers in an American accent.

There's no time to go to M&S now, I'll go on my way
home.

'Angela, can you get the PRs to bike invites to these people?
They're possible clients.' Designer Dormouse hands me a list on
the back of a napkin. 'Try and get them front row. And we need
some more pins. And the make-up artist has a brand sponsor, so
that needs to be added to the credits. Can you call them and ask
if they want anything in the goodie bag?'

'We'll start transferring backstage at five, you manage the
clothes, I'll take PR and hair and make-up.' Pandora sounds OK.
She's tough.

I ride with the courier van and make sure all the rails,
steamer, and samples are taken straight backstage at the venue.
The bland room is long and narrow but we soon fill it. We set up
the rails, a long row of tables and mirrors with lightbulb frames
for the hair and make-up, trestle tables at the far end of the room
for crates of bottles of water; while all the time the lighting crew
in their dusty jeans weave hundreds of cables across the floor.
My feet have consulted their union about going on strike.

Clothes are checked for any new creases. Seamstresses, stylists' assistants, and Pandora (*who knew she could sew?*) make final adjustments. The running order is pinned to the wall. We are ready.

'We're going for a drink, you coming, darling?' Ceci shouts.

How is it 10 p.m.? I'm sure it was six the last time I looked. I haven't gone to M&S. I haven't called Mr Darling. I'm late for his birthday dinner. Crap. 'Sorry, got to go!' I gather my bag up. Where did I leave my wheelie case? I need a cab. 'Taxi!'

I try Mr Darling's mobile. Straight to voicemail. 'It's me. I'm really sorry, I didn't realise the time, I've just left work. I'm on my way, I'll be there soon.' I hang up.

What am I doing? I call back. 'By the way Happy Birthday! OK. See you soon.'

The buildings that hug the Thames fly past as I stare out the taxi window. London always looks its best at night. Like a grande dame in her finest jewels, soft lighting suits her. *How could I not have noticed the time?* I feel like everything is conspiring against Mr Darling and me: his work, my work, his complete lack of understanding about the fashion industry. I hyperventilate a little when I think that maybe we're just not compatible. Maybe it's not going to work. Maybe I'm incapable of making a relationship work. I try to focus on looking at the river.

I knock on Mr Darling's flat door.

'It's open,' his voice calls from inside.

He's sat on the sofa, his tie loose round his neck, eating delivery pizza out the box in front of the TV.

'Happy Birthday!'

He puts down his slice of Texas BBQ. 'We need to talk.'

RESPONSIBLE ADULT

'Never in the history of fashion has so little
material been raised so high to reveal so
much that needs to be covered so badly.'

CECIL BEATON

I sit at the other end of the sofa, clutching my wheelie case. I
can't believe I've thrown away a good relationship just to run
around after Boho Bitch.

Mr Darling takes a small bundle of pink tissue paper out of
his pocket and hands it to me.

It's *his* birthday, why is he giving me something?

'Well, unwrap it then!'

I unfold the tissue paper. Inside is a Yale key cut from flowery
patterned metal. I didn't know you could get patterned
metal.

'It's a key for the flat. I know we've only been seeing each
other a few months, but we've known each other for years. I was
going to give it to you after dinner.'

'Sorry.'

'Doesn't matter, work's work.' He takes a swig from the bottle of beer he has open on the table.

'I thought ...' *you were going to dump me.*

'I got a patterned one because I thought it would be unusual. Quirky. Like you.'

'Thank you.'

'What do you say? Shall we have a slice of pizza to celebrate you moving in?'

Moving in? This is sudden. I thought we were coming to an end a few minutes ago. Shouldn't we have gone through months of agonising talks about whether we're ready to live together? Aren't I supposed to have launched a covert campaign to slowly work my way into your life, starting with subtly leaving my toothbrush in the bathroom and working up till I have my own drawer? I need to stop watching chick flicks. Mr Darling has asked me to move in. This will make it easier: we'll see each other every day. Work can't get in the way of that. *I live in London!*

I jump across and take a big bite of his slice of pizza. 'Happy Birthday!'

'Hey! That's my bit.'

'*Me casa es su casa, me pizza es su pizza.* And vice versa.'

Later, when Mr Darling's tidying in the kitchen, I text Mum:

> Good news! I'm
> moving out xx

***

The clock says: 05.00.

'Urgh.'

Mr Darling's bustling around. 'Good morning, Sleeping Beauty.' A kiss lands on my forehead.

'Urgh.' Why is my alarm going off? Moving to London should save me from early mornings.

Boho Bitch's fashion show!

Urgh. I sleepwalk backstage.

The noise crashes over me like a wave. Music, hairdryers, chatter, shouted instructions, ringing mobiles, clanging metal from the lighting rig. *This many people are up this early?*

A second wave of heat punches me in the face. *Damn my long rash-covering sleeves.*

The PR team are running around in head-to-toe black shouting into their headsets. The hairdresser and his team are working two at a time on the models sat at the mirrored stations. The girls' hair is being backcombed into privet hedges, and then smoothed over to create a helmet of hair. Those Virgin-Limobike crash helmets were clearly very inspiring. Make-up assistants kneel to paint the toenails of the models, making them look like they are bowing down to the Amazonian beauties. The glamour team operate like a tag-wrestling team. As the last hairbrush is pulled through a model's hair, the first make-up brush touches their skin. There is no time to pause.

'I'm so tired.' A red-haired model flops forward onto her hands, ruining the white eye make-up that's already been applied to her left eye. 'It's endless. My agent rang – I'm going to Milan straight after the show. I haven't packed.'

Milan – wow!

'I know, sweetie,' the make-up artist in multicoloured trainers replies. 'How about a facial massage? Would that perk you up?'

Can I get one?

'Got any coke?' sighs the girl.

I'm surprised models drink fizzy pop ... oh ... cocaine, you idiot, cocaine!

'After I've finished your make-up. Once your eyes dilate it's hard to balance the shadow.' The make-up artist puts her hand under the model's chin and tilts her face to the light.

Really?

'Angela! I need your help.' Designer Dormouse, wearing a bustle and a T-shirt, is fretting in the corner.

I wave at Ceci and Pandora who run past with armfuls of skirts.

'Put these on the girls.' Designer Dormouse passes me the M&S Long Johns I bought yesterday.

Hardly cutting-edge fashion.

'I need some scissors.' She waves the underwear about.

An assistant in denim dungarees passes scissors to her. Designer Dormouse snips quickly at each of the Long Johns.

She's lost it. Barking. Fruit loopy.

She signals at one of the models, who dutifully climbs into a pair. The torn Long Johns peak out from under the model's ethereal dress, like slashed jodhpurs. Combined with the ripped-bodice effect of the visible cups, and Boho Bitch's floaty clothes, it looks like Jane Austen meets punk. Clever.

'They look amazing!'

'They'll add contrast.'

'Five minutes!' shouts the head PR.

The models take their cue from the hard, deconstructed styling and stomp onto the catwalk.

Pandora and Ceci slump against each other. I lean against the cool wall. We've done it. Prepped a show in a day.

The stylist's assistants are fast. They strip the models from their first looks like they're peeling bananas. The models are pulled, pushed, zipped, laced and tightened into their next look in seconds. Cheers and clapping override the fading techno music.

A tsunami of fashionistas surge backstage.

'Who are all these people?' I press against the wall.

'Editors, buyers, bloggers, press,' Ceci exhales.

Faux-geeky guys with ironic bow ties wield microphones in front of cameramen. Women with Dictaphones and cameras swoop on Boho Bitch.

'One at a time!' the head PR shouts.

The models are stripping off in front of everyone! I've seen enough nipples to last me a lifetime's subscription to *Playboy*.

Energy crackles round the room. I'm sweating.

'Cheers,' Pandora hands me a mini Moët bottle with a straw poking out the top.

It's 9.20 a.m.

'Amazing. What an experience! It's thrilling being backstage!' Pandora bubbles.

I know! The post-show high. Everything's heightened. I'm soaking in colour, heat and sound. I'm drinking champagne backstage!!

'How did it go? Any orders?' Designer Dormouse touches the head PR's arm as she passes with her clipboard.

'Lots of orders. Only problem is they all want the *amazing* nude bodies and ripped leggings.'

… and not Boho Bitch's tulle dresses.

'We'll have to put them into production.' The PR signals to someone in the corner and adjusts her Bluetooth headset.

'Whoops.' Designer Dormouse glances briefly at Pandora and turns away with a smile.

The M&S magic underwear that saved, and then eclipsed, a designer fashion show. *Brilliant.*

'Let's celebrate!' Pandora grins. 'It's the Burberry party tonight, we'll have a fantastic time.'

'What me?' I point at myself.

'Of course, why not?'

Because you hate me? How many mini Moëts have you had? Why am I hesitating, it's Burberry! 'Great!'

'Fabulous!'

Pandora's been working toward this party for weeks. She's eaten even less than usual and embarked on a frenzied Thai boxing schedule. She's borrowed a dress and a clutch bag from the PR of the Accessories Queen, a designer with stores on Bond Street. She's going to look a million dollars and her outfit will be worth almost as much. I'll be wearing what I am now: skinny jeans and my high-necked Victorian shirt (which covers any lingering rash).

Another crazy day has passed, and Pandora and I are on our way to one of the hottest tickets of Fashion Week: the Burberry party. Half of London is gathered outside the store. The shop pulses with light. The red carpet is roped off to hold the catcalling paparazzi back. Members of the leggy elite fashion crowd, who may or may not be famous, strut inside. How did Pandora get an invite to this? *Don't ask. Hold your tummy in. Get past that velvet rope.*

Everyone's drinking champagne and being seriously glamorous. Pandora's bouncing like an overexcited schoolgirl. When did she last eat?

She rocks on her Louboutins and steps on the foot of a reality-TV star chatting to a drag queen.

Is she drunk?

'Hey!' the reality-TV guy yelps. His teeth are blinding.

'Watch where you're going,' she snaps.

The drag queen snarls, making her beauty spot quiver.

Uh oh. 'Let's go over here.' I steer Pandora's bony elbow away. 'What about some water?'

'It's Fashion Week!' She throws her arms above her head. Her dress rides so high she almost flashes her Brazilian. 'More champagne!'

Oh God. 'What about some food, there's probably canapés?'

'Mwah hah ha!' Pandora laughs in my face.

I'll take that as a no.

'Look! Strawberries!' She skips over to a chocolate fountain and piles of fresh fruit.

I thought you didn't eat in public?

She selects a strawberry, licks it, sucks it and makes suggestive eyes at a man the other side of the fountain.

She's molesting the strawberry. She looks like a porn star.

'I'm bored, let's go.' She drops the half-eaten strawberry into the fountain.

'Go where?'

'To dance!'

I thought fashionistas didn't dance? I want to stay here. I want to play celeb bingo. Full house for a supermodel.

Pandora staggers sideways into a well-known model.

I must have really pissed someone off in a past life. I can't leave her.

She drags me outside.

'Taxi!' Pandora screams.

Oh God, I can't look. *Please stop raising your arms so high! Oh what do you know? The cab stopped.*

Pandora is howling along to the radio. I'm getting a headache. It's possible she's singing 'I Will Survive', but I wouldn't want to insult Gloria Gaynor.

'LOVE YOU LONDON!' She screams out the window. 'Here, here.' She waves another invite at the driver.

Where is she getting them? A London Fashion Week invite counterfeiter? We pull up at a club. More velvet rope, more black-clad, ponytailed, clipboard-bearing gatekeepers.

'Panny, darling, you made it!' the gatekeeper cries.

Don't tell me, you went to school together …

Pandora and the gatekeeper air-kiss.

You're not going to introduce me? 'Hi I'm—'

'Go on in.' The gatekeeper guides Pandora through.

Oh for fuck's sake. I follow, quickly.

The club's packed. The music is loud r 'n' b, drum and bass.

Pandora starts grinding against a bloke with shapes shaved in his hair. Maybe she went to school with him as well.

Thank God the drinks are free. The crowd is very young and very fashion. It's not the usual glossy Voguettes I'd normally associate with Pandora. It's edgier. The club is full of quirky hairstyles, unique clothes, dilated pupils and glowing faces. Aren't those girls dancing on the table daughters of that rock star?

Pandora waves her mobile in my face and shouts over the music.

I can't hear you. I smile and nod.

She digs her bony fingers into my arm and pulls me through the sweaty bodies toward the front of the club.

Where are we going? Is that a stage? She wouldn't!

A spotlight flicks on and Dita Von Teese appears. The crowd roars. Pandora bounces.

There's a giant martini glass onstage. Oh my Coco! Dita Von Teese!!!

Everyone's holding phones in the air. Dita turns and dips and shimmies. She kicks champagne up with her feet, her skin luminous like the moon. Mental note: forget fake tan. Pale is more interesting.

***

I'm drunk. I'm hot. I'm dancing with a gay guy with pierced nipples. It's 3 a.m. I've been up for twenty-two hours. I want to go home to Mr Darling. 'Let's go.' I pull Pandora off the guy she's draped over.

'It's still early!'

'It's gone three.' I pull her past the free bar.

'It's nice and cold out here.' Pandora starts gulping in air.

'There must be a cab round here somewhere ...' I look up and down the empty road.

'Fuck!'

Did Pandora just swear? 'You all right?'

'My clutch, it's gone.' Her face has blanched so much you'd think she'd been told she only had five minutes to live.

'You sure?' The Accessories Queen's clutch she borrowed is worth a fortune. Where is it? You couldn't hide a peanut in the slip of the dress she's wearing.

'Fuck! What are we going to do?' She starts pacing.

We? How has this turned into we? 'Where did you last have it?'

'If I knew that, I'd know where I bloody left it. We've got to find it, we'll be in so much trouble.' She puts her hands where her hips should be and glares.

We? 'Calm down. It's probably still inside. We'll retrace our steps.' *She's drunkenly staggered all over the club. It could be anywhere.*

Where were we dancing? Did we sit at this table or that one? I move people's legs and arms and bodies out of the way. It's dark. It's loud. It's fucking 3 a.m. I can't find it.

Pandora's waiting outside, also empty-handed.

'No luck?'

'It's gone!' Pandora is shaking as much as Dita Von Teese's nipple tassels.

As juniors we're not supposed to borrow PR items. Stylists borrow samples for shoots. Magazine fashion editors borrow samples for shoots. If a fashion editor lost a sample it would be bad, but the PRs have an incentive to be nice to them: they give them free publicity. No one has an incentive to be nice to us. It doesn't matter that Pandora went to school with the PR of the Accessories Queen. A nobody junior has lost his irreplaceable sample in a north London club. 'I'm sorry, Pandora, what are you going to do?'

'What are *we* going to do? You were here. You were just as responsible as me ...'

'Now hang on a minute ...'

'You should have kept an eye on it. If I lose my job over this you lose your job too.' She spits out her words.

'Pandora!'

'I'll tell them I gave it to you to watch!'

Oh God. Why did I stay and look after her? If I'd just abandoned her tottering, drunken arse I wouldn't be in this situation. 'OK, keep calm. Is your phone in the clutch? I can ring it, hopefully someone will answer.' My hand shakes as I press dial.

We lean in to listen.

It's ringing.

I hold my breath.

'Hello?' A man's voice answers.

We're saved!

Pandora snatches the phone from my hand. 'You have my phone. Do you have my bag? Where—' The colour drains from her face.

Is she going to be sick?

'Yes,' she mumbles. And hangs up.

'What are you doing? Where is it? Let's get it!' This is not the moment to work on your phone manner.

'He has it.' Her voice is as flat as my hair.

What's she talking about?

'He found it in a pool of beer …'

A chill runs over my skin. 'He? You don't mean …'

She nods.

The Accessories Queen has found *his* sample clutch abandoned in a club.

We're dead.

Couture Meets Cool

'Too much good taste can be boring.'

DIANA VREELAND

'You're awake early for someone who came in so late!' Mr Darling rolls over. He looks slightly annoyed.

I've been awake since I got in, worrying about the Accessories Queen and my impending departure from the fashion industry. Is my fashion career going to be as short-lived as my retail one? 'I couldn't sleep.' *When I'm sacked how will I pay off my credit-card bill?* I won't be able to afford the little I said I'd contribute toward Mr Darling's rent. I've only been here two nights and I'll have to move back in with my parents. My life is over.

Pandora's the one who's done something wrong. I have to convince them I'm an innocent bystander.

'Want some breakfast?' Mr Darling is out of the shower and buttoning up his shirt.

I can't eat. 'No, thanks.'

'You never turn down food. What's up?'

My phone beeps. It's a text from Pandora.

> Meet me at work
> early. We need
> to talk.

She's come to her senses, she's realised I'm not involved! 'Nothing, just tired.'

The office looks weird at 9 a.m. Like it does at 10 a.m., but empty and quiet. Pandora's at her desk. Despite her liberal application of YSL Touche Éclat I can tell she hasn't slept either. Now she's sobered up and reflected on her actions she'll take responsibility and free me.

'What are we going to do?' she says.

Or maybe not. Why are you determined to take me down with you?

There's a knock at the door.

We both jump. This is like waiting for the executioner.

It's a motorcycle courier. He hands me a Jiffy bag. I sign the form. 'It's for you.'

Pandora rips it open. Her mobile, her keys, her Chanel lipstick and her black Amex fall out. The Accessories Queen has couriered her things back to her.

'Is there anything else? A note?'

She shakes the envelope upside down. 'Nothing.'

'This must be good? If he was going to ... do ... something he wouldn't just send this back.'

She's staring at her things.

'Pandora!' It's time to take control of the situation. 'Don't just sit there! Send some flowers or something. Apologise!'

She looks confused.

Have you ever apologised for anything in your life? 'It's the only thing to do!'

She picks up the phone. 'Hello, yes I'd like to order two bouquets to be delivered this morning, £150 each.'

£300 on flowers? Has she been taking tips from Elton John?
It's obscene. It might just work.

'Morning, ladies.' Georgina clicks in at ten. 'How are we today?'

'Fine!' *That came out high and squeaky.*

Georgina doesn't stop on her way to the kitchen.

I look at Pandora. She doesn't say anything. I'm not going to say anything. It's our secret. Who'd have thought it? My nemesis is now bonded to me.

***

It's a week later and all the girls are sitting in silence in the office. Ceci's staring at her computer; Georgina's archiving her call sheets; Pandora's pouting into a compact; Charlie's in her office meditating.

'I can't believe how quiet it is,' I sigh.

'It's always like this after London. Everyone's in Milan and then they'll be in Paris. Enjoy it while it lasts.' Ceci flicks back on to Style.com.

I stare at my suitcase, which is listing against the office wall. I'm slowly shuttling my possessions to Mr Darling's house. We've had to address the wardrobe situation. I have a few more hundred clothes than him. I've commandeered the main bedroom closet, chest of drawers and bedside tables. He has the cupboard in the second room. It makes more sense this way as he gets up at 6 a.m. every day. Without an alarm. He's a freak of nature. A throwback to the farmers in his family. I lasted about thirteen minutes of him crashing around our room before I threatened to move out. The second bedroom is now his dressing room.

An email from Mr Darling pings into my inbox:

> Really sorry going to have to cancel cinema tonight
> – stuck in office. Can you pick up milk on the way
> home? xx

Not again! He was supposed to help me get this suitcase home. And we have tickets for the most recent obscure French film. He must have known before today that he was too busy? And what a cheek asking me to pick up milk, like I'm his skivvy. Moving in together was supposed to make our relationship better. So far I've woken him up at night, he's woken me up in the morning and we've rowed over the size of my shoe collection. I deserve better than this – I'm booking an Ad Lee car home with my case and I'll ask Jen if she wants to come to the cinema with me. I take a few calming breaths. I need to remember how relaxed Mr Darling was when I had to work late on his birthday. Shit happens. This is all part of being in a mature adult relationship. So why do I still feel annoyed?

I look up. The girls are all still busy doing nothing. I'm so bored. The phone rings. I jump on it. We have a few artists working abroad at the shows, and while our involvement is minimal it's something to do. 'Hello, Charlie Monroe Management?'

'She is driving me mad.' It's Fraser. He's heading the hair team for a show in Milan tomorrow. 'Before we're allowed to eat or drink anything the designer insists it's blessed by a Kabbalah priest. At the end of each day she makes the whole team join hands and share a moment. Bloody waste of time … I've got to go. That stupid local assistant has just sprayed hairspray in the model's eye, doll.'

'OK, good luck!'

The models are still away, so there are no shoots taking place. The photographers have either gone abroad to the shows, or are recovering from London. *I'm bored*. We spend our days looking at pictures of the new collections online. 'Ceci, when does it kick off again?'

'As soon as they get back. All the mags want to shoot the best new-season clothes, *Vogue* gets first dibs, and the commercial clients all start shooting their campaigns and look books. Oh and everyone's sick.'

'Sick?'

'Yeah, all the editors and stylists and models. The four weeks of shows are hardcore, they're always travelling, don't eat properly, don't get enough sleep, so they all get sick. They call it fashion flu. They're all really short-tempered when they get back.'

'Sounds great.' I'm learning how the fashion industry undulates. It's frenetic, manic, intense, phones ringing, multiple productions, multiple problems, getting new clients, schmoozing old ones, soothing artists and dealing with the bodily functions of dogs. We work late, play hard and hardly have time to think, or eat, or pee. And then it's quiet. August. After London Fashion Week. Nothing. Silent. I should use this time wisely. Even if Mr Darling's too busy to chill with me, I can still recuperate. I should book a massage.

But before I can put any of those luxurious thoughts into action, Charlie appears. Today her Hermès scarf is tied in a wristlet. She reeks of patchouli oil. She's been smoking in her office again.

'We're busy over the next few months, so I think we need an extra pair of hands.'

A new member of staff? Not another Pandora to despise me and to blame me when things go wrong. Least it'll be a while till they start. There will be adverts, and interviews etc. Who has a say in the hiring process? Georgina and Ceci?

'Mia starts tomorrow,' Charlie says. 'I'm going to be working from home, but Mia is an experienced agent, a recommendation, so just show her where everything is.'

So much for the HR process. Apparently you can get hired in the snap of a clutch bag. Can you get fired as fast?

'Do you think it's Mia from Storm?' Georgina flicks through her Rolodex.

'Wasn't there a Mia at Flaunt Agency?' Ceci clicks through the diary.

'I deal with Tilly at Flaunt, I don't know,' Georgina answers.

'I didn't go to school with anyone called Mia,' Pandora adds. *No point asking me, I don't know anyone.*

I make an extra-special effort with my hair and outfit for Mia's first day. I have freshly painted nails and am wearing a ruched navy velvet pencil skirt, my red-white-and-blue-striped Vivienne Westwood shirt, my Gucci heels and a pair of Spanx. My life will be easier if Mia accepts me as a fashionista, and not the green newbie Georgina and Pandora think I am.

At 10.29 a tall, thin girl, with dyed-black angled hair, kohl-rimmed eyes and impossibly long legs, strides into the office in flat vintage boots.

'Mia?' Georgina stammers. She's pulled out the big guns and worn her mum's Dior today.

'All right.' Mia walks past Georgina and drops her bag onto the empty desk.

It's denim. And ripped. And dirty!

'This my place?'

Pandora bristles.

Georgina gives her a look.

She's clearly not what any of us were expecting. Mia doesn't have an air of insouciance; she has a tornado of it. She's *so* cool. Total girl crush.

'Hi, I'm Angela,' I leap forward and hold out my hand.

'All right?' She gives an amused smile. She speaks in a drawl, not the clipped RP of my other colleagues.

'I'll show you where everything is.' *Christ, I might as well just beg her to be my friend.*

Later, I even find myself talking about Mia to Mr Darling at home. I'm insisting we eat a proper meal together, like couples who live together ought to. 'I've told you Mia's from Manchester, haven't I?' I pause from chopping carrots.

Mr Darling nods and continues slicing a pepper.

'She used to be a big part of the underground club scene. That band she told me about weeks ago, remember, the one she saw in that weird café in Shoreditch? They were just mentioned in *Dazed*. She's ahead of the magazines!'

'Impressive. Pass me the soy sauce?' Mr Darling's shirtsleeves are rolled up and he has his tie over his shoulder to keep it out the way of the pan of boiling water.

I hand him the bottle. '*Dazed* is her favourite mag. Mia said she finds *Vogue* a bit corporate. It was hilarious – Georgina nearly fainted! Mia's like an anti-fashionista.'

'I'm really glad you've made such a good friend at work.' Mr Darling fiddles with the hob.

'Oh! And yesterday she ate actual pizza in the office. Can you believe it? Pandora was spraying her Chanel No. 5 round like air-freshener. You should have seen her face!'

'What's so special about eating pizza in the office?'

'Oh you know how the girls only eat salad or soup or coffee with a spoon. Mia's just so different. She has all these other interests. She blogs, she's directing a documentary about freerunners and she makes her own clothes. Perhaps I should take sewing lessons?' I drop the vegetables into the wok.

'You can't cut bread straight, my enthusiastic chatterbox. Why don't you blog? You'd be great at that.'

'Maybe. I wouldn't know what to say. I'm not in tomorrow night, by the way, Mia and I are going to some hip art exhibition.'

'That's fine. I'm going to be working over the weekend so feel free to make plans then too.'

I grit my teeth. This is ridiculous. I'm bored of wandering round the deserted Canary Wharf shopping mall at weekends on my own trying on clothes I can't afford. We see less of each other now than we did before we were living together. We're not ships that pass in the night: he's a cruise liner and I'm a hot air balloon. Some of my friends don't believe Mr Darling exists – he never comes out with me as he's always too knackered after work. He should try doing my job, it's manic during the day *and* I'm expected to socialise.

'We should all go for a drink, I'd love to meet this girl I've heard so much about,' he says.

I freeze. *Oh the irony. I didn't mean I wanted him to meet this friend.* Mr Darling with his suits and his City clients with Mia? The other office girls understand 'he works in the finance industry', it's Georgina's life goal to marry a hedge-fund manager. But Mia would think I was corporate, bourgeois, enslaved to The Man. 'Yeah, maybe.' *Be non-committal. Be cool.*

'You going to put that in?' Mr Darling nods at the ginger I'm holding over the pan.

'I'm waiting for the ideal moment. *This* is going to be the best stir-fry ever.'

'I'll settle for a good stir-fry that's ready now. Wine?' He waves a bottle of Sancerre.

'My favourite! Grab the plates, let's go.' *Hopefully he'll forget all about it.* Now is not the time to mention his long hours.

***

The exhibition is in a disused arch in east London. All the photos are black-and-white images of tarmac. Everyone here looks cool. *I really need to find an alternative word.*

There are free bottles of beer, stored in the ice-filled jaws of taxidermy animals. *I don't drink beer.* Everyone is ignoring the smoking ban and puffing on roll-ups. *I don't smoke.* There are bits of discarded car engine lying on the floor. *Are they art?*

Pretend this is normal: I spend every night hanging out in

decrepit buildings with people in multicoloured leggings and biker boots. *I'm cool.*

In the corner a girl has an electronic dog on a lead. *I thought that was a Hackney myth?*

Mia rolls her eyes at the dog. 'Try-hard.'

There are plates of cheese and ham on a table. I'm starving but I'm worried they're part of the exhibition. Is that a fire hydrant or a statement on global warming? *Keep looking nonchalant.* I'm getting a headache.

A guy in a faded white T-shirt that could be vintage or just washed in a dark load does a piercing wolf whistle. He stands aside as a giant inflated plastic ball is rolled out. Inside are two men. *They're naked! I can see their willies!* They strike a series of t'ai chi poses.

Everyone claps.

They roll off.

Another man steps forward, he has a quiff. A plaster is wrapped round one hinge of his thick-rimmed glasses. He is singing a Smiths' song in a Dutch accent.

My ears hurt. *This is raw. Cutting edge. I'm so middle class.* I fold my arms and rest one hand against my cheek in a thoughtful arty pose.

'You look very serious.' Mia grins. She's wearing a black rubber dress that could be a Gareth Pugh or a clever sex-shop find.

'You don't think this performance is good?'

'Nah, load of crap.' She sips her beer.

Oh.

'All right, Stan.' Mia nods almost imperceptibly at a man to her right with a diagonal curtain of hair across his face.

Stan shakes his curtain in greeting. 'What you make of Wolfgang's work?' He jabs his thumb at the photos of the road. His nails are painted black.

'Heart-warming,' says Mia.

'Premier model party tonight?' Stan's curtain vibrates.

'Yeah, I'm bored here.' Mia places her bottle on the cheese table and grabs a handful.

Damn, I could have eaten it!

We take a taxi to Premier's offices in WC2. People are gathered outside the glass front, smoking. Inside music is playing from speakers you slot an iPod into. I've never seen that before. Clever. Someone's standing on a chair to talk to one of the models.

'Darling!' Ceci, who's drinking a glass of white wine with two blondes, waves from inside the agency.

I wave back.

'Mia, you foxy minx you!' A camp guy in an army cap and fatigues approaches.

'All right, Pete.' Mia grips the army cadet in a hug.

'And you are?'

'Angela.' *Did that sound cool? Did I say it right?*

'Fab, we need more bitches.'

Thanks. I think.

'I'm totally over this. Shall we nick a crate and go?' Pete punctuates his speech with hand gestures.

We just got here. A key part of anti-fashionista socialising seems to be moving on to the next place. No wonder Mia's always been to places before the rest of the office, at this rate she'd hit eight a night.

Pete and Stan lift a crate of beers between them and casually carry it past the smokers outside.

Mia, Stan, Pete, the beer and I take another taxi back to east London. Pete knows someone who knows someone who's having a party. We end up with around a hundred people dancing on the roof of a Shoreditch warehouse. There seem to be a lot of models here too – I recognise their jutting hipbones.

'Whose party is this?' I shout at Stan over the techno.

'Some film director,' Stan's hair shouts back.

'Cool. Which one is he or she?'

Stan shrugs and carries on dancing.

'Isn't that the It girl who's always in the papers talking about her charity work?' With her edgy haircut and scruffy plaid she fits in perfectly with the anti-fashionistas.

'Fake,' snarls Mia. 'My friend went to prep school with her, says she's a tit.'

'A Tit girl,' I say.

'You're funny. You should write this shit down.' Mia claps me on the back.

'Got a bottle opener?' Pete opens the crate of beer.

We shake our heads.

'Got a bottle opener, mate?' Pete shouts to the dancing faces around us.

Nothing.

'Now what do we do?' Stan looks forlornly at his beer.

'I've seen people angle the top against a brick wall, hit the bottle with their hand and the lid pops off?' *Once*.

Pete angles the bottle against the small brick ledge that runs round the roof. He brings his hand down, as if he's smacking a ketchup bottle.

The bottle shatters and slices straight into his palm.

'Christ!' Blood pours from his hand.

'Oh my God, I'm so sorry.' What have I done?

'I'm going to be sick.'

'You all right, mate?' A lanky lad with a pretty face steps forward. 'I've done a first-aid course.' He pulls off his T-shirt off.

'I think I'm going to faint.' Pete stares at the lad's perfect six-pack.

'Don't I know you?' Mia prods the guy's shoulder.

'We worked together on an *iD* shoot.'

'That's right, you were the model!'

The model rips his T-shirt and ties a tourniquet round Pete's hand.

'You should go to the hospital.' The model stares into Pete's eyes.

'Probably ought to.' Pete stares back.

'Someone should go with you,' says the model.

Blood seeps through the fabric and drips onto the ground.

'Er, Pete? You really ought to go ...' Stan's curtain of hair is dishevelled.

'I'll take you.' The model puts his arm round Pete and helps him through the crowd.

It's my fault. He's probably going to be permanently scarred. I want to go home. Jesus, it's 4.43 a.m. I've got to pay closer attention to the time. 'I'm going. We get up for work in three hours,' I shout in Mia's ear.

She gives her amused smile.

Does she ever sleep? Is it uncool to sleep?

I push down the stairs. People are standing, sitting and snogging on every step. This is a fire hazard. *I'm so not cool.*

It's starting to get light. Where are all the taxis?

In the courtyard of Mr Darling's flat I pull off my heels. My feet are swollen. Ahhh. The floor feels deliciously cold. I tuck my stilettos under my arm. Where is my flowery key? I can never find anything in this bag.

The door opens.

Mr Darling is standing there in his suit. 'I was worried about you.' He looks angry.

He's ready for work and I'm coming home in my bare feet, after no sleep and with the beginning of a really bad hangover. 'I err ...'

'Are you hurt?' There's blood spattered on my elbow.

'It's not mine.' *I sound insane.* 'Someone cut their hand on a beer bottle.'

'Your idea of what constitutes a good night is so different from mine.' He doesn't smile. He steps past me.

'When will you be back from work?'

'Not sure. I'll call you later,' he says, without turning around.

Now I've done it. *I need to sleep.*

Beep, beep. My phone vibrates with a text message next to my head.

> Got your number from
> Mia! All stitched up now!
> Stopped on way to A&E
> to shag hot first aider!
> Had to hold hand in air
> throughout!!!!! Bitchin'
> night! Pete xxx

BLAST FROM THE PAST

'The fashion business is this legendary repository of young girls on their way to getting husbands.'

ALI MACGRAW

Mia enters the office just after me, a few minutes late, clutching a cup of coffee. She looks … cool. I bet she doesn't have to explain her behaviour to anyone. I need to find a way to make Mr Darling understand going out and networking is part of my job.

I'm so tired. Can I use Kirby grips to keep my eyes open? My head feels like it's full of Lucozade. A new email: the details of a job. I don't believe it. I rub my eyes. It's a charity shoot featuring Tit-girl. Is she as bad as Mia said? Organising this is what I need to get me through the morning. I'll sleep in the bathroom at lunch.

On the day of the Tit-girl shoot I stay late to speak to Daffodil. 'How was it?'

'Awful. She was two hours late …'

'No.' *She was probably out the night before dancing on the roof of a Shoreditch warehouse.*

'Yeah, then when she did arrive she didn't apologise, but demanded lunch!'

'How rude.'

'Then she threw her food on the floor, and said it was "gross". The stylist finally got her into the first outfit and she said she felt "physically sick" wearing it.'

'It's for charity!'

'She's a total cow.'

Mia was right.

***

A few weeks later Mia and I are hugging hot chocolates in the independent coffee shop round the corner. She's opened my eyes to another side of the industry, introduced me to fashionistas who are normal, balanced people, even if their haircuts are peculiar.

Then she drops a bombshell. 'I'm leaving,' she states matter-of-factly as she fishes a marshmallow from her drink and eats it.

'What?' *You can't go! You've made me see I'm good at my job and I don't have to be intimidated by the likes of Pandora. And I actually like you.*

'I'm going to New York.'

'When? For how long?'

'Next week. Not sure yet. A while. I'm going to work on a film about skateboarding graffiti artists.'

'You're not going to be an agent any more?'

'Fancy a change.'

'What about the fashion industry?'

She shrugs. 'Couple of the magazines are interested in a New York blog. I'll keep my hand in.'

'But …' *what about me? I'll no longer be cool by association. Don't leave me with the Pandoras of the industry.*

'It's an adventure.' She downs her chocolate.

'We'll keep in touch, right?'

'We'll email.'

I gulp.

'You can visit whenever.'

New York? Sounds amazing. But I can't see Mr Darling wanting to take the time off work. I could go on my own if it wasn't for the small issue of my whopping Visa bill. My hot chocolate suddenly tastes bitter. I need to go through and open my bills this weekend. I just keep shoving them in my handbag. I'm always so busy. And now Mia's leaving.

Back in the office I'm in a daze.

'Angela, it's Kristopher for you,' shouts Pandora.

Kristopher is a stylist who's working on a childrenswear shoot today.

I pick up the phone. It's quiet, no music, no chatter, no excitable kids. 'Kris, where are you?'

'I'm in the Gents.'

I've got a bad feeling about this.

'There's been an … incident.' His voice echoes.

'What's happened?' Mia waggles her fingers in her ears and sticks her tongue out at me.

'You know Sissy, the three-year-old model?'

'Yes.' My heart's pounding. I throw a pen at Mia to make her stop.

'I burned her with the steamer.'

'What! Is she OK?'

'She's fine, slight mark on her leg. They've got the first-aid kit now.'

Were the kids playing chase on set? 'What happened?'

'We were mid-shot. There was a crease on her dress and I didn't see the point of taking it off.'

'Oh my God. You steamed the dress while she was wearing it?'

Mia cracks up.

Georgina looks up alarmed.

'Well, yes, but she moved.'

'She's three!'

'The mother's not too thrilled.'

'I can see why!'

'Well, I thought I better let you know in case we need to do something?'

Do we have insurance? 'OK,' I manage.

'Super, thanks!'

It's my problem now.

I take it to Charlie.

'Bugger. I'll notify the lawyers. You call Hamleys and order the largest cuddly toy they have. Send a Selfridges' hamper to the mother.'

Hundreds of pounds later and the damage, if not the child's leg, is repaired. At 6 p.m. I storm out the office and don't wait for Mia to walk to the tube with me. It's been a crap day, and I know it sounds stupid, but I can't help feeling it's all her fault for leaving. As I barge past the tourists coming up the stairs at Baker Street I realise, oh the irony! that I feel sad she never got to meet Mr Darling. I wish he was at home tonight, but he's working late. Again. He's explained he's trying for a promotion at the end of the year. I just wish he'd make a little more time for me. I need a hug today. I get home. Eat cornflakes in front of the telly. Try calling Jen who goes straight to voicemail and then go to bed at 10 p.m. Mr Darling's still not home, so I wrap my arms round my knees and have a little cry.

***

I hold my mobile to my ear. 'Hi Mia, I've picked up Zane's book from that production company. I'll be in the office soon.' I'm dragging my feet this morning. Even though I went to bed early last night I feel knackered today. Mr Darling was up and out at some ungodly hour. I pretended to be asleep when he said goodbye.

'Cool. Georgina says can you go via Starbucks – she wants a double espresso, *someone had a late night*,' she adds in a whisper.

I laugh. I'm so going to miss Mia. I push open the door to Starbucks. Oh my God. It's Legally Hot. The noise of the cafe falls away. 'I've got to go Mia. Bye.' The sleeves of his tailored shirt are neatly rolled up. What is it about a man's forearms that makes them so sexy?

He fixes me with his hypnotic eyes. And smiles.

'What are you doing here?' I'm still holding the door.

'I'm buying coffee.' He lifts the paper cup he's holding.

'But why are you here, in Marylebone?'

'I didn't know I needed permission to come to Marylebone. Pretty necklace – Marc Jacobs?'

Yes, I bought it at the weekend to cheer myself up. I feel his eyes on me. *Don't blush. Don't blush.* I blush.

'And I love the hair, it's more honey, richer. You look well.' He steps back to let a woman with a buggy come through behind us.

'So do you.' Keep calm. My heart's beating so loud I'm sure the barista can hear it.

'What you up to nowadays, apart from getting coffee?' His hair is still a rich inky black. Like waves in the sea at night.

'I work at a creative agency in the fashion industry.' I try not to think about what he looks like without that shirt on.

'Not publishing?' He looks surprised.

'No. Why would you ask that?' And I try not to think about the things we've done together. Slut.

'You gave me a graduate scheme directory to give to my brother; you'd highlighted all the publishing companies. It made sense. You always used to talk about the books you read.'

Huh? 'Really, I don't remember.' When did I circle the publishing companies, before I broke up with Side-Parting?

'I'm on my way to a meeting, but it's been great seeing you. Really great. We should catch up properly. Go for dinner. Let me give you my card. It has my work and mobile numbers on for both London and New York. And I'll write my home number on it as well. And my personal email. Could you hold this?' He passes me his coffee cup.

Our hands touch. Electricity surges through me. *Remember to inhale.*

'You've got my number, my email, my fax. Contact me. Let's go out.' He hands me the card.

'Thanks.'

He kisses me on both cheeks. He smells of sandalwood. 'It's good to see you looking so happy.'

My cheeks tingle. The noise of the coffee grinder comes back. A man in baggy jeans catches the edge of my bag. I'm still staring at the door. *Why didn't I mention Mr Darling?*

At lunch I call Jen for an emergency powwow. 'Do you think bumping into Legally Hot is a sign?' I ask her.

'A sign of what? That you both go to Starbucks? You pass hundreds of people each day in Starbucks.'

'Yes, but I haven't slept with them. Don't you think it's odd that Legally Hot reappears just as Mr Darling doesn't have time for me? The universe is having a laugh.' I dodge a family of tourists with matching cameras who are blocking the pavement.

'You're being a bit harsh to Mr Darling. Doesn't he pay for most of that snazzy flat you live in? And take you out for posh dinners and stuff? He adores you, and of course the poor bloke has to work hard, he has to afford you,' she laughs.

'It's not funny, Jen. I feel like a corporate wife. I'm in my early twenties – I should be out having a laugh not waiting at home for my boyfriend,' I huff.

'Sorry, mate. I'm sure Mr Darling's just going through a busy time right now.'

I tut. I'm not so sure. I think he might be a workaholic. Nobody normal gets up at 6 a.m. every day, even on Saturdays, unless they have to.

'You're just being a drama queen. These things just happen to you, Ange. Your life is a soap opera,' Jen continues.

'Well, I don't want to watch any more. What do you think I should do?'

'About what?' Jen sounds distracted. I really ought to ask about her day first.

'About Legally Hot's card! Shall I call him? Shall I meet him?' He actually wants to spend time with me.

'Why would you want to do that?'

'I don't know. Is it rude not to?' That sounds reasonable.

'Have you told Mr Darling?'

'Of course.' Not yet. I will. *Maybe*.

'If this teaches us anything it's that Starbucks is evil. Do you know how many cups end up in landfill? You should support a local independent coffee shop ...'

Just what I need: a lecture from Jen on environ-MENTALISM and corporate evils. It's all the travelling. She's such a hippy. I read a great piece in a glossy about shopping being your patriotic duty to help the economy. That's what I need: retail therapy. 'Sorry, Jen, I've got to go, I'm just back at the office.'

'OK, but don't do anything rash, Ange,' Jen says.

'Of course not. Speak later.'

'And don't forget it's my leaving drinks this weekend!'

Christ, her trip to South America, that's come round fast. Why does Jen always sod off round the world right when I need her most? 'No problem. Love ya.' I hang up and duck into Zara. I spy a sexy gathered red jersey dress. I wonder if Legally Hot would like this?

***

It's November, autumn, or fall as the Americans call it. Jen's left for her big adventure and I'm looking at the latest photos Mia's emailed. Mia in a hot tub on a roof with skyscrapers in the background; her with a retro ghetto blaster in front of a yellow cab. New York looks amazing. I still haven't opened my visa bills. My handbag's getting really heavy now. It's like one giant faux-leather encased secret. Nestled in there as well is Legally Hot's card. He emailed me two weeks ago and asked again to meet up. I still haven't decided what to do. Mr Darling worked again this weekend, so I went out and got drunk with my non-fashion friends. I left Legally Hot's card at home so I wasn't tempted to text him when I was pissed. That would have been cringe-tastic. But least it would have made the decision for me. I wish Jen were here to talk it over. Thank Coco I've been so busy at work pretending to be just like the other girls, otherwise I think my head would have exploded trying to figure it all out.

'Angela and Pandora, are you free tomorrow night?' Charlie waltzes into the office, a Gucci scarf billowing behind her.

'Yes,' says Pandora looking up from her tear-sheeting.

Why?

'I want you to go to the *Tatler* Little Black Book party.'

'That's *the* party of the social calendar,' Pandora squeals.

Fantastic, but why do I have to go with Pandora?

'Ceci and Georgina are working on a production in Vegas so need to be in the office, and I have an awards ceremony to attend. It's difficult to get on to the guest list, I want the agency to be represented so I still get invited next year.' She hands Pandora a black invite.

The last time Pandora and I went out we nearly lost our jobs when she went batshit-crazy on champagne.

'I'm going to call in a dress to wear!' Pandora whips out her mobile.

Have you not learned your lesson? I give Pandora a look, which she studiously ignores.

The *Tatler* Little Black Book party is in Mayfair's legendary elite nightclub Annabel's. *Obviously*. I'm waiting on the corner of Berkeley Square. The grand white buildings loom over me. In the glow from the streetlights I can pick out trees and grass and benches in the gated garden. I'd love to explore it.

A cab pulls up. Pandora steps out. She looks incredible in a silvery slinky shift dress with wisps of ostrich feathers dancing off the shoulders. I'm wearing the red Zara dress I bought in case I decided to see Legally Hot. Even when I try really hard to look like a true fashionista, I don't quite measure up to Pandora and the others. 'Fantastic dress!'

'It's perfect for husband hunting.' She marches toward the club.

Oh God. I scurry to catch up with her. Mental note: don't run in front of the braying paparazzi. Two girls canter through in front of us. Didn't I see them in *Hello!* magazine, hanging out with William and Harry?

'You're not on the list.' The woman on the door's face is as flat and expressionless as the clipboard she's clutching.

We tried. Time to go back to my middle-class existence.

Pandora gives her Charlie's name.

'You should have said!' Clipboard's face lights up like Fortnum and Mason's window.

Pandora delivers her best disparaging look.

I'm glad she's here.

The club is dark and red and full of cushions. I guess that's what you get in posh nightclubs: upholstery. Pandora's well connected, but even she doesn't know anyone here. I mean, she knows lots of faces – she points out minor members of the royal family, aristocrats and society It girls – but no actual people.

'Bunners! Haven't seen you for yonks!' An eager-looking

ruddy-cheeked young man grips an eager-looking ruddy-cheeked young woman.

'Fabo, Harry!' The ruddy-cheeked girl claps him on the back.

I'm in a Jeeves and Wooster novel.

Pandora flutters her eyelashes at the ruddy-cheeked lad.

He looks fifteen!

She starts flicking her hair manically.

I assume he owns a castle.

Pandora goes into flirty giggly overdrive. Her life motto is: if in doubt, pout. She looks like she's auditioning for a 1950s pin-up poster.

He's not paying any attention.

I retreat to the Ladies.

Oh. My. God. Reapplying her make-up at the mirror is that Australian soap-star-turned-pop-star.

'Bit much isn't it?' she says.

Is she talking to me? I turn around. There's no one else in here.

'All these hooray Henrys and Henriettas,' she continues. 'It's all "Daddy this" and "Mummy that!"'

I giggle. 'It is a bit ... overpowering.'

'I came in here for a rest.' She blots her lips together.

'Me too! It's like a reunion of Ancestry.com.'

She laughs. 'It's like being invisible.'

'Or staff.'

'That's it!' She snaps her fingers. 'I knew they were looking at me funny! They probably think I should be serving them tea.'

'They think I should be cleaning their toilets.'

A famous, sexy, down-to-earth celebrity? How refreshing.

'Want some lip gloss?' She holds out a Juicy tube.

'Thanks.' OhmyGodohmyGodohmyGod. Best night out in a posh nightclub *ever*. Maybe I'm better at impersonating a fashionista than I thought.

'TIS THE SEASON TO
BE HUNGOVER

'If I'm going dancing, then I wear the highest
heels with the shortest dress.'

KATE MOSS

I've done something very stupid. It's all Pandora's fault. I've had
the odd drink with her and Ceci after work. They go to these
amazing bars, like the Sanderson and Claridge's. Everyone they
hang out with is gorgeous and well connected and it beats going
home to wait for Mr Darling to finish work.

It turns out Pandora has a talent for getting men to buy us
drinks. I'm not overly comfortable with the idea, but she
explained: 'Women spend all their money on clothes and make-
up and looking fabulous, the least men can do is buy us a drink.'
Which sort of makes sense after a bottle of champagne in the
office, and besides I'm skint.

Last night at the Soho Hotel we were hanging out with some
advertising guys Ceci knows, and this one bloke was flirting
outrageously with me. And it felt good. Mr Darling's always so
knackered when he comes home and the only thing he talks

about is the bloody economics project he's working on. I can't remember the last time he asked about my day. When I got home I was tipsy, and buzzing from the flirty talk, and I emailed Legally Hot:

> It was great to see you. We should catch up. xx

I feel really guilty. Mr Darling's gone in to the office today, even though it's a Saturday, and I'm just lying on the sofa rereading the message. My heart's racing. I also keep refreshing to see if he replies. What's wrong with me?

Oh my God! New message:

> So pleased you got in contact! I'm in New York
> with work at the moment, but back just before
> Christmas. I'd love to take you to dinner. I've
> missed you.
> xx

What have I done?

'I can't believe it's been two months.' I hug Jen. Carol singers murder 'Silent Night' behind us in the square of St Christopher's Place. 'No body piercings, face tattoos, dodgy-looking rashes or loss of limb that I can see. You've lost weight though, didn't eat enough guinea pigs in Peru?'

'I've lost weight – you've shrunk!' She steps back to look at me. In the glow of the Christmas fairy lights, I can pick out strawberry-blonde tendrils, highlighted by the sun.

'It's an optical illusion, I'm just dressing better.' I've spent so much time with fashion's skinny minnies I forget in the civilian world I'm slim. *Result!*

'You sure you're all right? You do have a habit of putting too much pressure on yourself.' She pulls her medical-professional face.

Maybe I've had a few too many nights out drinking with Ceci

and Pandora on an empty stomach. My face flushes at the thought of my message to Legally Hot. I grab Jen for another hug to hide my red cheeks. 'You're the one that's been backpacking across South America, sleeping God knows where and eating God knows who. We're worrying about you now. How was quarantine? Did they make you have a flea dip bath?'

'Shut up and let's eat, I've been fantasising about Pizza Express since Argentina.' She drags me into the restaurant.

'I love that you're back for Christmas! The Regent Street lights are up, the shops are full of happy present-buyers, there's a Christmas tree in the office ...' I don't mention Legally Hot.

'Fashion does Christmas? I'm amazed.' Jen sits at a table and salivates over the menu.

'We have decorations. A Scandinavian, wooden carved tree that cost Charlie the same as she pays me all year. And there's no tinsel. Or lights. It's very stylish. Minimal. I've recreated the look at Mr Darling's with a Perspex Paperchase tree.'

I want to show my friends and family how my taste has developed. I've taken a taxi with Alexander McQueen. I've shared a lift with Isabella Blow. I've borrowed an Australian pop star's Juicy Tube. I'm a fully fledged fashionista. I've spent three months working on Christmas shoots and then reading the magazines they've appeared in. I dream in magazine wish lists: stocking fillers for under a hundred pounds, unique decorations, charming wrapping paper and party dresses.

'A minimalist Christmas? Sounds a bit cold.' Jen buries her face in the garlic dough balls.

'That's not the best bit. I've been invited to fifteen parties in nine days.'

'Why?' Jen strokes her glass of wine lovingly.

'Because that's how it works in the fashion industry. Everyone throws parties. Model agencies, production companies, photographic agencies, magazines. We're expected to go, be seen and network.' This is to be done in the time-honoured tradition of drinking and gossiping. 'Work started dying down at the beginning of December. Every other photographer, stylist, fashion editor, hairdresser, and PR has flown off to Thailand.'

'Thailand is amazing.' Jen starts kissing the garlic butter dish.

'It is also the Center Parcs of the fashion industry. I bet they're all wafting around in Antik Batik kaftans and only talking to other fashionistas.'

'Thank you, this is wonderful!' Jen takes her Sloppy Giuseppe from the harried waiter.

'Fifteen parties in nine days. That's nine outfits. And nine hangovers.'

'Ange ...' Jen looks up momentarily from molesting her pizza.

'Don't worry; I've got a strategy. I've planned all my outfits, including underwear, and hung them up with Post-it notes listing which date they're to be worn on.' It stops me being bored while Mr Darling's stuck in the office.

'That's not obsessive at all.'

'It makes perfect sense. This way I can roll out of bed and not stress about what to wear. Maximising my sleep. And I've bought enough high-protein, slow-burning-carb ready meals and fruit slices from M&S to repair the hangovers.'

'Or you could just not drink?'

'That's not an option. It's expected.'

'I'm sure nobody's forcing you,' Jen tuts.

It's difficult to explain the inner workings of the fashion industry to civilians. If I don't drink I'll be marking myself out as different. 'Ceci said last year it got so bad Georgina actually ate a bacon sandwich.'

'So?' Jen looks confused.

'Calorie kamikaze.' Did I really just use the same phrase as the cake-sniffers? 'Apparently she then cancelled her plans to visit her family for Christmas and booked into a Balinese retreat to "purge" for two weeks instead.'

'The people you work with are unhinged,' Jen tuts.

'They're not that bad.' *And least they've been here for the last couple of months.* I tell myself off. Maybe I have got a bit too used to the way Ceci and Pandora talk, but I'm thrilled Jen's home.

'So does your incredible social life mean you're too busy to see those of us who haven't been invited to a million parties?' Jen raises an eyebrow.

'For the next week or so, yes. But we're still on for Christmas Eve, right? It's tradition.' I give her hand a squeeze. I'll talk to her about Legally Hot another time.

'Wouldn't miss it for a round-the-world ticket.' She smiles.

***

I've had to relax my budget a bit for Christmas. It's impossible to buy enough outfits and presents for everyone and not use your credit card. Luckily the shops are doing great offers on store cards. I've opened accounts with Topshop, John Lewis and Debenhams and got loads of discounts on my first purchases. It's great to tick present-buying off my to-do list, now I can give my full attention to surviving the marathon of parties.

DAY 1

'It's Christmas!' Ceci screams and pops a bottle of champagne.

It's a minute past noon.

By 3 p.m. we're jumping on the office Conran sofa in our heels.

By 4 p.m. we abandon the office to the answerphone and leave for the party. Another agency has rented a private room at Soho House. *I've always wanted to go to a private members' club!*

We reapply our make-up in the back of the taxi. The radio is turned up. Ceci and Georgina clink the champagne glasses they've brought with them.

Soho House is in a house. Which seems logical. I follow Georgina's Miu Miu-clad bottom through tiny corridors, up and down stairs. Are there any famous faces? The party room has loud pumping music and loud pumping patterned wallpaper. It's 4.30 p.m. *Everyone's drunk.*

'Angela! I'm Frannie! We speak all the time, so nice to put a face to the name!' A girl with short wavy blonde hair and a fantastic 1920s drop-waisted dress corners me. Frannie – this is fun! I wonder if there's any food? Oh! Bowls of almonds!

At home I down the two pints of water and the vitamin C tablet I left out earlier. I crawl into bed without disturbing Mr Darling. It's 2 a.m. I think.

One party, seven glasses of champagne, eighteen almonds, one heel blister.

DAY 2

Today there are *four* parties. Two at private members' clubs, one at a champagne bar and kicking it all off is lunch in a Michelin-starred restaurant. I ate my stomach-acid-neutralising melon and two paracetamol for breakfast. I'm wearing my latest Bang Bang find; a vintage 1980s Zandra Rhodes dress with geometric sequins on the shoulders. I have two gel insoles in my Gucci heels and I'm wearing Spanx. I am ready. Least there should be something more substantial than nuts to eat.

Legally Hot has sent me another message. He wants to meet on 17 December. I can't think about it now, I'm too hungover. I just need to make it through today.

Georgina and I have been invited to the Chelsea-based restaurant by a production company we've employed. The room is decorated in muted and expensive-looking grey tones. We pass through the eight round tables, all filled with pinstripe-suited City boys.

'Eight bottles of the Cristal, my man!'

All the men in here are ten or twenty years older than us. At each table sits a token woman. A colleague? A secretary? A mistress?

I'm relieved to reach our group. There are six of us in total, all women. All working that fashionista look of casually worn lavish clothes. We're the colour in the room.

'How you doing, darling?' Candy, who I've spoken to a million times on the phone, gives me a hug. 'Excuse the drones.' She rolls her eyes at the City boys. She's confident in her skinny jeans and black blazer with the rolled-up sleeves. Georgina told me shoulder pads are her trademark. 'Have some champagne!'

I take the glass. *And relax.*

By dessert I'm drunk.

By 9 p.m. I can no longer tell which club we're in. They all look the same: a quirky and expensive decor/a quirky and expensive crowd. Everyone's very 'med-yah!' *That's funny.* The mulled wine is delicious. Nobody wants dinner. Thank God for olives.

I'm crouching outside Mr Darling's apartment trying to get the key in the door.

It's 3.18 a.m. Key won't fit. I'm locked out. I'll die of hypothermia. Stupid ringing phone. 'Me. Keys. Door. Won't,' I hiccup. I have to go to bed. I have to get up. I have to get dressed again. I have to go to bed.

The door opens. Mr Darling's stood there in his pyjamas.

I'm on my knees, crying in a Zandra Rhodes dress.

Four parties, six glasses of champagne, four large glasses of mulled wine, two black sambucas, a sliver of carpaccio, a sniff of sea bass, an opulent trifle, a pot of olives and a purple bruise on my knee.

DAY 3

A buzzing noise. *Go away.*

… Sleep …

Beep, beep, beep, beep! My alarm's screaming. 'I've gone blind! I can't see!' Oh no, it's just the mascara sticking my eyes together. I can taste sambuca and lint. I try to roll out of bed. The floor undulates. My stomach's taken up acrobatics.

Mr Darling appears. He drops an effervescent Berocca into a glass of water. It sounds like a boiling kettle.

He places the glass and something small and dark on my bedside table. 'The taxi driver delivered this at 4.45 a.m. on his way home.' He sounds cross. 'I can't have my sleep disturbed like this; it's a very critical time at work. Can you try not to be so disruptive?'

I can't open my mouth to argue. I hear him slam the door on his way out. How dare he have a go at me, after all the times he's disrupted my sleep coming in late and going out early to the office. Last night was work. Why is his work more important than mine?

I turn my head, slowly. On the bedside table is my Mulberry purse. I sit bolt upright. *Don't puke.* Thank God, safe inside are all my credit cards.

Getting dressed hurts. My pink 1980s top, made from a cut-off dress, feels clammy. My skinny black cords are constricting my legs. I wince as I put my feet into my heels. I can't drink ever again. Just the thought of it makes me feel sick.

How can I survive tonight's parties? Nobody's sober. They'll think I can't hack the pace. It's passé. It's lame. It's unfashionable.

At St Paul's I get off the tube and steady myself against the wall. Try and stop the rising tide. My body's screaming for water. That's it! I'll drink tall glasses of water with lime wedges and tell everyone it's gin. Ceci said clear spirits have fewer calories than champagne. I'll tell them I'm worried about my waistline. They won't argue with that.

By the time I make it to the office I'm even more annoyed at Mr Darling. How dare he be so judgemental? I stomp past Ceci, who is resting her head on her desk, and switch on my computer. I open up the email from Legally Hot and hit reply:

17th is good for me. Can't wait. xx

It's only when my head clears an hour later that I remember Legally Hot's business card is also in my wallet. Did Mr Darling see it? A fresh wave of nausea hits me and I can't tell if it's alcohol or panic. I have nothing to hide. Legally Hot's just an old friend who wants to catch up. So why do I feel so guilty? I reach for another glass of water. I'll think about it later. I've got to get through today.

There was a flaw in my plan not to drink: I'm sober. I'm aware of what's going on. I feel responsible. This is going to be the Accessories Queen's clutch all over again. It's 8.30 p.m. We're in a private members' club. Again. Georgina, despite dating a viscount working in futures, is eating the face off a minor 1990s pop star. Ceci's been making the same joke for the last hour and falling off the sofa. Her bum doesn't have much padding – she'll be black and blue tomorrow.

'I think,' the fashion editor next to me grips my arm, 'I am adopted.'

This is the fifth time she's told me this in thirty minutes. The brown eye make-up that's spreading across her face matches her hair exactly. I'm running out of energy to nod politely. I'm running out of the will to live.

'Know how I know?' She prods me with a Rouge Noir fingernail.

Yes. 'No.' Where's Pandora?

'There are hardly *any* photos of me as a child. Don't you think that's odd?'

I haven't seen Pandora since she came back from the bar with that magnum of champagne she'd put on Charlie's card.

'*And* I've never felt like I connected with my mother. She works ...' The fashion editor glances over her shoulder and whispers, '... she works in a greasy spoon café.'

Your poor mum.

'So, I think I'm *adopted*!'

'I ought to go check on my colleague, I haven't seen her for a while.' I stand.

'Yes, yes, you do that. When you get back I've got something to tell you. Something shocking.'

Time to leave. I work my way round the table and climb over the assorted handbags. The fashion editor starts talking to Ceci. 'I think I'm adopted.'

Christ.

Pandora's not in the bar. I head to the toilets. Lying on the bathroom floor is a Chanel 2.55 handbag.

Fuck. 'Pandora?'

No answer.

I push the toilet door. The first one opens. The second is locked. I knock. 'Pandora, are you in there?'

No answer.

This does not look good. I bang on the door. 'Is anyone in there?'

A squeak comes from inside. A cut-glass squeak.

'Pandora, if that's you, make a noise.'

The same posh squeak.

'Can you open the door?' *Can I see her under the door?* I spy the red soles of Louboutins and a mass of patterned silk chiffon. It's her. 'Open up!'

She doesn't move.

I have an awful feeling in the pit of my stomach and it's not hunger. *She could have taken something. Fuck, fuck, fuck.* 'Open the door you stupid cow!'

Nothing.

TAKING ITS TOLL

'In difficult times fashion is always outrageous.'

ELSA SCHIAPARELLI

OK, don't panic. What would Coco do? Get some help. I run back into the bar. Georgina's still snogging the pop star who's past his sell-by date, and Ceci's wedged, in hysterics, between the leather sofa and the wall. They're no use.

I have to go to reception. *We'll get thrown out. Georgina and Ceci could lose their membership. Pandora might be …*

A tall, pinched brunette in a tailored and nipped-in trouser suit smiles at me.

'My friend's unwell and she's locked in the toilet. Can you open it from the outside?' This is karma for the time my friends had to remove the bathroom door at university to reach me.

'I'll call security,' the pinched and nipped-in receptionist says calmly.

A bulky man in a gangster suit arrives carrying a toolkit.

'This way!' I weave past the revellers staggering between the lounges and bars of the club.

I go in first. There's nobody else in here, just the closed door and Pandora's foot sticking out from underneath. 'It's all clear.'

The security man fills the space. 'Miss, can you open the door?' He starts at the hinges with a screwdriver.

Is there anything dodgy in Pandora's Chanel bag? Cigarettes, perfume, lipstick, tit-tape, a hairbrush. No pills, no powder.

The door creaks and the security guy lifts it off.

Pandora is lying on the floor in her Isabel Marant dress. Blinking.

Oh God. 'Pandora, can you hear me?'

She blinks.

'She's not responding to you?' The security guard crouches down.

'Yes, but that's not unusual.' I shake her shoulder. *Come on.*

Pandora lifts her head.

'Give her this.' He hands me a pint of water. 'Does she need an ambulance?'

'Where's my handbag?' Pandora starts.

'I think she'll be OK.' I hold the water to her lips. My hand is shaking. 'I've got your bag, Pandora.'

'Doesn't suit you,' she mutters.

'You'll have to get her out of here, love,' says security.

'Yes, sorry.' We need to stop making a scene. 'Pandora, can you stand?'

The security man pulls her up. I balance her arm across my shoulders.

'You sure you're all right?' He raises an eyebrow.

I'm pretty sure being carried from the building by a bouncer would automatically lose you your membership. *Christ, she's heavy for a tiny girl.*

'Where's my Chanel?' Pandora's icy tones are crystal clear.

Thank God for elocution. 'We're fine. She just needs to walk it off.'

He shrugs and starts to reattach the bathroom door.

'*Come on*,' I mutter as I part-walk and part-drag Pandora down the narrow hallway. *Oh no.* A handsome man is coming in the opposite direction. I stop and flatten Pandora and myself against the wall. *Casually*.

The guy passes. It's Jude Law. *Please let the ground open and swallow me whole.*

Pandora makes the cut-glass squeaking sound.

'Hi.' I smile. *It's entirely natural to balance a paralytic posh girl on your shoulder. I do it all the time.*

Oh the shame. Jude Law! Don't think about it – just get Pandora downstairs and into a cab. Tilt, step, tilt step, tilt, step. Across the street is a minicab office.

'I want another drink!'

'No, you don't.'

'Who *are* you?'

Give me strength.

'Where's my Chanel?'

'I've got it. Don't worry.'

The minicab office's door is open. The glow of strip lighting shows a small waiting room. I just need to persuade them to take her home.

I lean Pandora against the wall. 'Wait here, OK?'

Inside a man with bushy greying hair and stubble is talking into a radio mouthpiece.

I wait for him to finish. 'Hi. Can I get a car to Chelsea please? It's to drop my friend home.'

'Sure babe, the driver'll meet you outside in two minutes. Yankee, Foxtrot One, fare to Chelsea.'

Pandora's no longer leaning against the wall. *Fuck!* My head snaps left and right like I'm watching tennis. She's made it twenty-five metres down the road. 'Where are you going?'

'I need to find my Chanel.'

'It's on your shoulder! Pandora, get in the taxi. You need to go home.'

'I want to go to bed.'

'Good. This way.' I steer her back toward the minicab office. We're almost there.

She stiffens. Breaks free from my arm. Bolts and veers into the road.

I scrabble to catch hold of her. 'Pandora!'

A car swerves and honks its horn.

Pandora veers back to the left and runs into the minicab office.

What's she doing? Pandora vibrates, grabs the radio guy's wastepaper bin and vomits into it.

Goodbye cab home.

'This your friend?' The guy doesn't get up.

'Yes. Sorry. I'll pay for that.'

'Can't take her in that state, babe.'

'Please. She needs to get home. I'll pay extra. How much would it cost to get the cab cleaned, fifty pounds? How about I pay her fare *and* an extra fifty pounds?'

He sucks air through his teeth.

Please?

Pandora smiles.

'See, she's fine!'

The radio controller pauses. 'OK.'

There is a God! 'Thank you.' I help Pandora up. 'Come on, time to go home.' We wobble outside.

'Cab for Chelsea?' A driver with a kind smile holds open the door of a car.

'That's us!' I propel Pandora towards the back seat.

She twists and goes in backwards.

'All right there, love?' The cabbie leans over my shoulder.

'Are you going to rape me?' Pandora asks.

What the fuck? Who says that?! She obviously thinks this is an illegal minicab. *Have you ever taken anything other than Ad Lee in your life?* 'Sorry, she doesn't mean it. Bad joke!' *The poor driver.*

'It's all right, love. I'll get you home safe.' He smiles at Pandora.

'Thank you.' I grab Pandora's clutch. She must have some money in here? Twenty quid. Figures. I hand over my cash: my entire week's budget.

'Whereabouts in Chelsea do you want me to take her, love?'

'Pandora, what's your address?'

She emits a small snore.

I smile at the driver. 'Hang on.' I shake her leg.

'Wha?' Her eyes are sleepy.

'What's your address?'

'Chelsea. I live in Chelsea.'

'Whereabouts in Chelsea?'

'In Chelsea.'

This is no time for jokes. 'Do you have a flatmate, Pandora, someone I can ring?' *How can I not know whether my work colleague shares a flat?*

'I live in Chelsea.'

Two parties, four gallons of water, three packets of sea salt and balsamic vinegar crisps, half a sip of white wine and a fish-finger sandwich at home (eaten in the dark).

DAY 4

'Sweetie.' Mr Darling gently shakes my shoulder.

My skin feels plump again, no longer like a crinkle-cut crisp. I rub sleep from my eyes, that's better, now I can see his cute smile. *Why is he wrinkling his forehead like that?* The memory of my message to Legally Hot comes crashing back. I tense.

'There seems to be someone snoring in our spare room.'

Oh God, last night! 'It's Pandora.'

'What is a Pandora?'

'My work colleague, silly. I had to bring her back with me last night, she'd had too much to drink.'

'Bit of a shock when I went in to get my suit.' He doesn't look very impressed.

'Sorry! I was planning to get up before you and tell you.'

'When have you ever got up before me?' He raises his eyebrows.

That's uncalled for. 'I just didn't want to wake you when I came in. Again.'

'Right.' He stands and straightens his tie in the mirror. 'I'm going to put the kettle on.'

He could have offered me a cup of tea! What did he want me to do, abandon her in central London? Stick her on the night bus to Chelsea and hope for the best?

Twenty minutes later Mr Darling and I are eating Crunchy Nut Cornflakes in silence when Pandora appears.

Why is she still wearing the T-shirt I dressed her in last night? You can see her legs. All the way up. And whose hair looks like that first thing in the morning? Does she carry a hairdresser in her purse?

'Where am I?'

'In my flat. I brought you back here last night. You were unwell and you couldn't remember where you lived.'

Mr Darling smiles amiably at her.

Don't do that. Has he noticed that T-shirt barely covers her tiny arse?

'But where am I? I need to order a car home.'

'The Docklands, E14.'

'Oh my God! I got so drunk I woke up in east London. No one will talk to me ever again.' She flops onto the sofa. 'Aren't there gangs round here?'

'Pandora, we live in a gated apartment block with a concierge ...'

'To protect you from the gangs?'

'There are no gangs!'

'Hello.' She smiles at Mr Darling as if she'd just met him in a bar.

'Nice to meet you,' he says.

Don't look at her.

'Ladies,' he says, 'I'd love to stay and chat but I'm afraid I have to leave for work. Pleasure to meet you, Pandora.'

'You too,' she pouts.

I hate you.

'What is this?' She pinches the T-shirt she's wearing.

'It's mine, I thought you'd be more comfortable sleeping in it.'

'Your clothes are massive.'

Next time you collapse in the toilets at a private members' club you can stay there.

Pandora leaves in an Ad Lee and then arrives in yet another one at the office, looking refreshed and flawless. I've taken the underground and look wilted. I'm also beginning to think that maybe Mr Darling had a point, and it probably was a shock to walk in on Pandora this morning. I hope he was wearing more than just his boxer shorts.

'Morning, girls. Hope everyone had fun last night?' Charlie is handing out square red envelopes.

Christmas cards? I assumed they were too quaint for the industry.

I slice it open with my fingernail. It *is* a Christmas card. Filled with twenties. I *love* the colour purple!

It reads: 'Happy Christmas, thank you for all your hard work this year! xx'

'Thank you!' we all scream.

Georgina slips her card into her bag then visits the bathroom with it. *Clever.*

In the bathroom I count the twenties – it's five hundred pounds. Five hundred pounds! I've never held so much cold hard cash before. This would take a chunk out my Visa bill. I could start a nest egg. I slide the bulging envelope between the credit-card bills in my high-street handbag. I weigh the bag in my hand. Even full of money it weighs cheap.

A designer handbag is a symbol of maturity. It tells the world you are a sophisticate. It raises every outfit. It says: I've made it. I'm going to buy a handbag! After dealing with Vampira and Pandora, and all the late nights, I deserve a treat.

Everyone's buoyed by the cash bonus. After a model agency Christmas party, which is attended by a disturbing number of fat leering greying businessmen who seem to be nothing to do with the industry, we end up at Home House. Another private members' club. The novelty's worn off.

'But espadrilles are charming. All that rope. They're very peasant-chic,' Ceci waves her glass of red around.

'I know, but wedges were invented by Ferragamo. They're legendary,' Georgina counters. 'Plus espadrilles are often flat.'

'True.' Ceci nods.

I'm done. It's 11 p.m. Pandora's already left. I haven't seen Mr Darling all week. I want to go home and make up with him. I'm out of here.

'I'm sorry about Pandora this morning,' I say as I snuggle into his arms in bed.

'That's OK, I've just been a bit stressed about work,' he mumbles into my hair.

I feel bad for not thinking about the toll all his long hours are taking on him. This cuddle is nice; now is not the time to talk about work/life balance. I let myself drift off to sleep.

My ringing phone wakes me at 3.12 a.m. Unknown number. Something awful has happened. Mum? Dad? 'Hello?' My voice is shaking.

'Hi, this is Celine at Home House. We have a friend of yours here.'

Oh no.

Mr Darling groans. 'Fucking hell. I need to sleep. I have to leave at six.'

He never swears. 'Sorry,' I mouth and slide out from under the warm duvet. The lounge is cold and lit by the 24/7 light of Canary Wharf. 'Sorry, Celine, I don't understand?'

'Your friend has lost her bag. And coat. And she's a little confused. She was able to give us a number and it went through to answerphone and your number was given for emergencies.'

They must have called the office. This is not really the kind of emergency my number is meant for. 'Can I speak to her?'

'I'm afraid she's asleep in our reception.'

Great. 'Can you describe her to me?'

'She's wearing a fur jacket, and a pale green dress.'

'That's Georgina!'

'Do you have her mobile number? We were hoping to call it to try and locate her bag.'

I boil the kettle and make myself a fennel tea while I wait.

'We found it. It was behind a sofa. Does she have anyone at home we can call?'

'Try Rupert. He's her boyfriend, they live together. I'll hold.' I don't want another unexpected houseguest.

Rupert is contacted and a car is arranged to take Georgina home.

I open the bedroom door gently and tiptoe back into bed. The clock says 03:52. I may as well have stayed up all night drinking.

Two parties, four glasses of white wine, two pints of water, kebab-shop chips on the tube home, zero sleep.

DAY 5

In the office, I spend all day typing and deleting a message to Legally Hot. I don't know what to do. I wish Jen were going to one of these stupid parties. I just want to talk to someone normal. I try calling her at lunchtime but her phone goes to voicemail. I don't leave a message.

One party, one film-star sighting, lots of boring small talk, five glasses of champagne, two pumpkin-risotto balls, and one broken nail.

A MULBERRY
MOMENT

'Whoever said money can't buy happiness
simply didn't know where to go shopping.'

BO DEREK

A day of rest. Thank God for the weekend. It's midday
and I'm in bed. To my joy I discover Mr Darling in the
lounge reading the newspaper. 'Not going in to the office
today?'

'The report's finished, we're reading through on Monday and
sending on Tuesday.' He gives me a smile over the paper. He
looks tired.

'So is this the end of your long hours?'

'For this project, yes. So we can spend the weekend together,
unless you're partying?'

I'm caught a bit off guard. It's been so long since Mr Darling
and I have spent any time together I can't remember what we
used to do. I say the first thing that comes into my head. 'Do
you want to come shopping with me?'

'I don't really like shopping.'

This relationship is doomed. 'How can anyone not like shopping?'

'I don't like all the people. And it's boring.'

I snatch his newspaper up and sit on his lap. 'This isn't normal shopping; I'm going to Bond Street. The shops aren't busy. There are fewer hoi polloi, Your Majesty.'

He looks at me.

I really want him to say yes. I feel like he owes me after all the cancellations and the lonely hours spent here on my tod. 'I'll buy you a beer after?'

'Done.'

Thirty minutes later and we're walking the hallowed footpath of Bond Street. I think I'll cancel Legally Hot when I get home.

'That's a Lamborghini Murciélago,' Mr Darling points at a bright orange car. 'And that's an Aston DBS.'

'An orange car and a black car. How nice.' How can he be looking at traffic? I drink in the glistening storefronts. Even in the drizzly December rain it feels like the sun's shining on Bond Street.

'It's cleaner than the rest of London.' Mr Darling is looking at the pavement.

He's just not getting this. 'I can't believe you've never been here before. Come, meet my friends Prada and Dior!' I drag him into a shop.

A girl with a ponytail so severe my head hurts just looking at it approaches. 'Would you like a glass of champagne or a mince pie?'

'This isn't that bad.' Mr Darling eats his mince pie in one go, spilling crumbs down his jumper.

We're in Mulberry: the perfect place to buy a bonus handbag. I stroke the lovely leather goods. Timeless. Luxurious. Understated.

Mr Darling is trailing behind.

'This is the one.' I lift a chocolate brown tote, with a buckle strap running round the top. 'Ooh, look, it's called Jacquetta.'

'Why does it have a name?' Mr Darling pulls the same confused face he does when he can't get in to a microwave meal. For a smart guy he's got very little common sense.

It's big enough to carry my wallet, make-up, hairbrush, phone, a spare pair of shoes and several unopened Visa bills. I slide it on to my shoulder. It feels reassuringly heavy. 'What do you think?'

'Suits you. How much is it?'

'Four hundred and ninety-five pounds.' Cheaper than I thought. I'm actually on budget!

'Four hundred and ninety-five pounds! Is it made of actual gold? That's ludicrous. Put it down.' Someone's pulled the plug on Mr Darling, all the colour's just drained from his face.

'Shush! Jacquetta will hear you.' I hug the bag to me.

'You can't seriously be thinking of buying it? You could go on holiday for that.'

'Don't you think it looks nice?'

'Yes, it looks nice, but not five hundred quids' nice. You don't need to spend that kind of money on a bag. You look amazing in your pyjamas and they don't cost five hundred pounds! Wait, they don't cost five hundred pounds, do they?'

Legally Hot pops into my head. I think of the Gucci shoes he bought me. How he recognised the Marc Jacobs pendant I was wearing. He appreciates fine things. Maybe I was being hasty when I thought about cancelling our catch-up. 'It's a Mulberry. How much did you think it was going to cost?' *People are looking at us.*

'I don't know, a hundred, hundred and fifty max.'

Ridiculous. 'You could spend that on a Topshop one.'

'Well, why don't you get one from there then?'

'You don't understand. This is an investment piece.'

'An investment? What's that, Ange-onomics? A bag is not an investment, I've never heard anything so daft—'

'It is! It won't depreciate. I'll be able to resell it in the future.' That must be true. A designer handbag still costs a few hundred on eBay. *Why am I justifying myself?* 'It's my money. I can spend it on whatever I want.'

He takes a deep breath. 'Yes, you can. You're right; it's none of my business. Sorry, I won't say anything else.'

My cheeks are flushing. 'You're ruining a great moment for me.'

'Don't say that.' He gives me a squeeze and a smile.

I stroke Jacquetta. I don't want to fight today; it's the first decent amount of time we've spent together in months. It's not his fault he's not very fashion conscious. He's fashion unconscious.

'OK?' he says.

'OK.' I give him a weak smile.

The saleswoman places my Jacquetta into a tissue-lined box. The box then goes into a pleasingly huge paper bag. My first designer handbag, bought with money earned in the fashion industry. It's a threshold moment: I am a woman.

'Five hundred quid!' Mr Darling mutters behind me as we leave the store.

DAY 6

I step aside to let a lady with cropped red hair leave the office lift.

'Nice bag!' she says.

I knew it! Jacquetta's special. I just wish I could make Mr Darling understand. Sometimes I feel like we're talking a different language.

'*Amaaazing bag!*' squeals Ceci when I walk through the door.

Ceci gets it. Legally Hot would get it. It's only three more days till my date with Legally Hot. Not that it's a date. It's just two friends catching up, I remind myself. Maybe I should just double-check what Jen thinks? Her phone goes straight to answerphone.

One party, one unbelievably cool handbag, an unpromising venue, an unclear amount of alcohol, unpalatable canapés, unconscious in the cab home.

DAY 7

'How's it going?' Jen's voice drills through the phone.

'Can't talk.'

'You busy at work?'

'No, just can't talk. Tequila slammed all remaining brain cells last night.'

'Drink water!'

'Ughhh.'

Two hours later: I call Jen back. It goes to voicemail. Dammit. Dammit. Dammit. Only two days till I'm supposed to *meet* Legally Hot.

Two parties, two glasses of champagne, three glasses of white wine, one bowl of potato wedges, four paracetamol, two ibuprofen, one Tubigrip ankle support.

DAY 8

'Almost there, girls!' Ceci bounces into the office after me, gripping a bucket of coffee and wearing her Dior shades.

Georgina's not shown up yet.

How am I still alive? It's a Christmas miracle. It's 16th December. Jen, Mr Darling and all my civilian friends are starting to attend their work Christmas parties. Fashion is winding down. The agency closes tomorrow. Tomorrow I'm seeing Legally Hot. I gulp.

My mobile starts to ring, making me jump. It's Mr Darling. What's he doing calling? I blush as if he knows about my plan for tomorrow night. I take the phone down the corridor. 'Hello? You all right?' My voice sounds high and squeaky. My palms are sweating. This is it. He knows. He's going to confront me.

'I got the promotion!' he screams.

'What? Oh my God! That's fantastic!'

'They announced it first thing this morning. I'm a senior consultant. All the hard work was worth it.' He sounds so happy.

'Congratulations. We'll have to celebrate.' I feel a bit choked up.

'We are going to have a huge celebration, just you and I, look I've got to go, but I'll call you at lunch. I just couldn't wait to tell you.'

'Congrats again,' I say as the phone goes dead.

I walk back to my desk in a daze.

The doorbell buzzes.

'Who's that?' Ceci looks up from her coffee.

'I'll go,' I say on autopilot.

Standing the other side of the door is a massive bunch of red roses with legs. 'Angela Clarke?' asks the flowers.

'Yes.' They must be for an artist.

The roses rustle toward me, and a man, with one of those bolt earrings that look like a Polo mint, appears.

'Ohhh who are they from!' Ceci pads over in her bare feet. 'There's a card.'

> I couldn't have done it without you.
> Thank you for being so
> patient these last few months xx

Mr Darling! What a darling!

'How romantic,' Ceci exhales. 'You can't beat red roses. They're a classic.'

'I know.' I stare at them. I carry my flowers to my desk and open up my emails. A message appears from Mr Darling:

> Had to go before I could ask you something. Been
> trying to do it in person over the last few weeks,
> but we've kept missing each other. I know you're
> going home for Christmas, but would you like to
> come to mine at New Year's? It's about time you
> met my family.
>
> xx

A huge smile erupts over my face. He wants me to meet his parents. This is serious. This is real. This is the future.

I take a deep breath and open a new email.

> It was really nice to bump into you in Starbucks.
> Really nice. But I haven't been entirely honest
> with you. I'm in a long-term relationship, and after
> a lot of thought I don't think it would be
> appropriate for us to meet. I can't see you
> tomorrow. I'm sorry for leading you on. I wish you
> health and happiness with everything in your life.
>
> Angela x

I feel quite mean blowing Legally Hot off at the last minute. But it's taken me a while to figure it all out. Besides, it's better to do it now than when people might have really got hurt.

Mental note: try and think about things from Mr Darling's point of view and keep up the communication. I ignore the little voice in my head saying: what about telling him about your credit-card debt then?

'Where are you for Christmas, Pandora?' I ask. *I'm going to Mr Darling's for New Year!*

'I'm doing Christmas at the family estate, then New Year in Barbados with friends.' Pandora's wrapped in the fur coat she refuses to take off since a handful of snowflakes fell yesterday.

Bugger. Me and my big mouth.

'Lovely,' says Ceci.

'I'm thinking Vivienne Westwood, Barbour and tweed, English Heritage chic for Christmas, and Pucci meets Miami for Barbados,' Pandora adds.

'Lush! I'm spending Christmas at my friend's family's castle in Scotland and then New Year in New York. So McQueen for Christmas Day and Lanvin for New Year's.' Ceci leans over to smell my roses.

Don't ask me. Don't ask me.

'What are you doing, Angela?'

Sigh. 'I'm spending Christmas with my family in ... the ... er ... Home Counties and New Year at my boyfriend's family's ... er ... country estate.'

'And what are you wearing?'

Pyjamas for Christmas day and Topshop for New Year's. 'I'm weighing up several options.'

Ceci sips from her coffee bucket. 'It's best to get these things planned in advance, otherwise packing is a nightmare.'

I feel myself tense. I'm still not a true fashionista. Underneath my dress I'm wearing my Spanx; I imagine it feels the same as being partially digested by a boa constrictor. 'Don't you ever just wear something comfortable on Christmas Day? It is a holiday.'

'Fashion doesn't take a day off,' Pandora says.

I picture her shopping in Sainsbury's in a ballgown.

Ceci shrugs. 'The tighter the dress, the less likely you are to overeat. You don't want to be one of *those* who gain weight over Christmas.'

Everyone gains weight over Christmas, don't they?

'I knew a girl once who gained three pounds. Can you imagine? How awful!'

I probably fluctuate by three pounds every week. I wonder if they're monitoring *my* waistline? OF COURSE THEY'RE MONITORING MY WAISTLINE. One more day and I can hang out with the normal people who don't just photograph plum pudding but eat it.

I reply to Mr Darling:

> Congratulations again, Senior Consultant. What
> clothes shall I bring with me for New Year's?
> xx

Ping. Mr Darling's responded.

> Pack practical clothes. My family live in a small
> village. No need for anything fancy. x

Practical clothes. Jeans, ballet pumps, I can take the new pale-cream knit I snapped up in Topshop. There, I can plan in advance.

The door buzzer goes. 'I'll get it!'

'Sign here.' A courier wrapped up in scarf and gloves hands me a wine bag.

'Thanks. Merry Christmas!'

It's a bottle of Perrier-Jouët champagne, decorated with beautiful white flowers. The tag reads: Merry Christmas, Angela! Love Fraser xxxx

'Wow! Fraser's sent me a bottle of champagne!' Today just keeps getting better.

'Sweet!' cries Ceci.

'He sent us all one yesterday, he obviously forgot about you,' says Pandora.

Ouch. Remember it's the thought that counts. 'I didn't expect anything!'

'A good artist will always give you a Christmas pressie. I make a note of those who don't.' Ceci taps the pad on her desk.

I place the bottle next to my roses.

The door buzzer goes. It's a bunch of flowers for Pandora from a photographer.

The buzzer sounds again. Ceci and I have each been sent a Fortnum and Mason hamper from a stills photographer. Amazing! I'm loving today! It's like Christmas! It *is* Christmas!

Mid-morning, Daffodil pops in and presents me with a bottle of Chanel Coco perfume.

'You shouldn't have!'

'I got it free from the PR, sorry.' She looks embarrassed.

'It's Chanel! *Chanel*! I love it!'

She grins.

Designer Dormouse arrives in a fluster after lunch. Beautifully wrapped inside tissue paper and ribbons are two Nicole Farhi jumpers.

'I saw them at the sample sale and thought of you!'

I can't believe this! 'They are amazing. Thank you so much. You've just massively improved my work wardrobe.' I hold up a stripy jumper against me.

'What you talking about? You're always working the trends.'

I'm glowing. Pandora is glowering.

Another hamper, two more bottles of champagne, a ponyskin clutch bag, I'm overwhelmed. I'm going to need a taxi home.

Ms NY arrives. She's one of our highest earners. I've worked till gone 10 p.m. to get her back to New York when she's missed her flight. I covered for her when she was hungover and late to a shoot.

She places a gift-wrapped box in front of me.

It's rude to get too excited. What is it? Designer clothes, a limited-edition handbag, expensive make-up? I rip the paper off. *Casually.*

It's a supermarket-own-brand box of chocolates.

'How lovely.' I sound like I've just unwrapped a piece of coal.

She looks pleased with herself.

I open the lid to offer them around. *Hang on, there are four chocolates missing . . .*

'Someone gave it to me. I ate the strawberry ones, I don't like the rest.' Ms NY beams.

You didn't sniff these then? 'Thank you,' I manage.

One party, two mulled wines, three pomegranate martinis, one half-eaten box of chocolates, a taxi full of Christmas swag and a big snog with Mr Darling when I got home.

DAY 9

One Christmas lunch, three glasses of champagne, two suitcases, one train ticket home, a surprisingly warm hug from Pandora and a partridge in a pear tree.

CHRISTMAS WITH THE VON TRAPPS

'The essence of style is how you live your life.'

OSCAR DE LA RENTA

I stagger off the train with my bags like a donkey bearing the pregnant Mary, Joseph, the shepherds, the three wise men and their intricately wrapped gifts. Never pack at 3 a.m. after an excess of mulled wine. I've been in the fashion industry for nearly a year. Why haven't I mastered the capsule wardrobe?

I stare out the taxi window on the way to my parents' house. Everything looks so suburban. Small. Quiet. The same. It's a relief. I'm a fashion wreck. I have eye bags as big as Louis Vuitton trunks. I'm shaking from alcohol withdrawal. I'm so tired it almost dulls the pain of being apart from Mr Darling for a week. Almost. An unexpected thought pops into my head: will Side-Parting and his big-nosed fiancée be home for Christmas? There's a chance I'll bump into them in the local pub. Ugh.

'Hey Dad! Happy Christmas!' My dad's wearing his golf jumper. It's freezing outside, nobody can accuse him of being a fair-weather golfer. 'You haven't decorated the tree, right?'

'Nice to see you too. The tree's been left ready for you as per your instructions. I believe you called, texted and emailed your mum to make sure. You were tree-mendously specific.'

Dad joke klaxon. 'I'm going for minimalist Scandi-chic. All wooden decorations.'

'I like tinsel.'

'Maybe next year we'll do retro seventies.'

'You're turning into your mother. She hates decorations.'

'Because of the dust. I like decorations – but they must be stylish. Any sign of our old decorations? The angel I made when I was six?'

'I think your mum's managed to successfully throw them out this time. We shouldn't have let her store them in black bin bags last year.'

'Is she at work?'

'Yes, and I'm just going out. Need a hand with your bags?'

'Can we get them upstairs? Then I think I might have an afternoon nap.'

My bed. I savour the crisp clean sheets. Home.

***

'Good afternoon!' Dad's sat at the dining room table doing the crossword.

It's 11.15 a.m. the next day. I slept all the way through.

Dad's cereal bowl is in front of him. Mum's half-drunk cup of tea is at her place. They've only just got up too. I love my late-night, late-morning family.

'Morning, Dad.' I'm wearing my new loungewear. Comfortable *and* stylish.

'That's a nice top, where's it from?' Mum appears with more newspapers.

'Specialist shop. Only a hundred and fifty pounds in the sale.'

Mum grips the sideboard to steady herself. 'You spent *a hundred and fifty pounds* on a cardigan?'

I forgot I'm not talking to fashionistas. 'It's cashmere!'

'It's *immoral*!'

Welcome home.

***

Six days later the tree is decorated with simple wooden birds and snowflakes, I've consumed enough mince pies to fill my Mulberry, all my gifts are wrapped and I'm even beginning to fancy a drink. Dad did manage to covertly hang a number of gaudy foil ceiling stars when I went to get a manicure, but he looked so pleased with himself I resisted the urge to set fire to them.

In my old bedroom I lay *the* outfit on the bed: bouclé black-and-white shorts, cream vintage shirt, black opaque tights and my Gucci shoe-boots. Every year since we left sixth form there's been an unofficial school reunion in the local on Christmas Eve. I think it's only Christmas Eve. Maybe some people go every night? If Side-Parting and I had stayed together would we still live here? I can't imagine always going to the same pub. Missing London.

I check the mirror one last time. Expensive but industry-discounted highlights: check. Chanel nail polish: check. Gucci shoe-boots: check. Uniquely stylish outfit that says 'successful woman who hangs around with supermodels': check. I pick up Jacquetta. Butterflies at possibility of bumping into ex: check.

Mum corners me as I near the front door. 'You can't go out like that!'

Am I fifteen?? 'Why not?'

'You're wearing shorts. It's December.'

'They're bouclé, they're on trend.' I adjust Jacquetta.

'People don't wear shorts round here ...'

'Everyone'll be wearing them next season.' I grab my Burberry.

Mum shakes her head. 'You'll freeze.'

The taxi beeps its horn.

'I'm wearing thick tights and I'm taking my coat. I'll be fine. Don't wait up.'

'Angela.'

I stop. She has deployed the mum voice. I'm no longer an adult who lives and works in London, I'm four and I've just been caught eating the Play-Doh.

'That's a really nice bag.' Her blue eyes smile.

'Thanks, Mum.' I smile and hug her.

Jen's easy to spot at the bar. She's the white swan among the fake-tan tangoed masses. Everyone's dressed in jeans and vest tops, apart from those underage kids in the corner who are in full-on party dresses. *Oh well.*

'Mate, you look amazing. But aren't you cold?' Jen grips me in a hug.

'No, darling. You're looking pretty fabulous yourself. Is that nail polish?'

'I'm off work for a few days.' She shrugs.

We get a couple of drinks, a bottle of beer for Jen, a glass of what's supposed to be champagne for me, and find a table. The bar is dark and loud and smells of stale McDonald's. I can't believe we used to be so desperate to get in here.

We chat to old school friends. Several are married (*already!*), most work in insurance or management consultancy (*dull*), and many are fat (*pleasing*). Jen pops to the loo. We've been here for over an hour and there's still no sign of Side-Parting.

'Angela?' Someone taps me on the shoulder.

Oh. Just the popular boy in school, the one we all had crushes on. His hair's thinning a bit. 'Hi.' I turn back.

'I saw you when you came in, you haven't changed at all.' He gives me a grin.

I'm a dress size smaller, my hair is blonde and I'm wearing the kind of clothes that work in Mayfair. 'Mmmmm.' I glance at the door. I wish he'd go away.

'What are you up to nowadays?'

This is it, the killer line. Delivered to the wrong person. 'I work in fashion, darling.' *Where is Side-Parting?*

Popular boy pulls up a chair and sits backwards on it. *Classy*. 'You were always very stylish.'

No I wasn't.

'I work in London too, perhaps we could go for a drink?' He taps the back of the chair.

This is what all teen dramas centre on: the geeky girl getting the hottest guy in school. This is my moment, five years too late. Why is he even talking to me? The realisation hits me like the Selfridges door swinging into my face. He's talking to me because of how I look; I look like a fashionista.

'Sorry,' I smile. 'I don't think my boyfriend would like that.' *Mr Darling, remember him? Why are you even looking for, or hoping to see, Side-Parting?*

'Take my card and if anything changes, let me know?'

An accountant. I almost feel sorry for him. His twenties don't seem to be going as well as his teens. He peaked too soon. I shake myself. What am I thinking? I sound like Pandora. When did I start deconstructing what people look like and what they do for a living? I've got to watch myself: the more time I spend with the fashionistas, the more their attitudes rub off on me. I'm becoming bitchy by osmosis. It's just habit, I assure myself, like if you talk to someone with a really strong accent you start imitating them. I don't really think those things.

'What did he want?' Jen shimmies in beside me.

'Sex, I think.' Time for some humour.

'You're too sexy for your shorts!' she sings in a stupid voice.

I laugh. My outfit, and wanting to be seen at this bar, is feeling a bit fake now. The big reunion with Side-Parting, and his subsequent fatness/baldness/uncontrollable weeping at how amazing I am, hasn't happened. I never got to say any of the cutting pithy remarks I'd practised or swing my hair and strut off. Closure is an urban myth. What I really want now is to have a proper catch-up with Jen. 'Want to ditch this place and go back to mine with a bottle of wine?'

She looks around at the faces we used to be so desperate to impress. 'Yes.'

I lift my glass. 'Merry Christmas, darling.'

The next morning (*just*) I'm in my pyjamas, having a text conversation with Jen.

> Merry Xmas!
> How you
> doing? Jx

Mum and Dad are settling themselves on the sofa. My brother's distributing presents from under the tree. It's his job, he does it every year.

> A little ropey.
> Must have
> been that
> faux-champagne
> Ax

'That's from me, Mum!' My brother passes her the small intricately wrapped package.

'Pretty ribbon,' she says.

I paid ten pounds extra to have it wrapped.

'Oooh, a box.'

'It's not just a box, it's chocolates. They're really expensive truffles, flaked with real gold.'

Mum looks dubious. She pops one in her mouth. 'Bit rich. I'd have been happy with a bar of Dairy Milk.'

Right.

'Socks, thanks Angela. I could do with some more.' Dad's holding up his gift.

'They're cashmere, Dad.'

'Lovely.'

'Look at the pretty china pot your brother bought me, Angela! It'll match the bathroom perfectly.'

'Found it in a charity store.' My brother grins.

A charity store? You've got to be kidding?

> My parents
> don't like
> the presents
> I bought them!!
> Ax

Jen texts straight back.

> Sure they
> do really.
> What did you
> get them? Jx

> The *most*
> expensive gold
> leaf truffles and
> cashmere socks
> as featured in the
> best magazines. Ax

OK ... do your
parents read
those magazines? Jx

I watch my dad inspecting the bag of wooden golf tees my brother bought him. Something he really wants. *I've done it again – I've let the fashionistas worm their way into my head. I've bought presents for Pandora's parents. I'm turning into Pandora.*

***

It's the day after Boxing Day and I'm finally on the train. I had lunch with my family earlier. Mum tried to force-feed me all the leftover sprouts, because they were 'taking up space'. In her mind, leftover food is just another form of dirt to be disposed of. Then I had to pack, which should have been easy given that I'm just taking everything that I brought with me. But I couldn't fit everything into my suitcase; somehow my jumpers have gained weight over Christmas. They must have been at the brandy butter. In the end my brother had to sit on the case to close it. When I open it my dirty knickers will spring out like a jack-in-the-box. Dad gave me a lift to the station and I hauled my case back into and through London, a little later than I'd planned. I'm already exhausted and there's still two and a half hours till I'm due to arrive.

A lady in a fetching nylon uniform pushes a refreshments trolley past. 'Any drinks?'

I'm about to meet Mr Darling's family. 'White wine, please?'

London rolls away and is replaced by green and yellow fields and a pink sunset ...

Did I fall asleep? My face is pressed against the window. There's a line of drool spreading down the glass. Uber-classy.

The train's slowing down. We're here: Newport! Thank God I woke up. I scrabble to scoop Jacquetta off the floor and defy several laws of physics getting my case off the train. Mr Darling said he and his dad would meet me in the car park.

I try to smooth my hair. *Does my breath smell of stale wine?* I bet I have sleep creases on my face. I'm not ready to meet Mr Darling's dad. I need more time. I need a blow-dry.

Outside the station it's dark. I've grown used to the tall, lit buildings of London. You can see the stars here.

I spot Mr Darling and his dad. Mr Darling waves and comes forward to take my case.

'Hello, stranger,' he says, giving me a quick squeeze and a kiss. He smells of cinnamon.

I manage to giggle. His dad will think I'm a moron.

'Dad, this is Angela.' Mr Darling looks proud.

His dad's hair is completely white, but choppy and textured like Mr Darling's. His face is young, late forties, early fifties. I've never been good at ages. 'Hello.' He shakes my hand. He has the same laid-back, amused air that Mr Darling does. As if a laugh is about to bubble from his lips.

'Nice to meet you.' I relax a little, or maybe it's the wine. 'Do you mind if I sit in the front, I get carsick?'

'All yours.'

It's a further fifty minutes' drive. I can make out the dark shapes of mountains and the odd twinkling light of a lonely house out of the window. The sky is vast. London, the fashion industry, the constant effort to keep up, all feel a long way away. Why do I let it get to me, the worrying about fitting in, the worrying about impressing people? None of it matters. It's just when it's crazy and busy and I'm worn down I get confused. A little lost. Next year I'm going to change that.

Mr Darling's family home is halfway up a mountain. I can just make out the lights of the nearest farm. Music pours from the house. I hear the chatter of voices inside. Two soppy boxer dogs come bounding out to greet us.

'These are my girlfriend's.' His dad pats their heads. Mr Darling's mum died when he was eighteen.

We enter the kitchen. The place is packed. A party. All Mr Darling's family are here. Aunts, uncles, cousins, all up from the village. I'm on show. I shouldn't have had that last wine. I'm still in my hot and city-grimed roll neck. I've probably got dribble on my face.

'How you doing?'

'Good to meet you.'

'You've done well here, boyo!'

There must be thirty people sat round the edge of the lounge, all Mr Darling's family, leaning their backs against the wall. There's a plethora of blue eyes, rosy cheeks and the healthy complexion of those who don't suck the exhaust pipe of London each day. A few, including Mr Darling, have guitars. One has a tambourine. They sing. Really well. Halfway up a mountain, everyone singing – this family is the Von Trapps! Is that dress made from a pair of curtains? I keep an eye out for nuns. I clap along. I won't sing – I want these people to like me.

When it's time for bed I realise there's no streetlights outside and the moon is small. I hope I can find the bathroom if I need to pee in the night. Is that an owl hooting? Very ... *Harry Potter*. How lovely to grow up here. How far away London feels. I nestle against his warm body.

***

In the morning the view from the window is incredible. The Black Mountains. Picture-postcard. Mr Darling and I are sat under the Christmas tree in his dad's lounge. I'm sneaking forkfuls of the scrambled eggs he's made me for breakfast.

Mr Darling is grinning at the Paul Smith wallet I've just given him. 'This must have cost a fortune. You shouldn't have wasted your money on me.'

'Your own bit of Bond Street.' *These eggs are good.*

'It'll remind me of you every time I pay for something.'

I hit him with a cushion.

'Everyone's going to know it's from you. I'm such a scruff I would never have bought anything so stylish.' He starts emptying his old wallet.

'I hope you like it.'

'I do. Now, your turn.' He passes me a large heavy box covered in scrunched garish paper and what looks like a whole roll of Sellotape. 'Remember, wrapping is not my thing.'

I push the tray with the eggs on out of the way. 'It looks like you held the paper against it then continually wound the tape round.' I turn the package from side to side.

'Is that not how it's done?'

'I'm going to need scissors to get into this. Possibly dynamite.'

'I'll help.' He pulls at the tape.

I pull it the other way. The paper gives. It's an Apple MacBook. I stare at it. He's bought me a laptop. It's a thing of beauty.

'Your old laptop is so slow.'

'I've had it since I was at university …'

'You're not sentimentally attached to it?'

'No, it's dying. Technically, it's dead. I defibrillate it to get it going. Wow. This is such a … big present.'

'I know you've been using Macs at work. And you always talk about writing a book …'

'Do I?' *I didn't realise I'd mentioned that.*

'You should have a proper machine to do it on.'

I've only ever had slow second-hand laptops before. Grey plastic lumps of things. This is so new, so sleek; so thoughtful. 'Thank you. It's perfect.' I stroke the box.

'I'm glad you like it, I'll set it up while you finish your breakfast.' He lifts up the tray.

I'm grinning like a loon. I resume my assault on my breakfast.

Mr Darling has the box open and is reading the instruction booklet. 'I thought we'd go shooting this afternoon.'

I choke. *Shooting?* 'Like animals?' I'm not really a killing things kind of girl. I don't own anything tweed.

'No, clay pigeons. We do it on my gran's farm, down by the river.'

'That sounds very … country.'

'Worried about your aim?'

'I did rifle shooting at Guide Camp. Once. I was pretty good I'll have you know!'

'Come on then, Brown Owl, this needs to charge anyway.'

Shooting? Why not! It'll be good to get some fresh air after a week and a half of watching *Muppet Show* reruns and *Curly Sue* on the telly indoors.

As soon as we step out of the car I realise I've made a mistake with my clothes. The countryside is full of mud. *Does it rain all year in Wales?*

My bronze ballet pumps disappear into the goo. My skinny jeans are too skinny. My cream knit looks ridiculous. This is a disaster. I always thought I'd like to live in the country but I was wrong. Where's the tube? Where's Space NK? Where's my fruit smoothie? Where's the concrete?

'Want this?' Mr Darling hands me a spare blue fleece out the back of the car.

'Thanks.' My practical clothing is completely impractical.

Bang! *Christ that's loud.* The sound of gunfire ricochets off the hills. The clay pigeons smash as they're hit.

'Afternoon.'

'How do.'

Mr Darling's cousins keep their eyes trained on the 'pigeons'.

Oh pretty. One of his cousins has a man bag on the floor. The leather is incredible. 'Nice bag.'

'It's a shot pouch.' He grimaces.

'Oh. Sorry.'

He grunts and shows me how to hold the gun, how to anchor it in to my shoulder.

It's heavy. I glance at Mr Darling. He doesn't look worried. I won't make a fool of myself in front of his family.

'Pull!' shouts one.

'Now!' shouts another.

I aim and pull the trigger. The gun kicks back into my shoulder. My ballet pumps, which have no grip, fly out from under me. I hit the floor with a squelch. I'm lying in the cold wet mud! This top is dry-clean only!!!

'You hit it!' cries Mr Darling.

LADY IN THE RED

'You'd be surprised how much it costs to
look this cheap!'

DOLLY PARTON

After a week walking in the deserted Welsh mountains, returning
to demented London and Planet Fashion is a shock. But I'm
loaded into my magic knickers and ready to face my colleagues.

They all look very tanned.

Ceci pulls a miserable face, slumped in her skinny jeans and
mohair cardigan.

'It's not that bad being back at work, you'll soon get into it
again.' I give her little arm a little squeeze.

'I had a crap holiday, Danny and I broke up.'

'I'm sorry.'

'He was much more than my boyfriend; he was my
hairdresser. Who's going to do my roots now?' Her brown eyes
widen in panic.

'Erm, there's plenty more hairdressers in the sea, you can
always date another?' I look at Pandora imploringly.

She makes soothing noises.

'Never again. He kept more products in the bathroom than me. And once there was a spider in our bedroom and he screamed. I need a real man. Like a hot plumber.'

Ceci, you hang out in Chelsea and on your friends' yachts, where are you going to meet a plumber? 'New year, new start, eh?'

'Good idea!' She jumps up.

Huh?

'What are everyone's New Year's resolutions?' she cries.

Georgina and Pandora look rapturous. *I have a bad feeling about this.*

'I'm going to lose weight,' says the already tiny Georgina. 'I'm cutting out dairy.'

Georgina doesn't eat carbs, red meat, wheat, anything that was grown in the dark (negative energy) and now dairy. I think that leaves apples and macrobiotic lettuce.

'I've resolved to only date men with inherited wealth. They can work as well, if they want, but I'm not wasting my time on losers ...'

Way to go Pandora, resolving to be more bigoted.

'... and I'm only seeing people I'd consider marrying.'

Poor bastards.

'That's so sweet,' gushes Georgina.

Face-palm.

'I want to get fit,' Ceci continues. 'I've booked a personal Pilates teacher. He has all these amazing machines with straps and weights he attaches to your arms and your legs.'

'Sounds like a rack.' I open up my notepad. Time for work.

Ceci laughs. 'You're so funny, darling, what are your New Year's resolutions?'

Eat more chocolate, drink more wine and have more fun. 'I haven't really thought about it.'

'But it's the best thing about January,' Ceci enthuses.

'You could resolve to lose weight.' Pandora wrinkles her nose.

So I ate Christmas pudding for breakfast every day for the last two weeks, it's winter, that's what jumpers are for. 'I don't want to lose any weight.'

Pandora looks shocked.

Ceci looks incredulous.

'I might resolve to read a new book every week,' I push on.

'Why?' Pandora raises her eyebrows.

'Because it'll be good for me.'

'How? It won't make you thinner or fitter.'

Proof that starving the body of food starves the brain of oxygen.

***

A few weeks later Jen and I are drinking warming Cab Sauvignon near her current hospital placement in Euston. 'I thought the girls would keep their resolutions a few days but they're still going strong.'

'That's just not normal.' Jen taps her lighter on the table. She's resolved to quit smoking, and take up salsa. The two are not related.

My copy of *Madame Bovary* is still on the bedside table, untouched. 'Ceci eats half a chocolate button on Fridays. Then reseals the packet and leaves it untouched in her desk drawer. That's her weekly treat.'

'That's it?' Jen pulls the sleeves of her jumper down over her hands and pushes her thumb through where she's worn a hole. The woman wears high-street clothes, with holes in them, and looks as stunning as any of the fashionistas clicking around Harrods.

'That's it. Last Tuesday she was out at a meeting and I was so desperate for some sugar I took them from her desk and scoffed the lot. Had to run out and replace them. I am a bad person.'

Jen laughs. 'So how's things other than that?' She takes another sip of her wine.

'Totally stressful day, the model didn't show up for my shoot. I spent an hour on the phone before I reached the office. Then we were massively behind schedule. I was freaking out. I *really* need a massage. Or an assistant. Or a holiday. You – how's work?'

'I saw someone die today. An old man I've been working with a few months. He said he was tired. I was pushing him to do his exercises. Then he sat down on the bed. And died.'

'You totally don't understand stress till a model doesn't show up,' I squeeze her hand.

She gives me a weak smile.

'Sorry for wittering on about fashion shit.' I'm such an insensitive idiot. The world does not revolve around my next call sheet.

'It's fine, don't worry.' She tugs at her sleeves again.

'Is there something else?' Jen's never been any good at interrupting my stream-of-consciousness approach to conversation.

'I've met someone.' She pushes her hair behind her ear.

'Who?'

'A guy in my salsa class.' She blushes.

'I didn't know you were actually taking a class! That's great. What's he like?'

'He's bald with sticking out ears, his nickname's Mr Potato Head.'

'Sounds like a catch!'

'He's smart and funny and well travelled. And he's really into recycling ...'

'Ahhhh, I see ...'

'And he's tall. Really tall.' She's glowing.

'Taller than you?' This is important to Jen. At five foot eleven she towers over most men. I keep telling her it makes her look like a supermodel who's dating a millionaire but she wants, just once, to be the little lady.

'Taller than me in heels!'

'I think a toast is in order. To Mr Potato Head and wearing heels!'

We clink glasses.

When we come to pay the bill there's no cash left in my wallet. I've spent what I'd put aside for this week already. Time to put a stop to this. We're growing up. We've got jobs, responsibilities; one of us is dating a childhood toy. I'm opening the next credit-card bill that comes.

***

I have February's visa bill in my hand. I have nothing to fear. I've been a paragon of thrift.

1st February, Topshop: £120

That was emergency dresses I needed for work, technically that's my uniform.

2nd February, O'Neills: £57

This is outrageous! I'd never go to O'Neills – someone's cloned my card! Hang on ... that was the night I went out with Jen near her work.

2nd February, ATM withdrawal: £100

Same night. I must have done that tipsy thing where you take out lots of cash for a cab. I wonder what happened to the rest of it?

I scan quickly through the rest.

Boots: £47

Selfridges: £26

Strada: £42

Topshop: £45

They all seemed necessary at the time. They all seemed small. I've spent more this month than I can pay off. The amount I owe has increased to...

£6,324.25
!!!

My heart appears to have got lost and is bouncing around my head. That's virtually half what I earn in a year after tax. I'm going to be sick. Can I take anything back?

Hidden in the bottom of the wardrobe I find a Rokit bag I didn't want Mr Darling to see. Can you return vintage?

I hear the key turn in the front door. The Visa bill – it's on the coffee table!

I sprint past Mr Darling. 'What, no kiss hello?' he calls after me.

I ram the Visa bill into my Mulberry handbag. It's full of the damn things. Weighing me down.

'You all right?' Mr Darling comes into the lounge.

'Fine. Just wanted to put some lip gloss on before I kiss you!' *The lies just trip off my tongue.*

I snuggle into his arms, making a barrier between him and my handbag. I can feel it daring me to reveal its contents. I can't slow my breath. I owe six thousand pounds. I should've put my Christmas bonus toward clearing my debt. I shouldn't have bought so much crap.

'You sure you're all right?' Mr Darling pulls back to look at me.

I can't tell him. What would he think? He doesn't have a credit card, nor an overdraft. He's never borrowed money. He's too sensible. He'd think I was insane for racking up six grand on Topshop dresses and two-for-one offers on deodorant at Boots. I'm a liability. He'd leave me.

'Fine. Fancy a cup of tea?' If I grab my bag on the way I can get it out of here.

'Good idea, I'll make it.' He steps back.

'No, I'll do it.' I try to pass him.

We bump.

My hand catches the strap of my Mulberry. My nails scratch at the leather. The bag tips forwards and the Visa bills gush across the floor, dancing in all directions.

'What's all this?' Mr Darling crouches down.

'No, don't!'

He has one in his hand. His eyes and his mouth open in shock.

What's that sound? It's my world crashing down around me.

SNAKESKIN AND LADDERS

'I did not have three thousand pairs of shoes.
I had one thousand and sixty.'

IMELDA MARCOS

'I can explain ...' *I can't explain.*

With each bill Mr Darling picks up I feel him slipping away. I'm losing him one spending spree at a time.

'Are these yours?' He can't equate the massive debt with what he thought was his sane girlfriend.

I nod.

'How long has this been going on for?'

'I ...' I try to put it into words. The break-up with Side-Parting. The bags in Harrods. The hair. The make-up. The way Ceci, Georgina and Pandora look. The way they all live. The sample sales. The parties. The shows. The store cards. The pressure. The goddamn fashion industry. I'm bankrupt.

Mr Darling's face is dark.

'You ... don't understand ...' I stutter.

He's gripped the bills so tight in his right hand they're starting to crumple and tear. 'No, I don't. I can't believe you've spent so much money. What were you thinking?'

That I wanted to belong. That I needed to impress these people. I needed to prove I was good enough. I'm shaking. I open my mouth to try and explain.

'Don't. I can't get my head round this. I need to get some air.' He slaps the bills down on the table.

I wince. 'Can I come with you?'

'No, I need some time to think.' He grabs his keys from the table and storms out of the room. The front door slams, shaking the walls of the flat.

I look at the debris of my shopping sprees, my life for the last few years, scattered around the room. A fat tear escapes and rolls down my cheek. I sink on to the floor and cry.

***

Mr Darling's been gone for two hours. He hasn't answered his phone. I've picked up all the bills and put them in a pile on the dining table. I tried calling Jen but she didn't answer. She's probably off not spending money with Mr Potato Head. I thought about calling Mum but what would I say? She would be so ashamed of me. She repeatedly drummed in to me the importance of being financially independent. And, as ever, I ignored her.

I stare at the herbal tea I've let go cold. Next to it is the untouched one I made for Mr Darling. I start snivelling again. I've ruined everything. I've sabotaged my own life. Side-Parting was right, I'm stupid and out of my depth. I'm six grand in debt. I've been lying to everyone. I'm a fake. I've lied to the man who loves me, the man who bought me a Mac so I could write a book, the man I love.

I walk slowly into the bedroom and pull my case out of the wardrobe. It's over. It was only last month I was unpacking after our wonderful Christmas break together. I open it up and start heaping in my clothes. With each bundle of dresses I gather up I feel more anxious. All that money. I haven't even worn some of them. I feel sick.

'What are you doing?' Mr Darling's voice makes me jump.

He's standing in the doorway, watching me. 'I didn't hear you come back!' I manage, wiping quickly at my eyes.

He looks at me and sighs.

This is it. I should have packed quicker. I should have left. I don't want to hear him say it's over. I will not cry. I brace.

'I've bought you a Dairy Milk.' He pulls a chocolate bar from his back pocket.

'What?' I don't understand. Is it to sweeten the blow?

'I'm sorry I ran off. It was a hell of a shock.' He takes a step toward me.

'I'm the one who should be apologising. I'm so sorry. I've been so stupid. I should have told you. I shouldn't have spent all that—' I can't say it. I start to sob. So much for not crying.

'You're not leaving are you?' He signals at the case.

'I thought, I thought you wouldn't want me here any more.'

He puts his arms around me. 'Hey, come on now. We're in this together. We can sort it out.'

I'm getting snot all over the front of his jumper.

'It's OK.' He rocks me gently. Mr Darling drags the case off the bed, so I can lie down. He strokes my hair. 'Shush now, it's OK.' Exhausted I fall asleep.

When I wake Mr Darling is sitting at the dining table on his laptop. 'I've made a spreadsheet of what you owe and your incomings/outgoings.'

'Once an economist, always an economist.' I smile weakly. My eyes are sore and my throat is dry.

'Do you have any savings?'

'I had six hundred pounds.'

'Had?'

Full disclosure. No secrets. This is a new start. 'I spent it on a Marc Jacobs denim jacket.'

I see him bite his lip. 'OK. Anything else? ISAs? Shares?'

I shake my head.

'It's going to take some time to pay this off.'

I wince.

'Is there anything you have that could take a chunk off it?'

'The only thing I have of any worth is my clothes.' I swallow. 'I could ...' *Say it.* 'I could sell some of them.'

'Do you think you could do that?' He squeezes my hand.

'Yes,' I answer flatly.

My wardrobe is still open. All my shoes are in clear plastic boxes, unless they are designer, in which case they are still in their original boxes. All my dresses, skirts, shirts etc. are colour-coordinated. It's very organised for someone whose life is in chaos.

I pull out a pair of yellow shoes. From the English National Opera's costume sale. I queued with a friend from the early hours of the morning and fought off amateur dramatics enthusiasts to get these. I can't give them up.

Starting with shoes was a bad idea.

I take out my Alexander McQueen sample jacket. I frequent enough second-hand designer boutiques to know I could sell this for more than I paid for it. But it's McQueen! I shared a taxi with him. These aren't just clothes, they're bits of my history. I give myself a stern talking-to. This is how you got into this mess. Stop being stupid.

What about my Gucci shoe-boots? Legally Hot bought them for me. The first designer item I owned. I can't walk in them.

'How's it going?' Mr Darling appears.

I'm a grown woman. I need to take responsibility for my actions. 'I can sell these.' I show him the Guccis.

'Great! How much do you think they're worth? Thirty quid?'

'More like three hundred.'

'How much did they cost originally? Don't tell me ...' He rubs his temples.

'I'm going to sort it out. I'm going to let these go.' My voice cracks.

He sits on the edge of the bed. 'I've got a proposal for you,' he sighs.

He's going to make me sell the lot!

'With my promotion I got a bonus. I'll pay off your Visa bill if you cut up your credit cards and promise never to get another.'

Did he just offer to pay off my bill? All that hard work he put in for that bonus. 'I don't know what to say.'

His voice grows serious. His eyebrows almost meet. 'No credit cards, ever. That's the deal. You have to live within your means from now on.'

I nod. I can do this.

'Good. Let's cut up these cards.'

I take my Visa and store cards out of my wallet. Mr Darling hands me the scissors.

A little voice in my head cries: make a run for it. Take the Visa and go. Head to Selfridges, drink champagne you can't afford, wallow in new shoe purchases, ignore the bills, and push down the feeling of dread. No. I have to grow up.

I try and close the scissors over the card but my hand won't do it. I take a deep breath. The two halves of the Visa fall to the floor. Goodbye my friend.

I'm free. I'm relieved. I'm happy. I'm broke.

***

'Do you ever feel like university was a really long time ago? Sometimes I feel like a completely different person, as if I got lost on the way.' I flop on to the orange seventies sofa in Jen's new shared flat in south London. In a bid to save money we're staying in tonight and toasting her new home with Cab Sauv (two for one at Tesco).

'You think too much.' Jen doesn't look up from preparing her culinary *pièce de résistance*: baked beans on toast.

'I'm a feminist failure.' I slide down the leatherette back, until horizontal.

'Why, because you work in fashion?'

What?! 'No, because my boyfriend just paid off my Visa bill. I'm supposed to be an independent woman.'

'You didn't rack up loads of debt on credit cards because you're a woman, you did that because you're an idiot.'

'Cheers.'

'Hang on, I don't want to burn it this time.'

I study my wine while she painstakingly dishes up.

'Voilà!' She passes me a plate that does indeed look like baked beans on toast. It's a miracle!

'Looks delicious!' I'll reserve judgement. I've eaten her cooking before.

She joins me on the sofa. 'The problem with you, Ange, is that you think you have to buy all these things to keep up with those girls you work with.'

'I do! They would totally judge me if I didn't look the part.'

'But why do you care? Surely you don't want to be friends with people who judge you by what bag you're carrying?'

'It's not that simple ...' *Or is it?*

'I know you're expected to dress a certain way, in heels and whatever, but you're so stressed out about it you've run up a massive debt. Maybe fashion isn't for you?'

'But I love it!'

She gives me a look.

I just need to get the balance right. I can work in fashion and play at being a fashionista, as long as I don't get sucked in. As long as I keep it real, as the celebrities say. I can do that, right?

'I just need to be more careful going forwards. Stick to a budget.'

She laughs. 'I know you, mate, you'll stick to a budget till you see something you really want.'

'Totally unfair. Let's change the subject. Who would have guessed this vintage would so perfectly complement baked beans?' I pretend to swill and taste the wine like a sommelier.

Jen laughs. 'It really brings out the flavour of the grated cheese sprinkled on top.'

I'll worry about how I'm going to keep it real in the fashion industry later.

***

When I woke up this morning everywhere was covered in snow. I didn't think it actually snowed in London, except in Dickens books and Disney movies. It's up to my knees! The Docklands look beautiful. Clean. The snow's covered all the crap. The DLR is working but the tube, which is mostly underground, is cancelled. *Because that makes sense.* I'll have to walk from Bank. This constitutes an emergency worthy of breaking the fashionista rules: I'm going to wear flats.

The chiselled hunks of the City's buildings, which usually roar with the frenetic high-flyers of the financial companies, seem subdued under a fluffy white layer. The snow has made it quiet and still. Someone's built a snowman outside the Bank of England. Walking always helps me sort out my thoughts. I've been thinking about what Jen said about me thinking too much. I know, ironic. The fashion industry is intense. And insular, and crazy. Some people can rise above it, like Mia and Daffodil. They're down to earth. They don't freak out about what other people think of them. They haven't had to be bailed out of their credit-card debt by their boyfriend. Maybe there's nothing wrong with the fashion industry. Maybe there's something wrong with me. I just can't deal with it. Dammit, my boots are coming apart at the seams.

I need a new plan of action. Behaving like a fashionista at work is necessary to keep up with the other girls. In the warped fashion world, obsessing over what you wear and judging everyone you encounter is part of being professional. I just have to remember it's only an act. It's not the real me. I don't *have* to spend a fortune to compete, I don't *have* to sniff cake, I don't *have* to drink champagne, and I don't *have* to lose my head up my own Spanx-clad bottom. I need to learn to rise above it all, like Mia. I'll just develop a separate work persona, and take it off when I come home, like a uniform. I can do that. I think.

I reach the office just after 11 a.m. Not bad for an Arctic trek.

'They're not really suitable,' Pandora points at my boots, which now look like they've been chewed by a washing machine full of salt.

'They weren't built for this weather.'

'I don't mean unsuitable for the weather, I mean for work.'

Of course, you're wearing stilettos. 'Did you change when you got here?'

'No. I walked in these.'

'Didn't you fall?'

'No. Everyone knows there are two options in the snow: Chanel ski boots or stilettos. You dig the heel in like a crampon for grip.'

I see.

Ceci arrives, shaking snowflakes from her brunette hair and rabbit-fur jacket. She's wearing Chanel snow boots.

It's a set-up.

'Angela, you're here,' Charlie sticks her head round the door. Her neck's wrapped in woollen scarves today.

'Charlie, you made it!' I would have put money on snow being the perfect excuse to work from home.

'A word in my office please.' She beckons a fingerless-gloved hand.

I only wore flats because of the snow. I didn't know about the whole Chanel boot/stiletto thing. I got here as soon as I could. Please don't sack me – I've only just figured out how to survive!

I shake as I enter the office. Charlie has two electric heaters in here. It's small and stifling. I can't breathe.

'Take a seat.' She waves her hand at the Danish teak chair opposite her desk.

'Thanks,' I stutter. My cold skin starts to sting in the heat.

Charlie turns around and gives me a warm smile.

This is it. She's going to fire me. I close my eyes.

'I'm promoting you.'

'What?' I open my eyes. She's still there. Still smiling.

'I'd like to make you junior agent, give you your own artists to represent.' She picks up a pack of artist cards from the desk.

'Why?' I sound like a moron.

'Because you're good at what you do.'

'I am?' My brain won't function properly, my mouth's gone rogue.

'You're great at marketing, your productions come in on or under budget, I know I can rely on you. You've got the makings of a great agent.'

I've found it. My talent. My place in the world. I am an agent in the fashion industry. 'Thank you.' I wonder if I'll get a pay increase? I wonder how much those Chanel snow boots cost? No, I correct myself. Don't get sucked in. The Chanel boots are lovely. Very warm-looking, but I don't *have* to have them. I just got promoted without them, didn't I? I can do this. I can make it work. I'm a real fake fashionista.

***

Things move fast in the fashion industry and time flies like the latest It bag off the shelves. I'm settled. I'm happy. I'm promoted. Pandora still delivers me the odd catty comment, but I no longer give her ammunition. In fact I could give others a bit of advice.

How to be a successful agent in the fashion industry:

1. Make the artists feel special. (Despite how they behave.)
2. Make the artists and the boss lots of money. (Ditto.)
3. Don't trust anyone when it comes to production. Do it yourself. Cross every T-bar shoe and dot every eyeliner.
4. Look the part and work the party.
5. Always fly the client's dog business class.

How to fake it in fashion:

1. Always wear heels.
2. Always wear Spanx.
3. If necessary wear three pairs of Spanx.
4. Call everyone 'darling'.
5. Only eat salad in front of colleagues (if you fancy chocolate, go out for lunch).
6. Groom like Barbie i.e. get a professional to do it. Embrace time-saving treatments like three-week manicures (more time to live). Learn how to apply make-up in moving vehicles (more time to sleep).
7. Keep up to date with the latest diets: Atkins, South Beach, Dukan, whatever. Sound like a convincing participant of the thinspiration culture, without having to give up chips.
8. Keep an emergency drawer in your office containing hairspray, shampoo, make-up, tweezers, spare high

heels, tights, doggy treats. Nobody looks magazine perfect without a serious toolkit.

9. If in doubt, go to Topshop and buy a new outfit.

There you have it: a cheat's guide to making it in the fashion industry. My persona does all of the above, and the real me slobs about in my pyjamas, drinking cheap wine with my mates who've never heard of Gisele. It's a flawless plan. What could go wrong?

HOUSE-HUNTING

'Anyone who lives within their means suffers
from a lack of imagination.'

OSCAR WILDE

SEVEN YEARS LATER ...

'It'd take twenty minutes off our journey to work.'

'That's twenty more minutes in bed.' Mr Darling and I are
strolling home along the Thames discussing the new rental
apartment we've just viewed.

Mr Darling takes a sip of his latte. 'The second bedroom is
bigger than our current second bedroom ...'

'That's not hard.'

'I love the view of Limehouse Marina ...'

'We have always said we wanted to live there. Watch the
boats. Get coffee from the Italian deli.'

'I could get a boat and moor it outside the flat,' he jokes.

'A floating man-shed.'

'You can visit.'

'I'll wave from the balcony!' I toast him with my takeaway hot chocolate.

'What did you like about the flat?' he asks.

'The walk-in wardrobe.'

He laughs. 'I suppose I'll be relegated to the second bedroom again?'

'Yes, but it is bigger than our current second bedroom.'

'I could buy another shirt!'

'Don't go crazy there, Liberace, ease in slowly. Maybe a new pair of socks.'

We pause at Westferry Circus and look out over the Thames. To the west you can see the Limehouse warehouses we've just left, then the glass monoliths of the City, and then the river surges on out of sight under Tower Bridge, past St Paul's, past Tate Modern, past the London Eye. Behind us, Canary Wharf is burgeoning. We are in the middle of a property boom. Skyscrapers force their way up into the skyline like hungry shoots. We live in a giant building site. It's gritty, and noisy and exciting. The world is changing right before our eyes.

I take another sip. 'I don't think we should take the flat.'

'I thought you liked it?' Mr Darling shields his eyes from the sun with his free hand.

'I do like it. But it's a whopping amount of money to waste on rent. Why don't we buy?'

Mr Darling makes the annoying tongue-clicking noise he does when he's thinking. 'We'll need a deposit. I've got some savings. Have you?'

'A few hundred.' *In an Egg savings account once called 'Fashion Fund'.* 'I could buy the paint and wallpaper?'

'You can't mess about with a mortgage. Can you stick to your budget to help make monthly repayments?'

'That was years ago,' I huff. 'Can we stop going on about it now? I haven't taken out another credit card. I've reduced my overdraft limit right down. I'm not like that any more.' Then I feel guilty for snapping. If Mr Darling hadn't bailed me out, I'd have had to sell my soul at Cash Converters and been declared bankrupt.

'We're still young, maybe it's too risky.'

'But it makes sense for us to get on to the property ladder as soon as we can.' This is why Mr Darling and I work together. He tempers my extravagance, and I encourage him to be bold and take risks.

'OK!' He grins. 'Let's buy a house together!'

Together.

'Let's go look at that marketing suite for the new build just off the Marina?' He loops his arm round my waist.

'Right now?' *Now who's being bold and taking risks!*

The marketing suite is a temporary glass structure on Millwall Dock. It's full of 3-D models, floor plans, artists' impressions and sales guys wearing too much hair gel. To buy a cream shoebox of an apartment we need to place a thousand-pound holding fee and cobble together the 10 per cent deposit by the end of the month. Then we have a few months to arrange the mortgage before it's ready to move into.

We step outside for a powwow.

'We went out for a coffee and now we're buying a flat?' This feels surreal.

'Want to think about it?'

We're buying a flat. *Together*. 'No. Let's do it!'

Back inside I corner a shiny-suited salesman. 'You work on commission right? I'm looking for a good deal or I'll go talk to your friend with the lurid pink tie over there.' I point at another salesman who's swooping in on a couple with a baby. 'I want twenty grand off and free legal advice.'

Mr Darling grins.

'Do you work in sales?' The shiny-suit guy catches his fingers in his hair gel.

'No. I work in fashion, darling.'

As I turn around I notice Mr Darling take his phone out his pocket and start checking his messages. He seems to be doing that increasingly often lately. I'm sure it's nothing.

***

'We need to have a talk about the mortgage.' Mr Darling is clutching an A4 lever file; I've just walked through the door.

'I've had a hell of a day. The model missed her flight, by the time I got her sorted I was completely behind. Then a client kept me on the phone for nearly two hours giving me a detailed description of her latest colonic. They flushed out a metre of plaque. Did you know that was possible?'

He wrinkles his nose. 'Disgusting. Do you want to do this at the table or on the sofa?'

I sigh. 'Can we do it another night?' I want to watch American reality TV shows and marvel at their complicated lives and white, white teeth.

'It won't take long. I just need to run through some projections ...'

My phone starts ringing: Daffodil.

'Hold that incredibly boring thought.'

Mr Darling huffs.

'Hi, Daffodil!'

The noise of what sounds like a washing machine comes from the other end of the phone.

Has her bum called me? 'Daff, can you hear me?'

The washing machine pauses, sniffs and starts again.

Good God, she's crying! 'Are you all right? Where are you? What's wrong?'

Mr Darling looks concerned.

The washing machine pauses and spits out '… sacked!'

'You've been *sacked*?' Daffodil has been part of the make-up team on a prime-time TV talent show. It's a lucrative job. If she gets in with the winning contestant she could work on the album, promotional tours etc.

The washing machine is still whirring.

'OK. Take a few deep breaths. What happened?'

'I was sacked for being two hours late,' she dribbles.

'But that's so unlike you – did something happen?'

'I was set up!' The spin cycle starts up.

Mr Darling goes into the kitchen. I hear the kettle click on. Through the door I see him check his phone, again. Over the last few months I've noticed he never lets it leave his side. He's always been the type to leave texts and answerphone messages unchecked for days. It's a running joke between us. I get an uneasy feeling in the pit of my stomach.

Daffodil has slowed again. 'Hettie told me the call time was eleven o'clock. It was nine! I was asleep when the production assistant called. I couldn't get there quick enough. They had to get in someone else. And they sacked me.'

My attention snaps back to Daffodil. 'Hettie just needs to tell them she gave you the wrong message.'

'She swore blind to the producer she'd told me it was a nine o'clock call time. Then I found out Hettie's been telling people I have a problem with drugs. I don't do drugs!'

'Why would she do this? She's your friend! Didn't you get her the job in the first place?'

'Yes,' she says damply. 'There are rumours of cuts. She was the last one in, she thinks she'll be the first out.'

Stabbed in the back by your friend. I can't imagine Jen doing that to me. I can't imagine Jen doing that to anyone. 'I'm so sorry, Daff. I can call the producer tomorrow and explain what's happened?'

'Won't work.'

She's right. This job was organised through a record label contact of Daffodil's. The producer won't speak to me. At best I'll get the assistant.

'OK. But I can call round and let people know you're available. I heard rumours Sony are launching a new solo female artist. They think she's going to be huge in the US. The guys at Sony love you!' *You* will *be able to make your mortgage payments. You* won't *starve.*

I say goodbye and collapse on the sofa. I haven't even taken off my coat.

'Right! Let's do this.' Mr Darling reappears with that damn folder.

I groan.

'I know you don't like talking about finances but we're going to have to to get this mortgage.'

I bury my face in a cushion and groan again.

'I've started a new house and mortgage file. See this section is for the contract, this one is for—'

'I don't want to be the kind of couple that talks about filing systems,' I mumble from the cushion.

'No, but you want to be the kind of couple who own a flat.'

I sit up. 'I was thinking purple.'

'What?'

'For the bedroom curtains. Rich purple.'

'We can talk about interior design *after* we've secured the mortgage. I'm a little concerned about your, er, credit history.' He blushes. 'I've made us an appointment with the bank to start the process. In case we have to look around.'

I thought I'd left the great credit-card debt disaster in the past. Is it about to come back and screw up our new home?

***

I obsessively press refresh on my inbox. I'm waiting for a photocopy of an international pop star's passport to forward to my travel agent. Then I can get out of here and get to the bank for our mortgage meeting. I glance at the time. I'm cutting it fine. Mr Darling is probably already on his way with his A4 file and spreadsheet.

Organising the travel for the team isn't even my job. But the New York production team had allowed the glam squad, including my make-up artist, only twenty minutes to get from Hammersmith to Glasgow. They would have had to teleport. I had to step in.

I scan the online news reports of the international pop star's twenty-first birthday last week. Fresh-faced, pretty, blowing out the candles on a huge cake shaped like the number 21. Perhaps we can use some of the photos for my make-up artist's portfolio?

The email arrives. I press print.

Hang on. The birth date on the international pop star's passport catches my eye. That would mean she's actually … Well, well. She's not twenty-one, she's twenty-eight! She's a whole seven years older. That's my kind of maths. I shove the documents into the envelope and leave it marked up for the courier.

'See you guys later. I'm on my phone if you need me!'

'Angela, did you hear about Bonnie? She got signed by one of the top Paris agencies. Won a huge campaign,' Georgina shouts.

'Fantastic – I'll call her tomorrow.' All those years of working with Vampira paid off.

'Good luck!' cries Ceci.

I arrive breathless in the bank's sci-fi foyer. Mr Darling, after a seemingly endless study of interest rates, has selected a bank in Canary Wharf. They're probably more used to mergers and acquisitions than our measly mortgage.

We are whisked into a small cubicle room and Mr Darling hands his report to the puffy-faced bank manager. Her suit is one size too small and it doesn't look like she's brushed her dyed-blonde hair today.

'I'm afraid there's been an issue with your credit report.' She smiles.

Shit. My dodgy financial history has come back to haunt me, like the ghost of shopping trips past. *Did Mr Darling just shake his head?* This is the death knell of our relationship: the day my shopping habit cost us our home.

'I'm sorry, sir, but you've failed the credit check.'

'What!'

Mr Darling grips his folder tightly.

I can't believe what I'm hearing. 'You mean me – Angela Clarke – read it again.'

'No, madam, you passed. You have an excellent credit rating. Your partner has failed.'

I stare at him.

He stares at her.

Have we slipped into a parallel universe?

'But I've never had a credit card, an overdraft or a loan …' Mr Darling stutters.

'Precisely. You have zero credit history. You have never borrowed money and you have never paid it back. You have therefore failed a credit check.'

I bite my top lip. I mustn't laugh.

Mr Darling looks pale.

I cover my mouth with my hand. Try to smother my giggles. My eyes are watering. *It's NOT funny, stop it Angela.*

The bank manager offers me a box of tissues.

'Don't cry, baby!' Mr Darling takes my hand. 'It'll be OK. I just have to get a credit card. It's a formality. Then they'll give us the mortgage.'

'I'm not crying. I'm laughing!'

'Why?' Mr Darling looks confused.

'I'm sorry, it's not funny… It's just… Well, you should have gone shopping!'

PACKING IT IN

'Is there anything beyond fashion?'

DIANA VREELAND

'You will not believe what *she's* done!'

It's Fraser with the gossip about the latest pop star he's working with. 'What?' I flick through the artists' diaries for tomorrow's shoots. Mr Darling and I are finally moving into our flat and I want to double-check everyone has their call details. Daffodil is still touring with Sony's new solo female singer – I knew it would work out.

'*She* has hired actors to attend her child's birthday party.'

'What?' *Forget the diaries.*

'The kid's turning two or three or whatever, and has no friends. The poor little mite is just dragged around by the nanny all day. It never plays with other kiddies.'

'That's awful.'

'Super trag. One of the gossip mags wants to photograph his birthday party and *she's* fretting. *She* wasn't going to even have a party for him. Her plan is to hire child actors to pretend to be his friends.'

'The poor thing. I guess he's too young to realise.'

'*She'll* probably do it again next year, and the next. MTV will film his sweet sixteen but all the guests will be hired help.'

'Don't joke.'

'I'm not, doll, she's even bought fake gifts for the fake friends to bring. I wonder if he'll realise they're all wrapped in the same paper?'

'Stop, it's sad.' I don't want to hear about the unfortunate lives of celebrity offspring.

'That's nothing,' he says. 'Yesterday we were backstage with that girl group everyone's so excited about, and you know the northern one has had a sprog?'

I vaguely recall tabloid stories about how quick she's lost the baby weight. 'Yes.'

'Well, she and the others thought it funny to feed the baby McDonald's French fries. It's two months old!'

'Christ!'

'Don't worry, good ol' Fraser saved the day. I batted the chips away and told them they weren't suitable for babies. Do you know what they said?'

He loves an audience. 'No, what?'

He adopts a high-pitched voice. 'Yeah, you're right. Don't want her getting fat.'

I groan.

'I was like, fat, fat! The baby can't eat solids at its age!'

'Let alone all the salt!'

'Exactly! I should be given a medal, doll.'

'You should. Do you think the baby will be all right?' *What else are they trying to feed it 'for a laugh'?*

'It'll be fine, doll. It's with the nanny most the time. Missy's too busy eating her own Big Macs to care.'

I don't want to hear any more. 'Don't forget I'm not in tomorrow. I've sent you all your call sheets for the next three days. The girls in the office are up to speed on all your jobs. If there are any problems, you can call them. I'll have my mobile with me for absolute emergencies.'

'You focus on the move, doll. We'll be all right without you for one Friday.'

'Great, well, good luck with the show tonight and the shoot tomorrow and I'll speak to you when I'm back.'

I slide my 'New Flat File' out from under my notepad. I have a floor plan, a drawing to scale and twenty-three deliveries arriving tomorrow. I don't see the point in waiting till we move in and then ordering furniture. I can't go twelve weeks waiting for my bed. Dad, Mum and my brother are helping us move with a rented van. I've planned this like a production. I won't ever look like the girls in *Vogue*, but my flat can look like the properties in *Elle Deco*. By Monday, everything should be in and unpacked. The only thing left to do is finish packing tonight.

Ceci is conducting model go-sees on the sofa. I glance up just as a famous It girl walks in. Didn't she have her own TV show? What's she doing here? She has the requisite model components: height, weight, freakishly long legs – must have got those from her mum. The bad skin and yellowing fingers suggest too much partying – must have got that from her rock-star dad.

'Hi, do you have your book?' Ceci smiles.

The It girl stands looking awkward. 'Sorry, I don't usually do go-sees.'

She must have really pissed off her booker.

***

It's 10 the next morning and our flat is auditioning for a disaster movie location. I ran out of boxes last night. I've been filling black bin bags since then. Around 4 a.m. I collapsed on a pile of skirts. I'm turning into Designer Dormouse! Mr Darling's entire possessions fit in one suitcase and one cardboard box. Mine look like an Oxfam clothing mountain.

I carry a pile of books into the lounge.

Mr Darling's on the phone. He looks up. 'I've got to go,' he says and hangs up.

Am I imagining it or is he looking a bit shifty? 'Who was that?' I ask, trying to sound calm.

'No one, just someone from work,' he says busying himself with wrapping the dinner plates in newspaper.

He never takes calls from work on his mobile. He never takes calls on his mobile at all, unless it's from me.

'Good morning!' Mum shouts through the open front door.

I have to put all thoughts about Mr Darling and his mystery caller out of my mind. We're in the middle of moving into the flat we've bought together, for God's sake.

'Hello!' Mum shouts again.

'Looks like it's going to be a scorcher, London. Forecasters promise it's going to be the hottest day for over a decade, so "Relax" with Frankie Goes to Hollywood,' crackles the radio.

'In here, Mum,' I shout back.

She appears holding a box containing a kettle, tea bags, a bottle of squash and some loo roll. I feel better just seeing her. These are the essential things you need to accomplish any task. My dad is powered by tea.

'Your dad and your brother are outside in the van. We can start loading up.' She slowly takes in the jumble sale we call our possessions.

'We're running a teensy bit behind.' Sweat drips down my neck.

She purses her lips. 'I'll put the kettle on.'

I go to the window and wave. 'Hi Dad!' Dad and my brother, both modelling shorts, are opening up the back of the van.

My phone rings. Now there's nothing unusual in that.

'I'm worried about my portfolio, I want to talk about my editorial direction,' says Daffodil.

'We can definitely discuss that, in detail, when I'm back in the office on Monday.' *I've got a flat to move.*

Back in our bedroom, Mum is emptying my wardrobe into white bin bags.

'Mum, I'm using black bin bags for packing and white bin bags for rubbish.'

'I know. You've got too many clothes. You need to chuck some out.' A pair of Topshop jeans disappear into the bag.

'Wait! No, Mum! Those are my favourites.' I rescue my jeans and drop them in a black bin bag.

My phone rings. How many secret phone calls has Mr Darling made while I'm on the other line to work?

It's Designer Dormouse. 'Hello?'

'Morning! Can we chase my option for Tuesday?'

'No one needs this many clothes.' Mum is clearing my wardrobe into the white bin bags.

I have to get off the phone! 'I'm not in the office today, so I'll have to check when I get back in.'

'Sorry, I forgot! How's it all going?'

Mum holds up the Elizabethan costume I bought from the English National Opera's sale. 'What on earth is this?'

Fucking fantastic. 'Great, but I've got to get on. One of the girls in the office will chase it up for you. Speak Monday.'

'Good luck!' trills Designer Dormouse.

I'll need it.

Mum is shoving the ENO dress into her rubbish bag.

'Mum! That's Tosca's costume.'

'Well, she can either have it back or we chuck it. It's covered in white powder.' She rubs her fingers together and wrinkles her nose.

'It's plaster of Paris. It glows under UV light.' I make a snatch for the bottom of the dress but she's too quick.

'Why on earth would you want a dress that glowed in the dark?'

'I use it for fancy dress.'

'What's this?' She holds up a hot-pink leather skirt. 'Fancy dress too?'

'No, that's Harrods' own brand.'

'You can't possibly wear all of this.' She drops the skirt into the bag.

I need a new tactic. 'Mum, why don't you take Dad a cup of tea and I'll go through this really quickly?' It's amazing what the threat of being separated from the Zandra Rhodes dress hanging in the wardrobe does to one's energy levels. I shove everything into black bags in the time it takes for the kettle to boil.

Dad packs the van like a jigsaw.

Mum is happily bleaching everything in the flat.

We're on our way.

The boys travel in the van. Mum, me, and her box of necessities take the DLR. Mr Darling can't call or text anyone while he's with my dad.

We arrive before them.

'I'll put the kettle on.' Mum heads for the kitchen.

I walk through the light ground-floor flat. Our home. It smells of fresh paint. I slide open the doors that lead to a balcony overlooking the canal. A brightly coloured barge tugs past. A woman wearing a straw hat waves from the boat.

We're so lucky to live here.

My phone rings: Mr Darling.

'Problem. The back gate's broken, the concierge says we'll have to bring everything in on foot.'

Through the master bedroom's double doors I can see the van. Mr Darling waves. 'It must be 100 metres.'

'We'll carry it, you and your mum can take it over the balcony into the flat.'

'Mum, forget the tea, make orange squash!' The courtyard's white-hot.

My phone rings. Unknown number. 'Hello, Angela speaking.'

'I've got a delivery here for you. It's a bed.'

'I'm sorry but the gate's broken so you'll have to bring it down to the flat ...'

The delivery guy and Mr Darling have one end of the bed. Mum and I have the other. It is seesawing dangerously on the chrome balcony bar.

My phone rings. I contort myself to get it out of my pocket. It's Designer Dormouse. 'I've got to take this.' My end of the bed swings up.

'Not now, honey!' Mr Darling puffs.

I resist the urge to sarcastically mention his earlier 'work call'. 'It must be important. She knows it's emergency calls only. Hello?' I try to balance the bed against my shoulder.

'Thank God you answered!' Designer Dormouse cries.

'What's wrong?'

'I can't cope with this heat. What shall I wear?'

TIMES A-CHANGING

'In two weeks after giving birth to Lucas,
I was on the catwalk.'

NATALIA VODIANOVA

There is something odd about Georgina: she's eating carbs. I watch in fascination as she swallows wholemeal organic bread with her superfood salad. She looks calm. She looks normal. She must be an imposter. *What have you done with the real Georgina?*

Ceci's noticed too.

And Pandora.

We're all looking the other way, as if turning from a road traffic accident.

Ping! A pram-shaped light bulb goes off above my head. She's *pregnant*! It's the only possible reason she'd eat bread. This is not a diet lapse; fashionistas have an unnatural ability to stick to a regime. Ceci is still keeping her New Year's resolution from seven years ago.

A few months later Georgina goes out for a coffee with

Charlie. When she comes back she says: 'Girls, I've got an announcement.'

We all dutifully gather round.

'I'm pregnant!'

'Oh my God!'

'No way!'

'Congratulations!'

We all knew already. By my no-carb calculations she's about four months gone, though her tummy only has the slightest hint of a bump. Mine looks bigger after an Indian takeaway. Even in pregnancy Georgina is sticking to her tiny fashionista frame.

'This is a turn-up of events, hey?' Charlie corners me in the kitchen. 'Georgina's condition, I mean.'

You're making it sound like she's got a terrible disease. 'You never want children, Charlie?'

'The artists are my children. Plus I'm currently sleeping with two younger men; that's as disruptive as having a baby in the house.'

Then she really does surprise me: 'I'm promoting you to senior agent.'

'What?' I put my tea down.

'Congratulations.' Charlie pumps my hand up and down.

I'm a senior agent. I need to order new business cards! 'Thank you.'

'You'll need to take on more responsibility and look after Georgina's artists while she's otherwise engaged. And we'll need a new junior, to help you. Place an advert, go through the CVs and do the interviews.'

I've only been a senior agent for three minutes and you want me to hire staff? 'Sure.'

Georgina is on the phone to one of her photographers. She signals to me to take a seat next to her. 'I wanted to tell you my news … I'm pregnant!'

I lean my head against hers so I can hear. The photographer sucks his breath in. 'I have to say, I'm very disappointed in you.'

Georgina's knuckles turn white as she grips the receiver.

'Your timing is completely irresponsible. It's the busiest time of the season.'

Jerk.

'I can assure you everything's under control. Angela will look after you while I'm away.'

'You and I have a special relationship. I don't know Angela.'

I've been at the agency longer than you have, buster.

'Angela's a very experienced agent. She'll do a great job for you. In fact, she'd love to introduce herself.' Georgina passes me the phone.

I recite the usual reassuring titbits. 'I'm so looking forward to working together. I loved your shoot in *Marie Claire* last month. I was out for lunch with an ad agency the other day and think your work would be perfect for the next campaign they're working on.'

'Great,' he says enthusiastically.

That 'special relationship' didn't last long once I mentioned an ad campaign, did it?

'Wonderful, well, let's put a date in the diary for a coffee to have a proper chat. I'm looking forward to working together!'

I pass the receiver back to Georgina. 'Cheers for sticking up for me.'

'Don't fuck this up.' She drops the phone back on the cradle.

At the end of the day I rush home to tell Mr Darling about my promotion, but the flat's empty. That's odd: he didn't say he was working late. I think about the mystery phone calls, the constant checking of his phone. I'm sure there's nothing wrong, I'm sure I'm just imagining it. Side-Parting pops into my head for the first time in ages. The gap between him dumping me and taking up with Big-Nose was very short. Two days. Almost like they'd been seeing each other already. I don't know why I'm suddenly thinking of this now.

***

'What about HR?' Jen asks over the phone as I walk home a few weeks later.

I wanted to talk to her about Mr Darling's odd behaviour – he's going down the pub after work an awful lot – but we've got stuck on my promotion. I've been spending so much time in the office he could be up to anything. 'Agencies are only small. There are no guidelines. We all muck in and do a bit of everything.' I grab one of the last copies of the *Standard* outside Baker Street tube. It's been a long day.

'So how are you going to pick your new assistant? I still can't believe you have an assistant ...'

'Why shouldn't I have an assistant?' I say through gritted teeth. I had to fit the interviews round my other work. My to-do list has exploded *Mission Impossible* style. Each time my phone rings I have heart palpitations.

'Sorry, but you're hardly saving the world are you?' Jen laughs.

I don't find it funny. Everyone always thinks working in fashion is just sitting around and filing your nails. Georgina and the others are smart and hard-working. Is it so very wrong they like to look good while they do it? 'Anyway. The first girl was an hour late and squealed in recognition when she saw Pandora.'

'So *she's* out.'

'Exactly.' Shit, I forgot to confirm those flights for Vampira. I'll have to do it online tonight. Things are already stepping up and Georgina's only five months pregnant. 'The other two were both young, enthusiastic, and had similar levels of experience.'

'Tricky.' Jen sounds bored.

'They both held down jobs to pay the bills while they interned in the industry.'

'I still think it's dodgy you don't pay interns.' Jen has her public sector head on.

She's annoying me now. 'I'll pick the one with the nicest shoes.'

'Ange! You can't do that!'

'Fashion sense is a totally valid criteria for working in fashion. They have to look the part.'

'Stop joking.'

'I'm not.'

'You can't hire someone based on their appearance – Germaine Greer would throw *The Female Eunuch* at you!'

'Good thing Germaine doesn't want the job then,' I snap.

'Listen to yourself, Ange! You're talking like one of your bimbo colleagues.'

All the tension I've been carrying around comes to the surface. 'Don't call them that. Do you think I'm a bimbo too?'

'When you start hiring people because of their shoes, yes I do.'

'We can't all save the world in hospitals, Jen,' I spit. 'Fashion is a multinational business, it brings masses of money into this country, it creates jobs …'

'Oh yeah, it's really life-changing stuff,' she says sarcastically.

'Just because you have no interest in looking nice and buy all your clothes in Oxfam, it doesn't mean others have to!'

'Tell it to those stuck-up bitches you work with!' The phone goes dead.

She's hung up! How dare she! She doesn't know a thing about working in fashion, or the pressure I'm under. OK, what I said about Oxfam was harsh, but she called me a bimbo. I know the difference between my fashionista persona and reality. Don't I?

***

It's been three weeks and I haven't heard from Jen. I'm not ringing to apologise when she started it. I was looking at her Facebook profile to check she was OK this morning and there's loads of photos from some scabby festival she went to at the weekend. There's this girl with dirty hair and grungy clothes who has her arm over Jen's shoulder in most of the shots. They're waving beer cans around and laughing at the camera. Jen's clearly not bothered about our fight. I bet her new friend's been 'travelling' and sorts her recycling properly. They're welcome to each other. Maybe Jen and I have grown apart, maybe the only thing we have in common is that we once went to the same school. I miss her.

My junior places a cup of hot chocolate on my desk. I force a smile. She's keen, eager and has settled in fast. She knows her way round the kettle, the office and the sensitivities of my colleagues.

'Angela, phone!' shouts Georgina. She now looks like she has a grapefruit stuck up her Marni jumper.

I pick it up.

'I want a later flight on Tuesday. And Binky needs a new coat, call for a discount at the designer I did that Antigua shoot for.' Vampira immediately reels off a long list of instructions. I grab a pen. She always asks for me these days, it's a curse.

I type out a sneaky email to Mr Darling while she drones on:

> We keep missing each other this week, dinner
> together at home tonight?
> xx

Mr Darling confirms. I knew I was worrying about nothing. There can't be anything wrong if he's agreed to have dinner together.

'And my Eames sideboard needs photographing. It would be perfect for the campaign shoot in Paris. I want it here anyway.

This way the client can pay for the shipping. Send them photographs.' Vampira pauses.

'I'll get my junior to photograph it first thing tomorrow.'

'Good.' Click. She's hung up. *Finally*.

My junior appears with some magazines.

'Just the person. I've got a job for you ...'

I get home that night to an empty flat. Mr Darling must be running late. I unpack the M&S ready meal I bought and pop it in the oven.

Two hours later he's still not home. I've eaten my half of dinner and his. I flick aggressively between TV channels. It's either dire makeover shows where they make the participants parade about in greying pants or documentaries about the earwig population of Dorset. Utter rubbish. I've tried Mr Darling's phone but it's ringing out. What if something's happened to him? I pace up and down the living room.

I hear his key scraping against the door. I tense.

He staggers in, his tie askew, 'Hello my gorgeoush! Don't you look pretty today!' He tries to give me a cuddle, but I step out the way so he flops onto the sofa. 'Oooph,' he exhales.

'You're drunk!' I can't believe this. I was really worried.

'Tense day, went for a quick pint,' he slurs.

'We had dinner plans.' I scowl and cross my arms.

He closes his eyes and his breath deepens.

'Don't just come in and fall asleep!' Typical. The first time in ages we have to spend together and he gets wasted. 'Where were you?' I prod him with my toe.

'Out with Sandy,' he mumbles.

My heart stops. I can feel it freeze in my chest. Sandy? 'Who's Sandy?' I say as calmly as I can.

He emits a small snore.

I have to sit down. I need to catch my breath. The constantly looking at the phone, the mystery calls, and the late nights out:

it's got to be this Sandy girl. What kind of a name is that? I bet she's pretty and blonde and clever. She'd have to be if she's an economist. I've finally driven him away. He used to find my being late, or a bit frivolous with money, endearing, but now he's grown tired of me. It's taken us buying a house together for him to finally see it. Like those people who get married then realise it's a huge mistake and file for divorce the next day. I think I'm hyperventilating. Pull yourself together. Mr Darling wouldn't do that. Would he?

I shake Mr Darling's shoulders.

'Huh?' He half opens his eyes.

'Who's Sandy?' I sound calm, though I don't feel it.

'Intern, one of the interns,' he hnnnphs and starts snoring again.

Oh my God, she's twenty-one years old. I can't compete with that! I think I'm going to be sick.

I stand out on the balcony and take some big deep breaths of cold night air. I need to talk to someone. I need to figure this all out. I wish I was talking to Jen.

Mr Darling always keeps his phone in his front pocket. I just want to know. I hold my breath as I gently wiggle it free. He doesn't stir. I stare at it. Do I really want to be the pyscho paranoid girlfriend who checks her boyfriend's phone?

I unlock it and go to messages. My heart's pounding. Maybe I'm wrong. Maybe they're just friends. Sandy. Seeing the name is like a slap in the face:

> Great night.
> Great restaurant.
> See you tomorrow.

I feel dizzy. Sandy, again:

See you at
Holborn tube,
11 a.m.

Wait, when was that? Last Saturday. When he said he was working in the office.

I run to the bathroom and throw up. I sit on the cool bathroom floor and try to think. If I confront him, he'll just leave. It'll be Side-Parting and Big-Nose all over again. I can't be dumped again, I don't think I can take it. I need to stay calm. Perhaps if I give it time it will fizzle out. If we can just spend some more time together maybe he'll realise it's a mistake? We've just brought a flat together, he's probably having an early midlife crisis. That must be it.

I slide Mr Darling's phone back into his pocket. He looks so peaceful. I can't believe he'd really do this. I place a blanket over him and go to bed, where I lie awake for hours imagining how funny, sexy and perfect Sandy is.

SUSPICIOUS MINDS

'I will not retire while I still have my legs and
my make-up box.'

BETTE DAVIS

The next morning I hear Mr Darling whistling as he gets ready
for work. He clearly doesn't remember our conversation last
night. When he comes in to say goodbye I pretend I'm asleep.

I'm walking between the tube and my office when my phone
goes. Not Jen. Not Mr Darling.

International caller.

What does Vampira want now? 'Good morning, Angela
speaking.'

'I've never been so humiliated in all my life ...'

That's not Vampira's voice.

'... I hired your team in good faith.'

Uh oh. The only team I have anywhere at the moment are a
hairdresser, make-up artist and photographer in the Maldives.
This must be Rochelle, the magazine editor. 'Sorry the line's
bad, Rochelle, is that you?'

'Yes it's me. Can you hear me?'

'I can hear you. Is anything wrong?'

'Well, if you would describe your team getting so wasted they waded out into the sea and had to be rescued by the coastguard, then yes.'

Crap. I don't want to deal with misbehaving fashionistas today, I've got bigger things on my mind.

'They started drinking at eleven. We'd barely taken one picture. I've never worked with such unprofessional people before.'

'I'm so sorry to hear that. They usually work so well together.' I'm on autopilot. I wonder if Mr Darling is talking to Sandy right now. Maybe he brought her a morning hot chocolate.

'They are *too* together. It's cliquey. I've been spending the evenings on my own in my room while they drink in the bar.'

Poor girl. I know what it feels like to be Billy-no-mates. Stupid team. Who ostracises the bloody client? 'I'm so shocked this has happened. It's most unlike them. I'm so sorry, Rochelle.' *I'll kill them.*

'This has been the worst trip of my life.'

You won't be booking them again, then? 'I'm sure the photos will be worth it though.'

She snorts.

My phone starts making the incoming call noise. I hold it away from my ear: not Jen, not Mr Darling. It's my junior. She'll have to wait.

'God knows what I'll say to my editor if we don't have the shots,' Rochelle bleats.

'I know their behaviour has been disappointing, but I'm confident the shots will be amazing.' I cross my fingers.

'We'll see. I'll call you when we land,' she huffs.

My phone rings. It's my junior, again. 'Hiya!'

'Naked! She was naked!'

'What? Who?' I need a Starbucks.

'Vampira!'

'Vampira's in Paris.'

'She isn't. She's naked in her lounge.'

'What!'

'I'd let myself in and I was looking for the sideboard and I walked into the lounge and she was walking in from the kitchen. Naked.'

'No!'

'Yes! It was awful. She doesn't have any hair. Down there.'

Despite myself I find it funny. I must not laugh. I must not laugh. 'What did she say? What did you do?'

'She just said, "the sideboard's over there", and walked past as if being starkers in front of a stranger is totally normal. I took two pictures and got the hell out of there.'

I crack up. The lady in front of me gives me a funny look.

'It was awful.'

'You'll need counselling, readjustment to normal, clothed people. Was she rude?'

'No, the most pleasant I've ever known her to be.'

'This is obviously what's been wrong all these years. She clearly hates clothes.'

'Can't bear them.'

'Needs to be free as a bird, as naked as the day she was born. Oh my God, she's a naturist!' I see the woman in front of me smile.

'I need a drink.'

'Look, seriously, if you want to go via the coffee shop on the way in and just take a few moments to ... err ... clear your mind, do it.'

'No. I need to keep busy. I'll be in the office in about twenty minutes.'

'OK. I'll see you then. Deep breath, think of something else. Buy a paper, don't look at page three.'

'Ha ha,' she says before hanging up.

I like my junior. What would I have done if I'd walked in on a naked Vampira a few weeks into my fashion career? I would have called Jen, I think sadly. Then I'd probably have quit, fearing I'd be sacked. The thought sobers me. *Who would I be if I didn't work in fashion?*

***

I arrive home to find Mr Darling is working late again. Maybe he really is. It's not like he hasn't gone through insanely busy periods in the past. It's just that now I can't help but think he's with her, Sandy. I'm torturing myself. I've made a decision: I need to speak to Jen. I know things aren't great between us, but she's the only person who really knows me. She'll know what to do. The phone rings. 'Hello, it's me.'

'Ange! I'm so glad you called.' She sounds genuinely pleased to hear from me.

I nearly cry. A huge smile spreads across my face.

'Mr Potato Head and I got engaged! We're getting married!'

What? 'Oh ... wow!' I choke back my tears and everything I was planning to say. 'That's fantastic! Congratulations! How did he ask?' Now's not the time to mention Mr Darling.

'At the top of Ben Nevis!'

I didn't even know you were going to Scotland. 'A mountain ... romantic,' I manage. It's like I'm talking to a stranger. I feel small and very lonely.

'I'm so happy! Do you mind if I call you back later? We're busy ringing round everyone on the list,' Jen says excitedly.

Was I even on the list? Were you going to call and tell me? 'Of course, I'm really happy for you both.' I swallow the lump in my throat.

The flat is silent. I climb into bed, wrap my arms round my legs and cry.

***

Jen takes three weeks to call me back. Apparently she's been busy. I've been busy too. Pretending everything's hunky-dory. I've thrown myself into work, which has thankfully been manic. Whenever Mr Darling's working late or down the pub I say yes to drinks with Ceci and Pandora.

My phone rings. I jump. Every time my phone rings I jump. I can't remember the last evening I had without a work call. It's Jen.

'Hi,' I say. Things still aren't right between us.

'Hi,' she says.

I wait.

'I was calling, Angela …'

Cringe. Using my full name is a sign she's still cross at me.

'… to ask you a favour. I've always thought you'd be one of my bridesmaids, if you have time?'

That was the least enthusiastic invite to be a bridesmaid I've ever had. I wonder if her mum made her ask me? 'Of course I've got time.' It's not my fault I'm so busy at work. 'I'd love to.'

'It won't be posh, or very fashion so you probably won't like it but I'll email you all the details.'

Ouch. 'OK.'

'OK, then.'

'Bye.'

'Bye.'

It wasn't supposed to be like this.

***

'Guess which rich kid cut all the labels out of their designer togs when they were studying at university, so the other kids didn't pick on them, doll?' Fraser's voice is giggling down the phone at me.

'I'd love to, darling, but I really have to go. Tell me tomorrow.' I'm trying to get out of the office on time to help Jen look for wedding dresses. I only found out about it last night, when she texted me. It's been three months since she got engaged and she may as well have been travelling again the amount we've spoken to each other. The magic of Facebook let me know Grungy Girl is the other bridesmaid. If they suggest I get anything pierced, I shall scream.

'Ceci, darling, I'm off now. Tell the other girls "bye"'. Everyone, bar Ceci, is on the phone.

'Oooooh! Wedding dress shopping. Heavenly. Where's your friend going? Browns Brides? Vera Wang?' Ceci looks like she might dissolve into an almond sugary puddle.

'Something like that.' I can't bring myself to tell her the truth. Jen is buying her dress in Oxfam. The charity shop. I'm sure she's making a point about our row. This is taking the recycling thing way too far.

'I know a great florist who did, like, six of the Vogue girls' flowers – do you want her number?' Ceci starts rummaging in her Lanvin shoulder bag.

Jen has planted her own tulip bulbs. Her budget isn't really the same as a fashionista's. 'I think she's got something sorted, a specialist from Holland.'

'International. Dreamy.' Ceci closes her eyes and I assume imagines her own million, billion, trillion dollar special day.

'Got to dash, darling.' I can't face any more questions about Jen's cut-price wedding.

'Don't forget, drinks at Sketch tomorrow! Tootles!' Ceci waves her manicured fingernails.

I run down the stairs. How have I ended up being late again? I'll have to take a cab. Jen knows how busy I am – she's hardly making this easy.

I arrive at the address she gave me. The shop is large, and full of racks of musty clothes. A smartly dressed lady in her sixties standing behind the till points me in the direction of the changing rooms. I scan the ordered jumble as I pass. You never know when you'll find hidden treasure. My nose wrinkles. Jen's going to have to get this dress dry-cleaned.

"What will Ange think of it?"

I freeze at the sound of my name. They must both be in the changing room with the mustard yellow velvet curtain pulled across. How dare Grungy Girl call me 'Ange'. She doesn't know me. She has no right to shorten my name. She...

'Oh I don't care.' Jen's voice cuts through the heavy curtain and me.

I duck behind a rail of men's tweed jackets.

'Ange won't like it, she doesn't like anything that isn't designer,' Jen continues.

That's not true! I tug at my Vanessa Bruno dress.

Grungy Girl laughs. 'So we shouldn't tell her about your twelve-pound wedding ring, then?'

Twelve pounds? What's it made of, plastic? It'll break!

'She'd have a fit,' Jen laughs. 'Only Tiffany's would do, daaahlink.' Jen adopts a stupid voice.

I grit my teeth.

'I don't understand how you guys are mates – you seem so different?' Grungy Girls says. The mustard curtain bulges.

I hold my breath. There's a sound of rustling, as if Jen's sat down, wearing a huge meringue dress.

'She's changed.' Jen's voice is clear. 'She's different...'

I clamp my hand over my mouth.

'I hope it's just a stupid phase, but I'm not sure.'

I can't believe I'm hearing this. Tears spring into my eyes. How could Jen say that?

I back out of the shop, bumping into a table of shoes. The mustard curtain doesn't move. I run down the street toward the tube. Pausing only to send a text:

Going to miss
dress shopping.
Stuck at work. A

I haven't changed. Have I? I push the thought down. This is
Grungy Girl's fault; she's corrupted Jen. I'm the same as I've
always been. I am.

***

The office is empty. It's 10.05 a.m. Where is everyone? It's
August, but it's been so busy this year most of the girls have
postponed their holidays. No word from Jen. Whatever, she's
got Grungy Girl now and I'm too busy to care. I ignore the ache
in my stomach.

I follow the voices coming from down the hall. Ceci, Pandora
and my junior are gathered round the bathroom door.

'Georgina's locked herself inside. She won't come out.'
Pandora bangs on the door.

'What's happened?'

'We don't know. She came in and ran in here.'

Georgina's nine months pregnant. In the months since she
announced she's going to give birth to the latest designer baby
my world's fallen apart. 'OK, don't crowd her. Go back to your
desks. Someone make her a cup of herbal tea.'

They stare at me.

'The phone's ringing, go.'

They all file past.

I knock gently. 'Georgina, it's Angela. Would you like me to
get someone for you?'

She lets out a pitiful moan.

Christ. 'Are you OK? Are you hurt? Can you open the door,
hon?'

The door's unlocked. Georgina's mascara-streaked face
appears.

'Can I come in?'

She sniffs and nods.

I close the door behind me and lean against the sink. 'You all right?'

'No,' she whimpers.

'Have you had some bad news?' I ask gently.

She sits on the toilet seat. 'These jeans are size eight,' she blubbers. Her bump shakes with her sobs.

I wait.

She looks at me.

Is that it? 'Is that why you're upset?'

'Of course!' she screams. 'These are a size fucking eight.' She prods the skinny white jeans she's wearing. 'I've always been a size six. Look at my thighs – they're humongous.'

They're half the size of mine and I'm not preggers. 'I appreciate it's difficult when your body changes, but really, darling, you have nothing to worry about. You're tiny. Size eight is tiny.'

'Really?' She looks at me through matted eyelashes.

'Really. You look fabulous.' *Apart from the mascara Niagara Falls thing that's going on right now.* 'I'm sure this is just hormones, er, upsetting you.'

She blinks at me. 'I've been trying. I haven't been on the tube. I've been walking to work to burn fat.'

Georgina lives in Notting Hill. That's a forty-five-minute walk. Each way. 'OK, maybe you should ease off on the walking a bit. And you should take it easy for the rest of today. We can cover.'

'I am a little tired.'

'I could call you a car?'

'No,' she looks at her thighs again. 'I'd rather walk.'

After we've got her cleaned up and on her way home I reflect about what I've learned from the pregnant fashionistas I've known. Despite all being concerned with not gaining weight, they almost all look better during pregnancy. The tiny bit of weight they do gain plumps out hollow cheeks and softens stringy necks and chests. They look healthier.

They spend a lot of money on clothes. They invest in themselves and their bump. There are specialist maternity shops dedicated to designer clothes from the normal ranges: wrap dresses, empire waists etc. Being pregnant, it seems, is no excuse for not looking fabulous. Heels are a must.

Tales of fashionistas getting bikini waxes before their due date are rife. Apparently, the whole area becomes much more sensitive in the lead-up to the birth. But it's still preferable to have a landscaped lady garden than to be able to sit down for two days.

I've heard others stress about the hospital food. One persuaded her partner to book her into the Portland because, 'Then I'll be able to eat fish and steamed vegetables.' I'm no medical professional, but I'd wager a low-carb meal is the last thing on your mind after childbirth. Being a pregnant fashionista must be exhausting.

Georgina is a key member of our small staff and, like most agents, is planning to work until she pops. That's dedication to fashion. I hope her waters don't break in the office; delivering a baby is NOT one of my transferable skills.

All of this makes me start wondering. Do I want kids? There's no point even thinking about it. Mr Darling clearly doesn't know if he wants to be with me, let alone start a family with me. I'm growing increasingly obsessed with Sandy. I could go to the pub near their office and see if I could see her? I pinch myself, that's insane. That's stalking. I just have to hang on. He'll grow tired of her. Hopefully.

Georgina goes into labour that night. She leaves a message on the office answermachine; she's most annoyed she didn't get a chance to change into her planned birthing outfit before her son arrived.

And I found another text from Sandy on Mr Darling's phone:

> September sounds
> perfect.

Perfect for what? September's just a few weeks away. I'll find out soon. I push it all to the back of my mind. Thank God for Fashion Week.

ROLE REVERSAL

'What do I think about the way most people dress? Most people are not something one thinks about.'

DIANA VREELAND

'She's an absolute nightmare to represent, it's like having a five-foot-ten-inch child,' Amber moans.

I nod sympathetically. Amber, the booker of a diva supermodel, seems to be making the most of a rare night off by downing as much free champagne as she can. Her chiffon Marni dress looks like it's been scrunched up on the floor for a week. I hope she doesn't get papped tonight.

'I have to carry bloody Tabasco everywhere.' She teeters on her Manolos and flings open her Bottega Veneta knot clutch revealing a Chanel lipstick, a tampon and a bottle of Tabasco. 'She won't eat a damn thing without covering it in the stuff.' Between her fingers is an unlit cigarette.

I'm pretty sure they don't allow smoking in the Victoria and Albert Museum, even if it is a party.

'Is it a diet? Does she only eat lettuce, but covered in Tabasco for flavour?' My junior's wide-eyed at learning the supermodel's eating habits.

I'm about to assure her putting Tabasco on her cornflakes is not going to transform her into a cover girl, when her head spins in the opposite direction. She's staring open-mouthed at Vivienne Westwood as she, her husband Andreas Kronthaler and Sadie Frost pass us in a giggling cluster. My junior gawps at the white devil's horns protruding from Vivienne's dyed orange hair. She looks like she might just reach out and touch the back of Vivienne's red silk kimono dress ...

'Darling, why don't you go and fetch me another drink?' I stop her from ruining her career before it's really started.

She works her way through the sea of long legs and pinched faces surrounding us, glancing back to check where Vivienne is. Then she spots Erin O'Connor, whose pussycat-bow cream shirt and angular hair are visible above the heads of those near the bar, and picks up speed in her direction.

'I can't believe it's Fashion Week again, where does the time go?' I smile at Amber. I try not to think of Sandy's September text to Mr Darling.

'Last week she didn't show up for a campaign shoot. She fucked off instead to some ageing playboy's yacht. The client went mental, I thought they were going to sue.'

'Ghastly.' I drain the dregs of my glass.

'Nice dresh,' she slurs.

Oh dear, Amber seems to have tipped over the edge. 'Thanks. Dolce and Gabbana.' I sidestep another fountain of champagne as it escapes Amber's glass. I don't want a wet patch on my dry-clean only black satin pencil dress. Time to extract myself from the conversation. 'That's one of my hairdressers over there, I must go and say hello.' I wave a hand randomly at the masses of people around us. 'It's been really great to see you, darling, let's do drinks soon.'

We air-kiss goodbye.

I head to the marble steps dividing the room, eavesdropping on the screeching and gossiping cliques as I go.

'Did you see what she was wearing? She may have a different dog for each day of the week, but that's the same dress she wore to the Prada party.'

'We must do lunch, darling, when are you next in Cannes?'

'Well, I heard he slept with her husband while they were shooting in Miami.'

I stand on tiptoes in my red patent Miu Mius. The grand cavernous ceiling of the V&A embraces the noise of the fashion world, and more than a few oversized egos.

Pandora's energetically snogging a male model against the glowing neon oblong bar. I recognise his pale legs from the Comme des Garçons spring/summer show – I wonder if he always wears shorts? Poor love, she hasn't eaten a thing all day in order to squeeze into the dark-grey silk Isabel Marant dress she borrowed from the PR. No wonder she looks like she's eating the guy. I scan the crowd for someone to chat to. My phone beeps.

> Hen do 3 weeks
> today! Remember
> to get out of work
> early. Need to talk
> bridesmaid dresses.
> J

What's Jen doing texting three weeks in advance, checking up on me? This is ridiculous. I'm not looking forward to it. Things are still awkward between us. She and Grungy Girl seem to be organising everything together. They keep joking about Jen getting married at Glastonbury. I'm not sure I can be bothered with it all.

My junior appears clutching a vulgar-looking cocktail and waving enthusiastically. 'Elizabeth Jagger and Jerry Hall are here!'

I barely have time to take in Elizabeth Jagger's red lips and plunge-fronted polka-dot dress and the grey sequinned back of her mother's outfit before my junior tugs me in the opposite direction.

'Look, that's Tracey Emin right there,' she hisses.

I'm worried she might combust with excitement. Tracey is charismatically holding court to our right, in a spectacular floor-length eggshell-blue silk coat embroidered with flora and fauna and birds. I suspect it's Westwood.

'This party is so awesome. Do you think I can take photos?' my junior gabbles.

'Probably not a good idea. Did you get me a drink, darling?'

'Oh yes, I almost forgot. The barman said it's especially for tonight.'

She hands me the glass of alarmingly artificial red liquid. 'Lovely. I'll just pop it here to keep it safe.' I place it behind a nearby pillar. I have no intention of drinking that. Guaranteed hangover in a glass.

'God, can you believe that – someone's taken off their heels to dance?' She scoffs at the sliver of a girl dancing barefoot in front of the DJ.

I watch the girl's familiar dirty-blonde hair whip against her shoulders as she moves about. A column of tightly rolled material runs up the side of her green dress and drapes round her neck and down her back. It's a limited designer piece. I smile to myself. The dancer turns around. Those cheekbones are unmistakeable. 'That's Kate Moss, sweetie.'

The poor junior looks like she's going to cry.

'It's OK, hon, nobody heard you,' I whisper.

'Do you think we should take *our* heels off?' she says, stricken.

'No, I don't think that's necessary.' I wish I had another drink.

I spy a face I recognise, Frannie. I want to ask if the rumour I've heard that one of her photographers has landed the Gucci campaign is true.

'Sweetie, could you pop to the ladies and see if Charlie's still, er, powdering her nose in there? She seems to have been gone an awful long time.' I dispatch my junior.

She looks delighted at being able to suss out the party again.

My phone beeps. Jen's just not getting the message I'm busy.

> What do you think
> of me booking a petting
> zoo for the reception? J

She must be joking – who does she think she's marrying – Old MacDonald? I can just see all the guests dressed in their best pastel outfits and fascinators stroking pigs. That's exactly what you want in the background of your wedding photos: piles of animal shit. I tell myself off. I'm still hurt because she said I've changed. But I know that's not true. I'm exactly the same as I've always been – I've just got better clothes. I don't have time for this. I need to find out about Gucci.

I click down the steps and push into the crowd. The music is loud, the lighting dim. I can tell from Dale Chihuly's yellow and blue hanging glass sculpture, dancing in the light above, that I'm near the bar. There are so many people I can only take one step at a time. Sideways.

In the opposite direction a gentleman is moving in a similar manner to me, as we draw level he turns and we end up wedged, facing each other. He's in a dapper suit and a bow tie, with round-rim glasses balanced on his nose. It's Manolo Blahnik.

'Good evening.' He smiles politely.

'Hello.' I smile back.

There is a shift in the mass of people to our right and he is free. 'Have a nice evening.' He disappears into the crowd.

Some of my non-fashion friends queued for Manolo Blahnik to sign their stilettos. I thought it amusing at the time, like a rock star of shoes. I'll send a few of them a text, so they can remind me to tell them about it next time we catch up.

I just met Manolo Blahnik!

My phone beeps. Three new text messages. They all say the same thing:

Who??

Bloody civilians. I grab a glass of champagne from a waitress and head toward Frannie, and hopefully a slice of the Gucci account.

IN THEIR SHOES

'Give a girl the right shoes and she can conquer the world.'

MARILYN MONROE

I look at the white embossed invite again – there's only twenty minutes till Designer Dormouse's show starts. My taxi's surrounded by stationary traffic. I tap the invite on my knee. I can't believe I spent the morning inside a bin searching for a necklace. I'm an experienced agent now – this crap is beneath me. Despite showering and dousing myself in enough Chanel Coco perfume to render a pygmy hippo unconscious, I can still smell rubbish. I must be imagining it. It's not on my clothes. The Designer Dormouse rustled me up a replacement outfit: an oversized Katherine Hamnett T-shirt dress which bears the legend 'I USE A CONDOM' in huge black letters on the front. All the exquisite designer dresses she has in the office and this is the only thing I can fit into. It's passable with fresh black tights (from my emergency office desk drawer) and my Louboutins. Bin beggars can't be clothes choosers.

The time it took to visually recover from my trash trawl, answer my emails and field the usual frantic phone calls meant I left the office late. When am I going to find a second to plan my outfit for this stupid hen do? I feel like I haven't seen Mr Darling for weeks. I ignore the image of a small twenty-one-year-old blonde sinking her claws in to him.

I glance out the window, the taxi's near Aldwych. I only need to get to Somerset House. Eighteen minutes till the show starts. Sorry, feet, but it's going to be quicker to walk.

'I'll jump out here, mate.' I open the door.

'Fucking get out the—' screams a passing courier cyclist as he scraps his handlebar down the side of a bus.

I catch my heart in my Givenchy-lipsticked mouth and compose myself. Mental note: try not to kill anyone on the way to fashion shows. My legs shake as I make it to the pavement. Come on, stand tall, you work in fashion, the most exciting industry in the world, you can even carry off a T-shirt that's giving intimate information to all these strangers walking past. This T-shirt is fashionable, I am fashionable, my shoes cost six hundred pounds, repeat.

It's lunchtime and the Strand is clogged with tourists, shoppers, and workers out to get a sandwich. I walk as quickly as the crowds and my heels let me. My phone vibrates – I jump. It's an international caller, so not Jen, or Mr Darling. 'Hello.' Bright and cheery voice, only slightly breathless from my pace.

'It's me, doll,' hisses Fraser. He's shooting in Miami with a model famous for her blossoming film career. She no longer walks, which makes her sound like she's suffered some terrible accident instead of simply opting to stop doing catwalk shows. This campaign has been fitted round her latest movie.

Fraser mutters something.

'I can't hear what you're saying!' I push my mobile harder against my ear to block out the traffic noise.

'That's because I'm whispering. You will not believe what's happening here!'

'What, darling?' I prepare myself for a lament on long working hours and how they're only allowed a three-hour lunch break in the sunshine.

'In the middle of the set, she's on Skype to her boyfriend.'

'They probably don't get much time to talk, it makes sense for her to have a quick conversation with him when she can.' *I know how she feels.* I sidestep a group of leisurely ladies and find myself in the middle of a school field trip. Thirty little children swarm round me like blue-blazer-wearing ants. Children don't move in ways you can anticipate. I look for an escape route, but all I can see are kids. I try not to tread on any little toes with my pointed heels.

'Apparently, they don't have time for other things too.' There is a rustling sound, which I guess is Fraser shielding the phone with his hand. 'She's talking about sex.'

'Sex!' Thirty little expectant faces look up at me, the lady shouting rude words in the street.

'She said sex!' A little blonde thing points at me.

They all start squawking and laughing, their little heads bobbing up and down as they chant the word sex over and over.

'Really, how inappropriate!' A teacher in a cardigan decorated with knitted cats glares at me and my safe-sex T-shirt. 'This way, children. Come on.'

'Sorry, sorry,' I mouth as she shoots me death stares. I could explain I was shocked to learn a supermodel is talking about sex in public, but opt instead to blush the same shade of red as my nail polish.

'Are they just mentioning it in passing?' I whisper back.

'Noooooo. She's actually *talking dirty.*'

'Does she know you're there?' I've got visions of him bending down to hide behind his kit, trapped in a nightmarishly embarrassing situation.

'We're all here – me, the photographer, the client, the make-up ... Just standing a metre away while she discusses in detail what she wants to do to him.'

Gross. 'Does she know she can be heard? Has she got headphones on or something?'

'No. She's just sitting there, in the bikini for the first shot, her Mac on her lap, her hand underneath it, talking all kinds of freaky.'

Cheers for the unwanted mental image.

'I had to step away,' he continues. 'I'm a gay man – I really don't want to know about what goes on with her la la.'

'I doubt anyone does. What the hell is she doing?'

'I think she's getting off on it, I swear, doll, she looked at the photographer when she said she wanted to use her tongue to—'

'Stop! I don't want to know the details. Make an excuse. Say you have to use the bathroom.' I look left and right and run across the road.

He starts to snigger.

'This is a very serious matter, it is very unprofessional.' *I don't have time for this.*

'I'm only laughing because I'm so traumatised. I feel sick, actually. Do you think I could sue for sexual harassment?'

I can hear the dollar signs ping into his eyes. I look at my watch: fifteen minutes till the show starts. 'Her behaviour's inappropriate, but I don't think pursuing a sexual harassment case is a good idea.'

'But I could retire!' he says excitedly.

And miss out on moments like these? As if.

'Can you call a lawyer?' he pushes.

'You really want to accuse one of the world's hottest women of sexually harassing her gay hairdresser?'

'It's not going to convince a jury is it?' He sounds disappointed.

'Best to try and get through it. I'll have a word with her booker.' What am I going to say? *Oi! Your model is trash talking and touching herself up on set. Please give her detention.* 'You've worked with her before and always got on well. This is obviously some weird hormonal thing or something. Perhaps she took some bad drugs? I don't know. It'd be a shame to lose a big earner over one moment of madness.' I appeal to his bank balance.

'I'll just put my iPod on, drown it out. She can't keep it going much longer,' he says in a delighted manner.

No long-term damage seems to have been done. 'All right, darling. Good luck!'

I hang up as I draw level with Somerset House. Gathered there already are a disproportionate number of skinny people clutching bottles of mineral water. I no longer feel so uncomfortable in my bold T-shirt. This is where I belong.

In a drab rectangular room fifteen light-bulb-edged mirrors have been erected. Trestle tables and extra chairs are stacked against a wall and every available surface is covered in bags, coats, make-up, cans of hairspray and bits of paper. Backstage is chaotic, messy and hot as usual. The designer, who I call Mono after his monochrome outfits and monotone voice, is talking, flatly, to the PR team. My junior's trying not to catch her platform heel in the electrical cables covering the floor. Her dangly earrings swing as she distributes coffee among the thirty-odd people packed into this space.

'Here, let me help.' I steady the edge of the cardboard lid she's holding. 'This is a chai tea, which I believe is yours.' I pass the cup to the head hairdresser, who has a Prada shirt and a couple of brushes tucked into his belted jeans.

'Fantastic!' He takes the tea. 'Esme, don't pull it that way. You'll make her look like she's been caught in a wind tunnel. It's to look elegantly destroyed, the *other* way, the other way.' And he's off.

'Let the PR girls know their drinks are here.'

'Will do.' My junior gives an eager lip-gloss grin. This is her first time backstage. I remember mine. It feels like a long time ago, before everything became complicated.

Suddenly I hear Designer Dormouse's voice above everything else, she's not making audible words but a high-pitched squeaking sound.

'Oh, oh, oh, oh no!'

She's crouched down, and her jagged-hemmed poplin dress, from one of Mono's earlier collections, is splayed like a milky white flower.

'What's wrong?' I ask.

'Oh, oh. The shoes. They're slipping. Because of the little socks – the socks he says are vital to the look.' She gestures at Mono who's giving a pre-show interview to Style.com. 'They can't walk in them!'

The shoes are a sample size seven. Models who unreasonably refuse to have size seven feet are punished for their obstinacy by being made to walk in shoes that are too big or too small for them. Coupled with silky popsocks there's a strong chance these girls are going to trip down the runway with all the stability of a baby giraffe. I gulp.

The Designer Dormouse rocks in her crouched position. 'They're *all* going to fall. The press will have a field day. The designer will blame me. It's catastrophic. Disastrous. My career will be ruined.'

Not again.

'Will this help?' The model towering over her reaches into her YSL bag, which is hanging off the back of a make-up chair, and pulls out some sandpaper.

It takes a second to register why she's carrying around a DIY staple in her designer handbag – she's obviously used it to rough up the bottom of show shoes to give herself some grip. And people say models are dumb. Though I doubt it will solve the case of the slippery socks.

'Five minutes till show start!' calls one of the PRs.

Uh oh.

The Designer Dormouse shakes her head. She rises up, and I realise she's standing in a pair of the show heels. *Are you taking the saying: 'don't criticise anyone till you've walked in their shoes' literally?*

My heart has escaped my chest and is lodged beating in my ears. I'm constantly on edge these days.

Designer Dormouse's tone is unnervingly calm and cold. 'Stuff them …'

What?

'… with cotton wool, spray both the insides and outsides with hairspray, let's try and stick their feet to the shoes.'

Ah!

We fall to the floor and frantically cram the velveteen shoes with cotton wool. My Mulberry bag is still on my shoulder. We jam the sticky shoes on to each of the model's feet and fasten the straps as tight as possible. We are in the lap of the fashion gods. *Dear Chanel, Dior and Givenchy, the holy trinity of fashion, please don't let the models trip. I'll wear the hideous recycled peach bridesmaid dress Jen's found, I'll take 5 a.m. calls from Vampira, I'll stop fantasising about pushing Sandy into an office shredder if you just don't let them fall.*

'Two minutes,' calls the PR.

My junior and I brush dust from our knees and head to the catwalk entrance – it's the quickest way to our seats. I hear the PRs' walkie-talkies:

'Alexandra Shulman, editor of *Vogue*, is stuck in traffic. The eagle has not landed. Repeat: the eagle has not landed.'

'How does this work? Hello? Hello? Word is US *Vogue's* André Leon Tally is on his way. Over and definitely *out*.'

We step onto the protective-plastic-covered catwalk. I imagine what it must be like for the model; when the lights are on, everyone's staring and you're just praying you don't take a tumble. My junior and I elegantly scramble off the runway to find our place on the long white bench seating. We're not front row, and my junior doesn't have a seat, she's expected to stand at the back with the lucky fashion students who've managed to get inside. She's worked hard today and she's only small. I squish against the woman with augmented lips and the great Dries Van Noten jacket to my left and make room for my junior to sit.

'Is it going to work?' My junior clutches my arm.

'It'll be fine.' I don't sound convincing.

Jemima Khan, in a typically chic black dress, is settled on the front row opposite. The *International Herald Tribune's* fashion editor, Suzy Menkes, a London Fashion Week icon with her quiff-cum-victory-roll hairstyle, is sat near her. Some poor unfortunate is bumped off and replaced with a supermodel. There's a rustle at the entrance and Alexandra walks in. The show can now begin.

Two stagehands pull the plastic quickly from the runway and ball it up and away. The lights flare. Several people drop their sunglasses down over their eyes. The heat is intense. I have déjà vu. My phone beeps: another text from Bridezilla – *not now*. The music vibrates up through the floor and the first model appears. The photographers balanced on a plinth at the end of the catwalk set off a million flashbulbs. I cross my fingers and hold my breath. Please don't fall.

***

The first model strides forward confidently. A lovely sullen look on her face. I stare at her feet. *Was that a wobble, did her ankle just roll?* I look around me. No one has reacted – she's still upright – the audience are all watching the clothes. I exhale. The models gracefully stomp down the catwalk in skinny trousers and pedal pushers. The catwalk is awash with Mono's favourite colours: black and white. Dotted throughout are accents of charcoal grey: an asymmetric hemmed jacket, a shredded scarf. The lights highlight every considered stitch on the strong deconstructed jackets and tops. It's beautiful in its utilitarian simplicity, like a city skyline.

The models appear for their final walk and the crowd rise to applaud. Mono, in his immaculate suit, is clutching the hand of the last girl and waving jubilantly at the audience. All those months of sourcing, designing and stitching by Mono and his team, all those weeks the Designer Dormouse spent styling up outfits, deciding hair and make-up looks, all the hours taken to perfect the running order, all the money that's been spent on the show; it's all over in the time it takes me to pluck my eyebrows: six minutes flat.

The room is a mass of energy. People scoop up bags, coats, dogs, hurrying to the next show. There are shouts of hello and goodbye, air kisses, mobile phone calls – the air fizzes with good reviews.

'Awesome, incredible. Best experience of my life.' My junior is bubbling away next to me as I drag her along.

We ride the wave of cameramen and press onto the scuffed catwalk. Bursting into the backstage area I look for the Designer Dormouse. Models are stripping off, pulling on jeans and jumpers, ready to head to the next show. Cameras, microphones and tape recorders are thrust into the face of Mono. His head PR is showing the buyers the rack of samples, as they appear back on the rail, still warm from the models. I grab a mini bottle of Moët from a tray. I need something to steady my nerves. I see the Designer Dormouse, pacing in the corner.

'Wonderful show, Alexandra Shulman was front row!' I grab her for an air kiss.

She pulls away and looks at me with moist worried eyes. 'Did any of them fall?'

I give a big relaxed smile. 'No darling, none of them fell.'

SOMETHING'S GOTTA GIVE

'I'd like to grow old with my face moving.'

KATE WINSLET

It's eleven o'clock that evening and I'm still in the office. Eleven o'clock. I want to cry. But my voice is calm. 'I'm sorry, Alfie, but I can't get you a pink painted elephant by tomorrow.'

'But it's fucking vital to the shoot.'

It's not vital to the shoot. It's some mad over-the-top idea. 'I've tried everything I can, but there are no available elephants in Johannesburg tomorrow.'

'Then I may as well not show up!'

That's it, act maturely. 'What about a giraffe? I can get you a giraffe.'

'I don't want a fucking giraffe, who wants a fucking pink giraffe.'

I'm pretty sure you can't paint a giraffe, but that doesn't seem important right now. 'What about a monkey? I could get you some monkeys.'

'No.'

It's like talking to a fricking five-year-old. 'A snake? You could do some really cool shots with a snake.'

'Forget it. We'll do it without the animals. If I can't have a pink elephant then I don't want anything.' He slams down the phone.

I should call him back. Or maybe let him cool off. I just want to go home. I close down my computer, switch off the lights and lock up the office.

The street is full of people laughing, drinking and smoking outside the pubs. I wonder where Jen is tonight. Off with her grungy bridesmaid, probably.

I hail a cab. All I had for dinner was muesli. I'm exhausted.

I let myself into the dark flat. The bedroom door is closed. Mr Darling's gone to sleep. I change out of my clothes in the hallway and brush my teeth in the kitchen sink so as not to wake him. I use the light from my phone to pad across the bedroom. I'm getting too old for this. Gently I lift the edge of the duvet.

He moves and sighs.

I freeze.

'We need to have a talk,' he mumbles.

A talk? This is it. It's September.

'In the morning.' He rolls over. His breath deepens.

He's going to tell me about Sandy. He's going to ... I'm no longer tired. I can get you two monkeys, a giraffe and a snake in Jo'burg tomorrow, but can I make a relationship work?

***

It feels like I've been asleep for a few minutes. My alarm can't be going off already.

Mr Darling stirs beside me.

Mr Darling? He's never here when my alarm goes off. That's not my alarm. I sit up straight. It's my mobile. It's still dark. What time is it? My bedside clock flashes 05.01 at me. Christ. Something's wrong.

'You OK?' Mr Darling mumbles.

I hold the phone to my ear. 'Hello?'

'I want to move my meeting to Thursday.'

Vampira. 'What?'

'Do I have to repeat everything? I want to move the meeting to Thursday.'

Am I dreaming? I pinch myself. 'Ouch!'

'Pardon?' she snaps.

'Nothing, sorry. Are you all right? It's a little early.' *I fucking hate you.*

'I am waiting for my flight and I have time to run through a few things …'

You have got to be kidding me! I flop back onto the bed.

Mr Darling groans and swings his legs over the side. 'I'm going to the spare room,' he hisses.

'Sorry,' I mouth at him. He wants to have a *talk*. My stomach lurches.

'… and I want to see that stupid woman from Spanish *Vogue*. I think I could do something with them.'

'Mmm yes.' I use the pad next to my bed. My photographer's calling me at 5 a.m. because she's bored. If she called anyone else at this time they'd tell her to stick her to-do list up her liposuctioned bottom. I've got to start switching off my phone. *But what happens if there's a real emergency? My artists rely on me.*

I hear the shower start. Mr Darling's obviously given up on sleep and decided to get ready for work. *Crap.* I've got to get Vampira off the phone. Didn't Side-Parting say we needed to talk just before he ripped my heart out and put it in a blender?

'… they are making an announcement,' Vampira says.

I can hear what sounds like French through the airport tannoy. What are they saying? Damn me for not paying more attention in languages at school.

Mr Darling's work shoes click across the wooden floor. The last thing he does before leaving is put his shoes on. Is that his keys jangling?

'I land in two hours. Have the car waiting for me.' Vampira hangs up.

I stumble out of bed, dragging the duvet halfway across the room.

I fling myself into the second bedroom. He's not here.

The bathroom door's open. Empty.

I fly across the hallway and slide into the lounge in my bedsocks.

Mr Darling is drinking tea on the sofa.

This is it. 'Sorry about that: Vampira.'

'I guessed. Sit down. I wanted to talk.'

That horrible word again. I twist the hem of my pyjamas.

' … we've both been so busy lately, and we haven't spent much time together.' His face is serious.

Please don't say it's not working out.

'We need to make some changes.'

I brace.

'I think we should have a date night once a week.'

What? 'A date night?'

'We need to spend some quality time together. How are you fixed for next Thursday, Miss Clarke?'

Vampira's out the country. Alfie's shoot will be over. 'That would be perfect,' I stutter.

'I'll book dinner or something.' He stands and picks his keys off the coffee table. 'Have a good day and don't work too hard.'

Quality time? Is this a test? One final date to see if he wants me or a twenty-one-year-old economics pop tart? Well, I can guess who's won that competition already. We're one of those couples that *schedule* time to see each other. The romance is dead. I go back to bed. But I can't sleep.

DIAMONDS ARE FOREVER

'Big girls need big diamonds.'

ELIZABETH TAYLOR

Tonight is date night. I've bitten down all my nails worrying about it. I wanted to call Jen but things still aren't great between us. She above everyone else should be able to see the difference between my fashionista persona and the real me. Maybe we really have drifted apart? I contemplated talking to Pandora about Mr Darling, but she'd only want to know how much he earned before she gave an opinion. In the end I decided the best thing to do was to be the very best me on our date. Remind Mr Darling of why he fell for me in the first place.

I promised I wouldn't be late. He hates that. I've spoken to all my artists. They all have their call details. I've answered all my emails. I've visited the bathroom and reapplied my make-up. I tap my nails on the desk. 5.58 p.m. That's close enough for me. I'm off. The office phone rings. Ceci and Pandora are both on the other line. Charlie's already left and my junior's collecting portfolios from a magazine. I could let the answerphone get it?

I sit down again. 'Charlie Monroe Management, Angela speaking.' This better be quick.

'Thank God, doll!' Fraser hisses.

It's 6.01 p.m., not the time for gossip. 'Fraser, I've got another line holding for me.'

'You've got to help – they're going to cut my finger off!'

'What? Who?' What the hell is he talking about?

'I only did it as a joke ...' he babbles.

'Fraser, stop. Did what? What did you do?'

'I tried on a million-pound ring on set and now it's stuck on my finger.'

I let my head fall onto my arm on my desk. 'Why would you do that?' I say into my elbow.

'It was a joke, you know, oh look at me, I'm wearing a million-pound ring. But now I can't get the bugger off.'

Probably because it is a piece of women's jewellery!

'They're going to arrest me,' he starts to snivel.

Why *now*? Why, when I've arranged to meet Mr Darling and our relationship hangs by a thread, can't they keep their fingers to themselves? 'Calm down. They're not going to arrest you. Who knows?'

'Just the stylist, she's in here in the gents with me.'

Lucky girl. 'Have you tried Vaseline?' Which goes on the top ten things you never want to ask your gay male artist.

'Yes! It's still stuck!'

'OK, run it under the cold tap and then put your hand in the air. Your fingers are probably swollen. I'll call the client and let them know what's happened so they don't think you're trying to sneak out the bathroom window with the ring.'

I speak to the client, stop the client from hyperventilating and cancel the ambulance Fraser's called. At 6.45 he finally gets the ring off, and keeps all his fingers. I'm late. Very late.

The weather's bleak. A few spots of rain fall. It takes ten minutes to find a cab. I should have taken the tube. Finally I reach Mr Darling on Old Broad Street. This is where Vertigo is.

'I thought we'd have our first official date night where we had our first date.' He's wearing his best suit. Looks like he's had a haircut. He won't look me in the eye.

I've let him down, again. *This is it.*

He stalks through the metal detectors and is out the other side before I catch up.

We ride up in the lift with another couple. They are all giggly and hugging. Is he like that with Sandy? We stand in silence.

The lift doors open and the other couple skip off round the corner.

Mr Darling hands our coats to the maître' d. The view takes my breath away. It doesn't matter that I've seen it before, that I've lived in London for eight years, that I walk these streets every day; it is beautiful.

The maître d stops at the table that overlooks St Paul's. There's a bottle of champagne, two glasses and a little red ring box.

I stare at the table. 'What about Sandy?' I half whisper.

'What?' He looks bewildered.

'Sandy, the twenty-one-year-old blonde girl.'

'Who?' He's beginning to look annoyed.

'Sandy, the intern in your office.'

'What are you talking about? Sandy's not a girl. He's a thirty-five-year-old rugby player from Australia,' Mr Darling furrows his brow.

'But you met her on a Saturday, when you told me you were at work.'

'How do you know that?' He raises his eyebrows.

I look at the floor. 'I read your text messages. You lied to me.' I meet his eyes.

'What have you got yourself worked up about this time? You're right, I did meet Sandy, the *man*, on a Saturday and I did lie to you about it. He took me to the same jeweller's he got his wife's wedding ring from in Hatton Garden.'

'What?' My head's spinning, and it's not from vertigo. 'So you haven't been having an affair with Sandy?'

'He's not really my type,' Mr Darling laughs.

How have I got this so wrong?

'I've been talking to him about the Formula One, and how best to plan tonight. September seemed good because you're always so busy with Fashion Week. I didn't think you'd guess what I was up to.' He grins.

'I ... so you ...'

All this time I've been worrying about nothing. I'm an idiot. I'm a fool. Oh my God I'm ruining the big moment! 'Sorry!' I put my head in my hands and screw my eyes up. How could I doubt Mr Darling? Have I got so lost in fashion I've lost sight of reality? Has the fear of being caught off guard like I was with Side-Parting made me paranoid? I open my eyes. I gasp.

'Angela, will you marry me?' Mr Darling is down on one knee.

Oh Coco, Christian and Yves. 'Yes!'

Mr Darling takes a ring out the box and slides it on my finger.

A solitaire diamond.

'Don't worry, it's insured.' He winks.

'I *love* it!'

He grins then coughs nervously. 'I hope you don't think it's too old-fashioned, but I asked your dad to give me his permission to ask you to marry me.'

'When?'

'The day we moved into our flat.'

The day I first thought you were up to something! I am such a numpty.

'You don't mind, do you?' He looks worried.

'No, it's romantic. I assume you would have asked me anyway if he'd said no?'

'Naturally. Though he seemed quite delighted to be "getting rid of you".'

'Hilarious.' I roll my eyes. I bet if I'd just spoken to Jen she would have told me I was being silly. She would have assured me I was worrying about nothing. How have I pushed away one of the people who looks out for me the most?

I throw my arms around Mr Darling. 'Let's tell people!'

My parents are on holiday, on a boat sailing round Turkey. The call goes straight to answerphone. I don't leave a detailed message, just ask that they call me back.

What about my brother? His answerphone message informs me he is in Canada on business.

Mr Darling's brother and his wife? We get their answerphone too.

'Where the hell is everyone?'

'Let's leave it an hour and see if any of them get back to us. If not we'll start calling other people.' Mr Darling takes the phone from my hand.

'OK.' I can't stop grinning. 'I'm just going to pop to the loo. It's obviously the excitement of it all!'

'Hurry back!'

I'm busting to tell someone. I walk into the Ladies, where a group of women are waiting in a queue. 'I just got engaged!' I scream.

The tiny room erupts. I'm hugged, they coo over my ring. I'm so excited I want to tell the world.

Walking back to our table I feel a ripple through the bar. The women from the toilets are telling their work colleagues, their partners, the people they are out with.

Mr Darling and I are enveloped in a wave of emotion. Men in suits shake Mr Darling's hand and clap him on the back. I'm hugged and kissed.

'Congratulations!'

'We got married this year – it was incredible!'

'Good job, man!'

'Let's see the ring.'

'These guys just got engaged!'

There's a cheer and clapping. Someone buys us a bottle of champagne. The bar presents us with another. Slowly the crowd subsides and the two of us are left with our fizz.

'Couldn't wait then, my little blabbermouth?' Mr Darling laughs.

We get marvellously and deliriously drunk.

Staggering around looking for a taxi, we cling to each other screaming with laughter.

'I did ask you when I was sober,' Mr Darling says.

Just so I knew he really, really meant it.

A NEW CHAPTER

'Above all, be the heroine of your life, not the victim.'

NORA EPHRON

There is a lot of screaming in the office. If there's one thing fashionistas are good at it's screaming about diamonds.

'You are so lucky!' coos Ceci.

'It's so romantic.' My junior strokes my hand.

'Gorgeous,' sighs Charlie.

'Angela, line three, it's Trina from Saatchi,' says Pandora.

Oh well, you can't have it all. Back to reality. Or back to my persona. I thank them all graciously. I'll tell my artists later. 'I'm doing a breakfast run,' my junior whispers.

I pick up the phone and hover my finger over the connect button just long enough to say, 'Egg white omelette. Take the money out of my Mulberry.' I slide my handbag across the floor to her.

'Hi Trina, how are you? How was Miami?' All thoughts of my own wedding will have to wait.

The afternoon passes in a blur. My phone just won't stop ringing.

My mobile beeps. It's a text from one of my stylists:

I'm pregnant!!!!!!!

What crap timing. I've just landed her a huge high-street brand, a mortgage-paying long-term client for her. A pregnant stylist and a new mother is not what the client is expecting. I text back:

Fantastic news! Congratulations!!
When's it due? Kisses xxx

Something niggles in the back of my mind. Isn't that how the jerk photographer responded to Georgina's pregnancy? Well, this is different, I'm only watching out for my artist's needs. I'll email the client, take them out for lunch and reinforce the relationship. My mobile beeps again:

April. I haven't told
my husband yet! xx

April, that's when they shoot their main campaign. Bugger.

'Angela, line four, it's Frannie,' shouts Pandora.

Gucci, Gucci, goo! 'Frannie, darling, how are you?'

'Fabulous, it's one of the agency girls' birthdays – we're having macaroons and champagne.'

'Delightful!' I wonder if I can fit a manicure in before the weekend? Really show off my ring.

'We're doing birthday drinks at the Sanderson after work, you should come with?'

I imagine my stylist going into labour during the middle of an ad campaign shoot. I have a massive to-do list. I had promised

Mr Darling I'd be home at a reasonable time tonight, but this could lead to a slice of the Gucci goldmine. He'll understand. 'Sure, I need a drink.' I'll make it up to him next week. 'Whose birthday is it?'

'Gabi's, she's thirty, we gave her Botox vouchers.'

I see the reflection of my face in my Mac, ironically, frozen. *Botox vouchers for her thirtieth birthday? Subtle.* I shall be twenty-nine next birthday. Which leaves me with just over a year till I'm thirty. That's two seasons. That passes in a flash. I'll be thirty and the industry expects me to have Botox. I feel as if the poisonous liquid's been injected into my forehead and is trickling cold over my face. 'I've got another line holding, Frannie.'

'Go darling, I'll speak to you at the bar later. Ciao ciao.'

Ciao.

'You all right?' My junior, with her smooth unlined twenty-year-old forehead, looks up from her desk.

'Just a little dizzy. I'm going to the bathroom.'

Inside I lock the door and stare at my reflection in the mirror. Receiving Botox vouchers for a thirtieth birthday present doesn't feel like a gift, it feels like an instruction. What's next? Being prescribed a facelift at thirty-five? I know loads of people have work done, but I assumed it was their own personal choice. Like opting not to eat carbs; nobody wrenches the bread from their hands. I smooth my dress over my size eight figure. I'm under no illusions as to how the fashion industry works, but while I was whizzing through my twenties, drinking champagne, scoring designer freebies and partying with celebs, I never thought about growing up. Growing older in this industry.

I think about all the times I've been late to meet Mr Darling. Even on the night we got engaged, when I was seriously worried about our relationship, I still arrived late for our date. All the early morning phone calls I've taken. I've come to fear the ring of my mobile phone. Text messages make me jump. I think about Georgina's hysterics over her size eight thighs, Pandora's competitiveness. All the money I've spent. I reflect on my horror at learning my stylist's pregnant. It *was* exactly how the jerk photographer responded. I'm a jerk. Do I even know my junior's name?? How many hours do I spend in my work persona and how many do I spend being the real me? Oh Jen, you were right. I have changed. I *have* disappeared up my own Spanx-clad bum. After everything we've been through together. I didn't want to listen. I haven't grown up, I've grown into a walking, snarling ball of anxiety. How did I get here? I try to picture myself, still working in fashion in twenty years' time. All I can see is a pinched, stretched, surgically enhanced me, with a great wardrobe and few friends. Do I want to be that person?

Only my junior is left in the office when I come out. 'Can you do me a favour, Liv? Call Frannie for me and tell her I've gone home sick.'

***

I open up the flat door. Everything's quiet. It looks like Mr Darling is still at work. For once I'm relieved. There's something I need to do.

I rummage inside the cupboard in the spare bedroom, moving aside old *Vogues* and last season's clothes, which I've vacuum-packed. I know it's here somewhere. Bingo! I pull out an old pencil case. Among the chewed pencils and dried up biros is a strawberry-scented pen.

I sit down at the dining room table and write at the top of a clean page in my notepad:

To-Do:

1.   Sort my life out

I stare at it. Now what?

I turn the page over and start again.

Pros about working in fashion:

1. The parties.
2. The freebies.
3. The gossip.

Hmmm, that looks more superficial than it really is. Try harder.

4. Some of the people are lovely.
5. I'm good at my job.

Alongside it I write:

Cons about working in fashion:

1. Some of the people are a bit dubious.
2. My feet always hurt.
3. I'm always hungry.
4. I've given Net-A-Porter 97% of my annual income.
5. I haven't slept properly for months.
6. Each time my phone rings my heart races at the prospect of a fashion emergency.
7. I use the phrase 'fashion emergency' without irony.
8. I don't get to spend any time with the people I love.
9. I'm not very nice to the people I love.
10. I HAVE TURNED INTO A GIGANTIC STUCK-UP TWAT.

A fug lifts from my head. I can see clearly. It's definitely the strawberry-scented pen. I swallow. I know what I have to do.

'Good morning, bride to be!' I sing into my mobile the next day.

'Hello!' Jen sounds surprised to hear my voice. 'You're up early,' she says.

I imagine her arching her eyebrow at me.

'Yeah, well, I've got some making up to do to a good friend of mine. Turns out I've been a bit of a tit.'

There's a pause.

I cross my fingers.

Jen laughs. 'It has been known to happen.'

We're good. 'Anyway, I wanted to let you know I've made a decision. I'm going to hand in my notice.' I check my skirt isn't tucked into my knickers as I pass the florist on Marylebone High Street.

'What! Why? What have those girls in your office done now?' Jen goes up an octave.

'Nothing. I've just decided I want to change direction. I want to be a writer.' *I like the way that sounds. Smart, creative, interesting.*

'You can't just wake up and decide to be a writer, Ange!'

'Why not?' I sidestep a busload of commuters that are emptying on to the pavement.

'For one thing you have no experience.'

'I had no experience of fashion, but I made it, didn't I?' I pause outside the office building.

'And what are you planning to write?'

'I'm going to write a book about the fashion industry. Listen, I've got to go. I'll see you Friday for the hen do, I'll be there *early*.' And for once, I knew I meant it.

ACKNOWLEDGEMENTS

I'm grateful to so many people for getting me to this point, that I fear this is all about to get a bit 'Oscar-winning speech'.

You'll have to imagine the big poufy dress and the over-emotional tears.

To Diana Beaumont for believing in me, encouraging me, advising me and generally being an all-round kick-ass agent. To my editor, the ever charming, ever wise, ever reassuring Hannah Knowles and her floral wine. To Shona Abhyankar, Kay Hayden, Jen Green, Han Ismail, Beccy Jones, Vanessa Milton, (and Rose Alexander), Justine Taylor, Jacqui Lewis and all the wonderful talented and hardworking team at Virgin. To Paul Donnellon for his enchanting illustrations. To Lucy Stephens for designing such a stylish cover, and, even if it was only fleetingly, making people believe I look like the girl on the front.

To the incomparable Debra Daw, and the consummate Deborah Arthurs, Tamara Abraham, Maysa Rawi, Sadie Whitelocks and all the team at the *Mail* Online, without whom this book wouldn't have existed.

Thank you to Li Armstrong, Jenny Jarvis, and Hayley King for years of support, hand holding, cocktail drinking, and for not laughing too loudly when I said I wanted to be a writer. And thanks to Fleur Sinclair for aiding me with endless drafts and existential angst.

To the many people who've given me advice, feedback, help and general leg-ups along the way: Rupert Heath, Dan Bourke, Ann Stenhouse, Caroline Natzler, Jean Thomson, Catherine Headley, Joyce Ferguson, Helen Phillips, Renee Tyack, Margaret Yiannaki, Keiko Itoh, Kathy Montgomery, Sarah Day, Kate McNaughton, Jamie Mitchinson, Tom Sears, Claire McGowan, Paula Goldstein, Deborah Dooley (and Bob), Deborah Wright, Solvej Todd (and all the team at the Literary Consultancy), Elina Jansson, Ness Guinsberg and Dani Guinsberg. I owe you all a drink (or two).

For doing the impossible and making me look great in a photograph: Tim Wheeler, photographer, Dani Guinsberg, make up, and Terri Capon, hair.

Thank you to my eternally patient family, Mum, Dad, Chris, Sam, Guy and Hannah. I love you all.

And finally to all those I worked with, partied with, gossiped with or met in the fashion industry: thank you for the memories, the experiences, the hangovers and the laughs. If you want me, I've gone into hiding.